ASTON MARTIN

ASTON MARTIN
THE POST WAR COMPETITION CARS

Anthony Pritchard

Foreword by Roy Salvadori

Aston Publications

Published in 1991 by
Aston Publications Limited,
Bourne End House, Harvest Hill,
Bourne End, Bucks., SL8 5JJ

British Library Cataloguing in Publication Data
Pritchard, Anthony
   Aston Martin
   1.   Racing cars, history
   I.   Title
   629.228

   ISBN 0-946627-48-7

Designed by Chris Hand

Printed in Hong Kong

Sole distributors to the
U.K. book trade,
Springfield Books Ltd.,
Norman Road, Denby Dale,
Huddersfield, West
Yorkshire, HD8 8TH

Contents

Foreword

I am pleased to have the opportunity to write the foreword to this detailed account of post-war Aston Martin competition cars. I drove works Aston Martin cars from 1953 to 1960 and again in 1963 and John Wyer, who masterminded their success, became one of my closest friends. David (later Sir David) Brown, owner of Aston Martin, commissioned John Wyer to create one of the world's finest sports car teams from scratch at a time when, Jaguar apart, Britain was not considered as a serious contender in international motor racing. Works Aston Martins finished second at Le Mans in both '55 and '56, won there in 1959, won at the Nürburgring three years in succession and won the Sports Car World Championship in 1959.

The success of the Aston Martin operation was brought about by John Wyer and David Brown's meticulous choice of personnel: designers, engineers, mechanics, team personnel and racing drivers, all true professionals, and with the incomparable Stirling Moss as lead driver the full potential of the cars and team organization was ably demonstrated. (There was no room for poseurs in David Brown's équipe.)

Before the 3-litre formula for World Championship events was brought into being in 1958 Aston Martin, because of their policy of racing with engines comparable to their production road car, restricted engine size to 3 litres and on some of the faster circuits such as Le Mans we had a hard time competing against Maserati, Ferrari and Jaguar who were using larger capacity engines. Notwithstanding this handicap Aston Martin finished second in both the 1955 and 1956 Le Mans races which, to my mind, was as great an achievement as winning

the 1959 race, which of course was restricted to the 3-litre formula. Also, on the slower circuits of Europe Astons won a great many international races against larger capacity cars by virtue of their vastly superior roadholding and brakes.

In the course of its history the Aston Martin Company has been through difficult times but, because of the illustrious name, has found saviours: initially with David Brown and more recently the combination of Victor Gauntlett and Peter Livanos who now, together with the Ford Motor Company of America, will ensure the future of this great marque.

John Wyer's contribution to the success of Aston Martin cannot be overstated, it did not stop at the development of the successful competition cars. Not only was Aston Martin one of the best organized of racing teams (and John's book on the subject, *Motor Racing Management*, is now a classic), but in addition he created a team spirit second to none, a happy atmosphere and an informal club to which it was a privilege to belong; he resolved problems within the team with a firm but paternal hand, and in post-race celebrations he enjoyed himself as much as any of the drivers. During his years running the Aston Martin, Ford GT40 and Gulf-Porsche teams he made history and earned a reputation that remains unmatched. The name Aston Martin to me reads John Wyer and David Brown and I am indeed proud to have played a role in some of their success.

Roy Salvadori
Monte Carlo
February 1991

Introduction

For me it has been a great pleasure to write this book, refreshing my memories through my own records, the people I have talked to and the authorities which I have relied upon. Above all I have relied on the *Aston Martin Register*, published by the Aston Martin Owners Club biannually. The 'bible' has expanded my own records (which I have kept, as an enthusiast for Aston Martin, Jaguar and Lotus, since the 1950s), corrected errors for me and, on occasion, convinced me that I am right and that the Register is wrong. As a member of the AMOC and eternally grateful for the efforts of Jane Archer, Neil Murray, Jim Young and Alan Archer, I resent deeply those writers (including some distinguished names) who cheerfully pillage this work of research without so much as a brief acknowledgement. In this context I would add that while I have referred freely to chassis numbers, I have not referred to engine numbers of competition cars, and seekers after fuller information should refer to the Register.

I have always been a great admirer of John Wyer and David (now Sir David) Brown and their achievements. Wyer's *Motor Racing Management* (published by The Bodley Head in 1956) is a superb motor-racing book. It has become almost customary to denigrate the efforts of Brown and Wyer, accusing them of muddled thinking, bad planning, ill-conceived projects and concentrating on minor at the expense of major events.

From the very early post-war DB2, that so cleverly combined the Lagonda 2.6-litre twin-cam engine with features of the Claude Hill-designed Aston Martin 'Atom', there followed a succession of ever-improving sports-racing cars. In a manner that was totally logical for a company with, by international standards, very modest resources, the von Eberhorst-designed DB3 was evolved into the much more competitive DB3S; during its four-year life as a works competition car, the DB3S itself was developed and substantially modified and followed by the space-frame DBR1 that won at the Nürburgring three years in succession, at Le Mans in 1959 and the 1959 Sports Car World Championship. If Aston Martin competed in minor races at Silverstone, Goodwood and Charterhall and missed major international events, there was a tight budget to consider, and the continual duels between Aston Martin and Jaguar brought great publicity at a British National level.

The truly great mistake, but not folly, was the Lagonda V12, which suffered a major design fault, rarely ran well and developed lower power than ever anticipated. The idea to build an advanced and charismatic V12 to rival Ferrari in sports car racing and to power a luxurious Lagonda was a not unreasonable ambition. It was a great sadness that once so much money had been expended on the initial design and construction of the V12 there were no funds for a redesign. The adaptation of the revised 1955 Lagonda chassis for the DBR2s of 1957 was an inspired idea and the DBR2s were cheap to build, and in their battles with the Lister-Jaguars brought Aston Martin great publicity, even if they were never fully developed. However much David Brown wanted Aston Martin to be the dominant team in sports car racing, everything depended on the sale of production cars, and a win with a 3.7-litre 'special' in a minor race at Silverstone had a better effect on sales than a failure at Sebring or in the Targa Florio.

Aston Martin's real error lay in their approach to Formula 1. After dithering for a number of years, the team completed a Formula 1 car in late 1957, decided to miss the 1958 season and raced the cars in 1959. The mistakes were many. It was a mistake to miss a season and lose any competitive edge, it was a mistake to detract from the 1959 sports car programme in order to run Formula 1 cars, it was a weakness not to get the cars sorted more quickly and it was a blunder to continue the Formula 1 programme in 1960. David Brown was racing for his own satisfaction and fulfillment and most of his mistakes he could well afford. The Formula 1 programme was a blunder in a different league, but one much easier to appreciate with hindsight than it was at the time.

In Appendix 3 I have listed the racing histories of individual competition Aston Martins. Of especial interest to me was to follow the fortunes of competition Aston Martins in the second-hand market (together, in particular, with Jaguar, Lotus and certain specialist road cars). An afternoon's cycle ride (later a trip at the wheel of venerable Sunbeam-Talbot) could encompass

Cooper at Surbiton, Anthony Crook's Bristol showroom (initially at Esher, later at Hersham), AC Cars at Thames Ditton, Alta at Tolworth and HWM at Walton-on-Thames. Other regular trips were to Lotus at Tottenham Lane, Hornsey, Performance Cars on the Great West Road at Brentford and, later, The Chequered Flag in the Chiswick High Road and the Chequered Flag (Competition Cars) at Edgware. Regular visits to Silverstone Club meetings also helped the enthusiast keep abreast of car movements. Cars often remained on the showroom floor for many months. There was little demand for an obsolete DB3, an ex-works DB3S flogged round the Club circuits (and probably badly maintained) by a private owner or even an immaculate low-mileage production DB3S that was not suitable for either competition or road use. Well-healed, far-sighted enthusiasts were few and far between.

Anthony Pritchard
Ruislip
May 1991

1   DB1 and DB2, 1948–52

David Brown acquired Aston Martin after he had read an advertisement in *The Times* in late 1946. For the sum of £20,000 he obtained the prototype 'Atom' car, some rather ancient machinery, rented premises at Feltham and the services of designer Claude Hill. The sum paid was substantial and the purchase was no bargain. Shortly afterwards he purchased the rights to the Lagonda name, the new design with 6-cylinder twin overhead camshaft engine which was the work of 'Willie' Watson under the overall supervision of Lagonda Chief Engineer W. O. Bentley, five prototypes and the machinery, but not Lagonda's premises, which had been sold separately. Accordingly all the Lagonda material was moved into hangars formerly occupied by the Hanworth Flying Club at Hanworth Air Park, Feltham. The Hanworth Air Park premises remained the home of the competition department throughout its long history and was only finally vacated in 1964.

No immediate decision to run a works sports car team was made by David Brown, and initially the company concentrated on development of the 'Atom'. In 1948 Hill asked Brown whether he would consent to the construction of a car to compete in the Spa 24 Hours race in July. David Brown agreed with reluctance, for he considered that the race was too close, a matter of a few weeks, for that job to be done adequately, and that the 1970cc (82.55 x 92mm) 4-cylinder push-rod Aston Martin engine, said to develop 90 bhp at 4750 rpm, was insufficiently powerful. The Spa car featured the 'Atom' engine in tuned form (it may have developed as much as 95 bhp), David Brown 4-speed gearbox, the same square-section tubular chassis, coil spring front suspension with short trailing arms (and a transverse torsion bar) and, at the rear, coil springs and a rigid axle located by a Panhard rod and parallel linkages. The body was a stark two/four-seater with cycle wings. At Spa the car was driven by Leslie Johnson and St John Horsfall. The team also used in practice a light blue DB1 that had been completed in a frantic rush.

The entry of 39 cars was a very mixed bag that included the 2-litre Tipo 166 Ferrari of Chinetti/ Lord Selsdon, the 3-litre Delages of Louveau/ Gérard and Breyre/Transenter and a trio of 3.6-litre Delahayes, Metcalfe's 8-litre Bentley and, in the touring class, works entries from the Czechoslovakian Skoda and Jawa factories. Much of the race was run in wet weather; the Ferrari led for 4½ hours before retiring and much of the faster opposition crashed. The race had started at 4 pm on the Saturday and by 9 am on the Sunday morning Horsfall/Johnson headed the field and stayed in front to score a remarkable victory. Of the works Aston Martin in this race, *Motor Sport*'s 'Spa Correspondent' wrote: 'The winning Aston Martin was most impressive to watch, and the suspension was so soft that it moved as the driver climbed out of the cockpit. It ran complete with silencer and was indeed quiet. A three-sided aircraft-type aero screen was used, complete with diminutive windscreen wiper. J. Eason Gibson presided over the pit work and signals.' By any standard it was a remarkable and unexpected victory and did much to influence David Brown with regard to the team's future competition activities.

Originally numbered SPA/48/1, the 24 Hours winner became LMA/48/1 and was rebuilt by the 1948 London Motor Show as the 'Spa Replica', but no further examples were built, mainly because of the high price of £1998 plus purchase tax. Also at Earls Court was the 'Two Litre Sports', first seen in practice at Spa and the first post-war production car, based on the 'Atom' and with a very curving body designed by Frank Feeley. Fourteen of these cars were built and they were retrospectively typed the DB1.

DB2, 1949

By late 1948 David Brown had decided that all future Aston Martins would be powered by the Lagonda 2.3-litre engine. Claude Hill was more than a little upset at this decision because he was working on a 6-cylinder version of the 'Atom' engine. Brown and Hill argued furiously and Hill decided to leave the company.

The cars raced by Aston Martin in 1949 were very much interim models between the DB1 and the DB2 and prototypes for the DB2, so they are normally regarded as prototypes in the DB2 series. The chassis was very similar to that of the DB1, but the wheelbase was reduced to 8ft 3in from 9ft 0in. Frank Feeley designed a new two-seater body

At Le Mans in 1949 the 1970cc DB2 of Mathieson and Maréchal laps the DB1 of Lawrie/Parker, a private entry which finished 11th. *(Geoffrey Goddard)*

of classic lines that, modified and improved over the years, remained in production at Aston Martin until 1958. Two of the cars constructed, LMA/49/1 and LMA/49/2, retained the 4-cylinder 1980cc engine, whilst the third, LML/49/3, was fitted with the 6-cylinder Lagonda engine, now enlarged to 2580cc (78 x 90mm); with two SU carburettors, power output was said to be 116 bhp at 5000 rpm. They were painted matt green.

Only two races were entered that year and once again John Eason Gibson was team manager. The first race was the first post-war Le Mans 24 Hours event in which the cars were driven by T. A. S. O. Mathieson/P. Maréchal (LMA/49/1), A. Jones/N. Haines (LMA/49/2) and L. Johnson/C. Brackenbury (LML/49/3). It proved a disastrous race for the team; the 6-cylinder car retired after only six laps because of water pump failure and LMA/49/1 was crashed by Pierre Maréchal at White House on the Sunday morning – the car rolled, Maréchal suffered severe injuries and died the following day. Maréchal's car had been running without brakes for a very considerable period. The surviving car of Jones/Haines took seventh place at an average of 72.52 mph, but had lost over an hour in the pits because of starter motor problems. The race was won by the Ferrari of Chinetti/Lord Selsdon.

After Le Mans it appears that LMA/49/1 was scrapped and only the surviving two cars were entered in the Spa 24 Hours race, LMA/49/2 for Lance Macklin/Nick Haines and LML/49/3 for Leslie Johnson/Charles Brackenbury. A pre-war 2-litre Speed Model was also entered by St John Horsfall for himself and Paul Frère. Although the Aston Martins ran well, they were never in contention for the lead and, with a different Ferrari from the one that had won at Le Mans, Chinetti/Lucas were the winners from Louveau/ Mouche (Delage 3-litre). Johnson/Brackenbury finished third (second in the 4000cc class), whilst Macklin/Haines took fifth place (third in the 2000cc class). It was rather humiliating for the David Brown team that Horsfall, driving solo, finished fourth overall (second in the 2000cc class).

DB2, 1950

For 1950 David Brown decided to put the DB2 into production, as well as re-launching the Lagonda, and the DB2 was exhibited at the New York Motor Show in April. The lines of the car had been 'cleaned up' but initially production cars retained three front grilles as on the DB1 and side grilles. Early in the year David Brown had asked John Wyer, formerly of Sunbeam, Solex and the famous Monaco Motors in Watford, to run the works team and the initial agreement was for one year only. Wyer's first and prime task was the Le Mans entry.

A 1949 car, LML/49/4, which had been used for works development purposes, was made available to Lance Macklin with works support early in the year. Macklin competed on 26 March in the Inter-Europa Cup at Monza. This was run as two two-hour events, one for sports cars and one for touring cars. Macklin led the sports class for some while, but eventually finished second to Consalvo Sanesi's Alfa Romeo 2500. After the race a *Concours d'Élegance* was held for finishers and this the Aston Martin won. Macklin stayed in Italy to compete in the Targa Florio on 2 April, but crashed into a ravine.

For the 1950 Le Mans race Wyer prepared three cars, LML/50/7 (VMF 63), LML/50/8 (VMF 64) and LML/50/9 (VMF 65), and these were in fact the first three production cars. All three cars had the early LB6E 2.6-litre engine with SU 1¾in carburettors and the only modifications were a

moderately raised compression ratio and twin-exhaust system. Other changes included a larger 32-gallon fuel tank, larger battery, quick-action radiator fuel filler flaps flush with the roof (on the 1949 cars the fillers protruded above the roof) and another flap in the bonnet with a quick-action filler for a tank in the bulkhead holding a reserve of one gallon of oil released to the sump as needed. Power output was 125 bhp at 5000 rpm. Al-fin brake drums were fitted. The cars were now finished in a polished dark green, and all sound-proofing and the interior trim were removed. The team also took to Le Mans with them LML/49/3 (UMC 66), the 1949 6-cylinder team car. Macklin, Brackenbury, Abecassis, Fairman, Parnell and Thompson had been signed up as drivers.

The cars were driven to the race on the road, and not far south of Rouen Jack Fairman crashed LML/50/9. Fairman's pregnant wife was in the car, suffered injuries and had to be taken to hospital. LML/50/9 was too badly damaged to

Another view of LMA/49/1 which Maréchal crashed with fatal results later in the race. This was the only fatality in the long racing history of the David Brown team. *(Geoffrey Goddard)*

In 1950 David Brown entered Le Mans for the second time and this DB2, LML/50/8, driven by Macklin/Abecassis finished fourth overall, won the 3000cc class and, more importantly, the Index of Performance. *(Geoffrey Goddard)*

race, so LML/49/3 was substituted and John Gordon was brought into the team, as it was thought that Fairman was in no state of mind to race. Although Thompson/Gordon retired after eight laps because of a broken crankshaft, the other two cars enjoyed relatively trouble-free races to finish fifth (Macklin/Abecassis, first in the 3000cc class and first in the Index of Performance), and sixth (Brackenbury/Parnell, second in the 3000cc class and third in the Index of Performance). Macklin/Abecassis, much the faster pair, had been delayed for a short while

Raymond Sommer at the wheel of DB2, LML/50/8, finished tenth overall in the Production sports car race at Silverstone in August 1950 and was second in the 3000cc class. Rather embarrassingly the Aston Martins were beaten by Duncan Hamilton's very well-driven Healey Silverstone. Sommer was a superb driver – note the beautiful balance of his four-wheel drift.
(Guy Griffiths)

In the 1950 Tourist Trophy on the Dundrod circuit in Northern Ireland, Reg Parnell with LML/50/7 finished fourth overall and won the 3000cc class. *(Geoffrey Goddard)*

because of a sticking throttle. Talbots took the first two places ahead of an Allard and Nash-Healey. Following the Le Mans success Wyer joined Aston Martin permanently as Chief Development Engineer.

On 20 August the three 1950 works cars ran in the One-Hour Production Car Race for cars over 2 litres at the International Trophy meeting at Silverstone. Because Macklin had injured a foot, his place in the team was taken by veteran French driver Raymond Sommer and the other DB2s were driven by Parnell and Thompson. Overall the race was dominated by works-entered Jaguar XK120s and the Aston Martins were pipped in the 3-litre class by Duncan Hamilton, driving superbly with a Healey Silverstone. The Aston drivers finished tenth (Sommer with LML/50/8, second in the 3-litre class), 12th (Parnell with LML/50/7, third in the 3-litre class) and 15th (Thompson with LML/50/9, fourth in the 3-litre class).

That the DB2s were simply not fast enough became evident once more in the Tourist Trophy run on the Dundrod circuit in Northern Ireland on 16 September in torrential rain and a gale. The results of this 3-hour race were decided on the basis of target lap speeds and Stirling Moss

with Tom Wisdom's Jaguar XK120 was the winner on both the road and on the handicap calculated on a percentage basis. The three DB2s finished as follows:

4th, General category, 4th on handicap, 1st in 3-litre class, R. Parnell (LML/50/7), 72.72 mph (95.93 per cent)
5th General category, 5th on handicap, 2nd in 3-litre class, G. Abecassis (LML/50/9), 72.38 mph (95.49 per cent)
7th General category, 8th on handicap, 3rd in 3-litre class, L. Macklin (LML/50/8), 71.78 mph (94.69 per cent).

The following Saturday the works Aston Martins competed in the Shelsley Walsh hill climb, in which they ran in the 1501–3000cc class for Production Cars. Frazer Nash Le Mans Replicas took the first three places in the class followed by the DB2s of Parnell (LML/50/7, 48.07 sec), Abecassis (LML/50/9, 48.73 sec) and Brackenbury (LML/50/8, 50.46 sec). Anthony Crook's Frazer Nash team won the Team Award (Production Cars), although the *Aston Martin Register* suggests otherwise.

The final outing by the works in 1950 was at Montlhéry, just before the London Motor Show,

Another view of the 1950 Tourist Trophy with Macklin (LML/50/8) leading an Allard J2 and Abecassis (LML/50/9). *(Geoffrey Goddard)*

results and in November engaged former Auto Union and ERA designer Professor Robert Eberan von Eberhorst to join Aston Martin to design a true sports-racing car, but the appearance of this would be some way in the future.

DB2, 1951

Because the planned DB3 sports-racing car was taking so long to develop, Wyer, despite opposition from von Eberhorst, built two lightweight DB2s, so that there would be something for the team to race and to keep his staff occupied during 1951. It should be added that, as deliveries of the DB2 to private buyers did not start until 1951, there were still very good reasons to attract publicity for the model through racing.

The two new cars were LML/50/50 (XMC 76) and LML/50/55 (XMC 77), on which a weight saving of 450 lb was achieved. The chassis were extensively drilled (saving 32 lb), lighter 18-gauge (instead of 16-gauge) alloy was used for the

when LML/49/3, with a team of drivers consisting of René Bouchard, Charles Brackenbury, Lance Macklin and Eric Thompson, made an attack on the 3-litre 24 Hours record. The record attempt was abandoned because of a broken chassis on this very hard-worked car, but the official reason was given as fog, which had threatened to end the attempt.

David Brown was well pleased with the year's

The Aston Martin DB2s during scrutineering for the 1951 Le Mans race. *(Geoffrey Goddard)*

At Le Mans in 1951 DB2s LML/50/50 driven by Parnell/Hampshire (No 24) and LML/50/55 driven by Abecassis/Shawe-Taylor lined up in front of the pits before the start. *(Geoffrey Goddard)*

bodies, the side and rear windows were made in Plexiglas and with an 8.2:1 compression ratio and, initially, running on two SU carburettors, the power output was 128 bhp at 5000 rpm.

In the Mille Miglia at the end of April Tom Wisdom, partnered by Tony Hume, drove LML/50/8, loaned by David Brown and prepared by Aston Martin's Service Department. Wisdom turned in a brilliant performance, finishing 11th overall and winning his class.

Aston Martin first entered the lightweight cars in the Over 2 Litres One-Hour Production Car race at the International Trophy meeting at Silverstone on 5 May. Jaguar XK120s took the first five places, with Rolt's Nash-Healey sixth, but Parnell finished seventh with LML/50/50 and won the 3-litre class at 81.42 mph. The second car was driven by Abecassis, but retired at Woodcote early in the race because of a seized gearbox.

Wyer had built only two lightweight DB2s because he had been hoping that at least one DB3 would be ready for Le Mans. This was not the case

In the race Macklin/Thompson with LML/50/8 finished third overall and won the 3000cc class. *(Geoffrey Goddard)*

and so the team entered the two lightweights, together with LML/50/8. All three cars were now fitted with aluminium cylinder heads, three Weber twin-choke 35 DCO carburettors and developed 138 bhp at 5500 rpm. In addition two private DB2s were entered at Le Mans.

Le Mans provided a magnificent British triumph, for the new Jaguar C-type driven by Peter Walker/Peter Whitehead won the race, while the Aston Martins finished in the first three places in their class and a Jowett Jupiter won the 1500cc class. Lance Macklin/Eric Thompson with LML/50/8 were third overall (fourth in the Index of Performance), George Abecassis/Brian Shawe-Taylor with LML/50/50 were fifth overall (sixth in the Index of Performance) and Reg Parnell/David Hampshire were seventh overall (ninth in the Index of Performance). The Aston Martins enjoyed a totally trouble-free race. The private cars of Nigel Mann/Mortimer Morris Goodall (LML/50/59) and Peter Clark/Jack Scott (LML/50/57) finished 19th and 22nd overall.

The DB3 eventually appeared in the Tourist Trophy at Dundrod on 15 September, but the team also entered the two lightweight DB2s, back on SU carburettors. The race was now run as a scratch event and the works C-type Jaguars of Stirling Moss and Peter Walker took the first two places. Both the DB3, driven by Macklin, and LML/50/55, driven by Abecassis, retired (the DB2's retirement was caused by clutch failure), but Brian Shawe-Taylor drove LML/50/50 into seventh place overall and second in the 3000cc class behind Baird's Ferrari. Eric Thompson drove LML/50/9, which had been acquired by Rob Walker, into eighth place overall and third in its class.

DB2, 1952

Although Aston Martin's main efforts were concentrated on the DB3 in 1952, the team ran the DB2s in a couple of events. A full team of three cars was prepared for the Mille Miglia, inspired by Wisdom's performance in 1951 and

David Brown supported the Aston Martin Owners' Club meeting at Silverstone in July 1951 by sending along two DB2s for Abecassis and Parnell. *(Guy Griffiths)*

A rare photograph – Geoff Duke at the wheel of Parnell's DB2 in practice for the Prix de Berne in May 1952. In the race Duke with LML/50/55 finished fourth and Parnell with LML/50/50 fifth. *(Geoffrey Goddard)*

Tommy Wisdom with LML/50/50 in the 1953 Mille Miglia. He retired at Ancona with rear axle problems. *(Geoffrey Goddard)*

One of two 1970cc push-rod cars, LMA49/2, was sold to P.B. Whitehouse and raced by him during 1951. It is seen in the 2-litre Production Sports Car race at Silverstone in May 1951. *(T.C. March)*

reconnaissance in strength'. Abecassis retired LML/50/55 because of clutch problems (Abecassis seems to have been rather hard on the clutches of the cars he drove), but the other two drivers performed magnificently. Tom Wisdom, again partnered by Hume, finished 12th overall with LML/50/8 and won the over 2000cc Touring class, whilst Reg Parnell, partnered by Gerboli, was 13th overall and second in class. The race was won by Bracco (Ferrari) from the Mercedes-Benz 300SL of Kling.

Later that month, on 18 May, the team fielded two cars in the Prix de Berne, the sports car race accompanying the Swiss Grand Prix. Geoff Duke, newcomer to the team, finished fourth with LML/50/55 behind a trio of works Mercedes-Benz 300SL cars and Parnell finished fifth. Remarkably, the same day Duke won the 350cc Swiss Motor Cycle Grand Prix on a Norton.

At Le Mans, the privately entered DB2 of Peter Clark/Mike Keen (LML/50/57) finished seventh overall and third in its class.

Postscript

There was only one works entry with a DB2 in 1953, Tom Wisdom with LML/50/55 in the Mille Miglia, but that year he was out of luck and retired at Ancona because of rear axle failure. Private owners had raced and continued to race DB2s with success in minor events, but a private owner was destined to achieve another major success with the DB2. Lyndon Sims, partnered by J. Ambrose, with LML/50/X2 scored a magnificent victory in the 1956 RAC British Rally. This was one of five very late cars 'additional to the Production sanction'.

Lyndon Sims partnered by John Ambrose drove this DB2 to victory in the 1956 RAC Rally of Great Britain. *(John Ross)*

2 DB3: 1951–53

Von Eberhorst's brief at Aston Martin was to design a sports-racing car using the existing LMB 2.6-litre twin overhead camshaft engine and a David Brown 5-speed gearbox. The DB3, as the new model was designated, was to prove an inadequate car for a number of reasons, quite apart from the fact that its development was protracted. The concept was insufficiently advanced, the DB3 was too heavy and the engine insufficiently powerful for the DB3 to be truly competitive.

The basis of the DB3 was a ladder-type, substantially braced chassis constructed from 16-gauge 4-in. tubes. Chassis weight was 141 lb. At the front, suspension was by trailing links and transverse torsion bars, while at the rear there was a de Dion rear axle; the de Dion tube, constructed from three steel sections welded into one, was located by a Panhard rod and parallel links that connected with the suspension and acted as torque members. The upper rubber-bushed parallel links were symmetrical, but of the lower links, that on the nearside was at a greater distance from the upper components. Each lower link engaged by serrations with a transverse torsion bar. The two torsion bars were mounted parallel, one above the other. Armstrong double-piston-type dampers were fitted. Al-fin brake drums were fitted front and rear (13in. front and 11in. rear), with those at the rear mounted inboard. The wheels were wire-spoked with Rudge Whitworth-type knock-off hubs. The wheelbase was 7ft 9in., and front and rear track 4ft 3in. The simple aluminium-panelled body with the lines of a touring car, rather than an out-

Lance Macklin at the wheel of the prototype DB3 in the 1951 Tourist Trophy at Dundrod. He retired because of engine problems. *(LAT)*

The date of this testing session at MIRA is unknown, but it is believed to be in 1951 after the DB3 was first raced. The team was trying to resolve a final drive problem. The track was waterlogged and driver George Abecassis's expression sums up the misery of that day. When the car was first tested at MIRA before the Tourist Trophy it was unpainted and the bonnet scoop was a later addition. *(Guy Griffiths)*

and-out sports-racer, looked very much like an open version of the DB2, but with a 'portcullis' radiator grille.

As first raced, the 2.6-litre DB3 was fitted with three Weber 35 DCO carburettors and developed 133 bhp at 5500 rpm, which was totally inadequate. Transmission was by a single-plate Borg & Beck clutch to the special David Brown S527 gearbox with overdrive top gear and synchromesh on the upper four ratios. Overall length was 13ft 2.5in. and dry weight 2010 lb.

1951

After Wyer had hoped in vain that the DB3 would be ready for Le Mans, the first car, DB3/1, was tested in primer at MIRA by Lance Macklin. Apart from twitchy handling, all seemed well and Macklin drove the car in the Tourist Trophy on the Dundrod circuit in Northern Ireland. Both at MIRA and Dundrod Macklin was handicapped by a broken toe, the result of an accident on his motor launch. Because, apparently, of a strike at the Aston Martin works, the DB3 arrived in Northern Ireland still in primer, but before the race it was given a hasty paint job. Macklin was

timed at 113 mph over the flying kilometre (compared with the 125.8 mph of the fastest Jaguar C-type driven by Peter Walker) and held fifth place before making a pit stop because of a trailing exhaust pipe. The DB3 eventually retired because of what was said at the time to be 'a broken exhaust system'. Onlookers in the pits, however, noted that the exhaust note was unchanged. The real reason was that an oil leak had caused run bearings. It was a problem easily rectified for 1952. In this race only the DB3 ran with an experimental aluminium cylinder head.

1952

Over the winter four more DB3s were completed, DB3/2, which was built for David Brown's personal use, and DB3/3, DB3/4 and DB3/5, which were in effect the Le Mans team cars. Changes to the car were few, but Weber 36 DCFS carburettors were adopted, a few more bhp were gained during the year, the gearbox was now the S527S with a lower overdrive top (0.885:1 compared with the 0.83:1 of the S527), and there were louvres in the front wings to help dissipate under-bonnet heat and a bonnet-top air-scoop for the carburettors. Team drivers included Abecassis, Peter Collins (newcomer to the team and a member of the HWM Formula 2 team), Geoff Duke (World Motorcycle Champion), Pat Griffith (another newcomer and an HRG and Lester driver), Macklin, Parnell, Dennis Poore and Thompson.

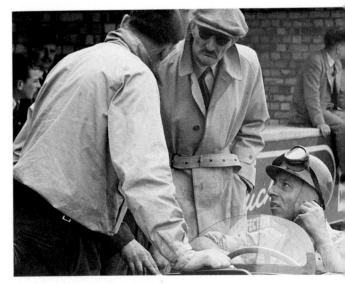

At Silverstone in May 1952, Abecassis reports to Wyer (left) and von Eberhorst (centre). *(Guy Griffiths)*

Partly because the team ran DB2s in two races, it was a limited season of racing with the DB3s. The sports-racers first appeared in the Production Sports Car race at the International Trophy meeting at Silverstone in May. A team of four cars was entered. The race was won by Moss (works C-type Jaguar), but of the other two Jaguar entries, Walker dropped back because of a pit stop and Rolt retired because of a broken drive-shaft. Parnell (DB3/3), Abecassis (DB3/4) and Macklin (DB3/5) finished second, third and fourth, took first three places in the 3000cc class and won the team prize. Macklin had been badly delayed because his engine refused to fire at the Le Mans start. DB3/1 was driven by Duke, but he went off at Stowe Corner on oil dropped all over the track when Mayers's Lester-MG blew up its engine, rejoined the race and retired at the pits with deranged steering.

After the DB2s had run in the Prix de Berne, DB3/1 was dispatched to the Isle of Man for Geoff Duke to drive in the handicap British Empire Trophy race. Duke knew the circuit intimately and, in one of his few inspired drives with a car, came through to take the lead on the road and had real prospects of a win on handicap as well. Sadly, Duke's run came to an end when the crankshaft broke.

In 1952 the Monaco Grand Prix was held as a 195-mile sports car race (it had last-been held as a Formula 1 race in 1950). Aston Martin entered three DB3s, all with the engine enlarged to 2922cc (83 x 90mm) and developing 147 bhp at 5000 rpm. Because each pair of bores on the LB6 engine was siamized, enlarging the engine was a major problem, but 'Willie' Watson had overcome this by increasing the bores eccentrically so that the centre-lines of each bore were moved further

In the Silverstone race Macklin drove DB3/5 into fourth place overall and third in the 3000cc class behind winner Stirling Moss (Jaguar C-type) and team-mates Parnell and Abecassis. *(Guy Griffiths)*

At the end of May, Geoff Duke drove DB3/1, the sole Aston Martin entered, in the British Empire Trophy on the Isle of Man. He drove very well, but retired because of a broken crankshaft. *(Geoffrey Goddard)*

With the help of the Manx constabulary Duke pushes the DB3/1 away after the engine broke. *(Geoffrey Goddard)*

apart. Von Eberhorst off-set the connecting rod on the gudgeon pin to overcome the problem that the centre-lines of the bores were no longer in line with the centre-line of the crankpin. The cars were driven by Parnell (DB3/3), Peter Collins (DB3/4, his first drive for the team) and Macklin (DB3/5). The race was led by Moss (works C-type Jaguar), whilst the three Astons were overheating and constantly stopping at the pits to take on more water.

On lap 24 Manzon (Gordini) overtook Moss and what happened next was brilliantly and lucidly described in *Autosport*: 'Reg Parnell's engine emitted great clouds of smoke and he came to rest at Ste Devote corner. Realizing that he was partially blocking the road, he manhandled [the car] to a space between the straw bales. The marshalling was pathetic, and no one attempted to warn approaching cars. A waiter from a nearby restaurant rushed out and began to wave a tablecloth and the crowd in the tribune gesticulated with programmes.

'Fuel leaking from Mascarenha's Allard had softened the tar, causing the corners to be extremely slippery. Parnell shouted to officials to help him get the Aston Martin further off the road, but they insisted that a crane was required. Reg said a few rude words, and lifted the tail of the Aston.

'At that moment Stagnoli (Ferrari) spun round on the soft tar and hit the Aston Martin. Manzon, approaching at high speed, dodged the Ferrari, but also crashed into Parnell's car, and Moss, right on his tail, did likewise. Tony Hulme (Allard) also became mixed up in the mêlée, and there were five cars littering the corner. Parnell was pinned against a straw bale and suffered a severely bruised leg, whilst Hulme damaged his hand.' Moss rejoined the race, which was won by Vittorio Marzotto's Ferrari, but was disqualified.

The cause of Parnell's engine failure was a broken crank-pin, which resulted in broken connecting rods. The same problem affected both Macklin and Collins, but the latter finished seventh, eight laps in arrears, as his engine did not break until after he had crossed the finishing line.

John Wyer's immediate problem was that the three cars raced at Monaco were the Le Mans entries and he had intended them to be driven on to the Sarthe circuit. The crashed DB3/3 was dispatched by train for repair at the premises of coachbuilder Henri Chapron in Paris, two production engines were flown to Nice in Brown's executive de Havilland Dove, so that the other two cars could be driven to Le Mans, and DB3/1, now fitted with a coupé top incorporating a rear 'hatch', and competition 2.6-litre engines were dispatched from Feltham to Le Mans. More

At Le Mans in 1952 Parnell/Thompson drove DB3/1 with coupé bodywork (incorporating a 'hatch' round the back window, a feature later adopted on the production DB2/4). Unfortunately DB3/1 retired after only ten laps because of final drive failure. *(Geoffrey Goddard)*

problems followed at Le Mans when Pat Griffith crashed DB3/4 during the first day's practice. An urgent telephone call to Paris ensured that repairs to DB3/3 were completed overnight, although this meant that the car featured a much stumpier tail and it was substituted, contrary to the race regulations, for the damaged car.

The Le Mans race proved yet another débâcle, for all three Aston Martins retired with failure of the hypoid bevel final drive, a bad batch with a higher ratio used at Le Mans only. The first retirement, after only ten laps, was Parnell (driving the DB3/1 coupé with Thompson) and this was soon followed by the Poore/Griffith DB3/3. The third car, driven by Macklin/Collins (DB3/5), ran swiftly and reliably and was holding fourth place after 20 hours when it too retired with the same problem.

John Wyer has commented, 'We then sent two 2.6-litre cars to Jersey and Boreham, really to

gain more experience with the hypoid gears and satisfy ourselves that we'd overcome that problem.' Both, however, were important British races and for Aston Martin *not* to have entered would have been remarkable. For all entries after Le Mans the team used the S430/6SR 4-speed gearbox with second and third mainshaft gears running on needle rollers.

The Jersey Road Race, run for the fifth and last time ever, was held on the 3.2-mile St Helier road circuit in two 10-lap heats and a 20-lap final. In the first heat Abecassis (DB3/4) finished third in his heat behind Ian Stewart (Ecurie Ecosse C-type Jaguar) and Ken Wharton (Frazer Nash Le Mans Replica). Parnell (DB3/5) had a stiff fight with Dobson's XK120 Jaguar in the second heat, eventually getting ahead to finish second to Oscar Moore's HWM-Jaguar. Oscar Moore retired in the final and the order was Stewart, Wharton, Abecassis, Parnell.

In the same race Poore/Griffith drove DBR3/3 with abbreviated rear tail, but they retired after 31 laps with water pump failure. This was the car driven by Parnell at Monaco, hastily repaired by Chapron in Paris. No 6 is the Talbot of Chambas/Morel. *(Geoffrey Goddard)*

At Boreham at the beginning of August an International meeting was sponsored by the *Daily Mail* and the programme included 102-mile races for sports cars up to 2000cc and over 2000cc. The larger-capacity race was divided into classes for cars up to and over 3000cc. The race was won by Stirling Moss (works C-type Jaguar), with Duncan Hamilton (private C-type) in second place. Parnell (DB3/5) drove a strong race to finish third overall, winning the 3000cc class and defeating a brace of Tipo 225 2.7-litre Ferraris driven by Roy Salvadori and Tom Cole. Abecassis with DB3/4 had held second place in the class until slowed by a blocked fuel filler and this resulted in his retirement.

Aston Martin's last race of the year, on 16 August, was the Goodwood 9 Hours, the first in the short-lived series, starting at 3 pm and finishing at midnight. The 'bob-tail' DB3/3, driven by Parnell/Thompson, was powered by the 2922cc engine, but this had been modified by using connecting rods with offset big-ends and no

At Boreham, at the beginning of August 1952, Parnell drove DB3/5 and won the 3000cc class of the sports car race, finishing third overall. *(LAT)*

further problems with the bottom end of the engine were experienced. Power output of the 3-litre engine, running on three Weber 35 DCO carburettors, was now 163 bhp at 5500 rpm. DB3/4 (Abecassis/Poore) and DB3/5 (Collins/Griffith) retained the 2.6-litre engines in what was the now standard 141 bhp form. The main opposition came from a strong team of works C-type Jaguars and the private 2.7-litre Ferraris of Baird/Salvadori and Cole/Graham Whitehead.

The race started on a wet track, which gave the Aston Martins a decided advantage and at the end of the first hour Parnell led from Rolt (works Jaguar), Abecassis, Moss (works Jaguar), Baird and Peter Whitehead (works Jaguar). As the track dried out, the Jaguars moved into the first three places, but Whitehead crashed his C-type, Parnell/Thompson held third place and Baird/Salvadori were in fourth place ahead of the other two works Aston Martins. Disaster struck for Aston Martin just after 6 pm. The Parnell/Thompson DB3 had been lapping with smoke pouring from the rear end (it was in fact caused by a leaking oil seal). When the car stopped to refuel, Wyer and mechanic Jack Sopp pulled up the seats to investigate. Fred Lawn was refilling the fuel tank from churns and spilt a good quantity of the last churn; the fuel ran down the tail, on to the rear undertray and was ignited by hot oil. The DB3 became enveloped in columns of flame and black smoke, both Wyer and Sopp were badly burned and Lawn rather less so. All three were rushed to hospital, and Parnell took control of the Aston Martin pit. Shortly afterwards Poore came in for a routine refuelling stop, complaining that he had lost all gears except top. Abecassis took over, but the starter jammed. This was freed by the mechanics and then Abecassis found that he could not even engage top gear. Eventually he forced the lever in and the car staggered away. This DB3 fell right out of contention and eventually retired because of clutch failure.

Behind the two leading Jaguars came the surviving Aston Martin of Collins/Griffith, and Salvadori/Baird moved up into fourth place with their Ferrari. The Rolt/Hamilton Jaguar retired because of a broken half-shaft, the Moss/Walker Jaguar lost a lot of time in the pits while the rear suspension A-bracket mounting was changed, and by this stage Salvadori/Baird led from Collins/Griffith. Despite everything, however, it was to be Aston Martin's lucky day. When

Salvadori made a routine pit stop with the Ferrari to hand over to Baird, who was to drive for one lap only, the battery was completely dead. After a change of battery the car rejoined the race, its one-lap lead turned into three-lap deficiency. At the finish Collins/Griffith crossed the line in first place. Tom Cole/Graham Whitehead finished second, two laps in arrears and Salvadori/Baird, after a magnificent chase of the leaders by Salvadori, finished third, five laps in arrears. It was Salvadori's drive at Goodwood that led John Wyer to invite him to join the Aston Martin team in 1953.

On 30 August Abecassis drove DB3/4 at Shelsley Walsh Hill climb, recording 42.28 sec to finish second to Wharton's Frazer Nash in the 3000cc Production Sports car class.

So far as David Brown was concerned, the 1952 season had been disastrous. Apart from mechanical calamities, the cars were very much down on power – and this was to plague Aston Martin throughout the team's racing history. John Wyer has written: 'Throughout the fifties we were keeping pace with Jaguar – there was very little to choose in bhp between their engine and ours – but we always had the disadvantage of half-a-litre ...' Unfortunately this is not supported by the facts:

	bhp/litre
Jaguar C-type (3442cc, 200 bhp approx, 2072 lb dry)	58.11
Mercedes-Benz 300SL (2996cc, 175 bhp approx, 1918 lb dry)	58.41
Aston Martin DB3 (2922cc, 163 bhp approx, 2012 lb dry)	55.78

Whilst he was still in hospital following the Goodwood fire, Wyer was asked by David Brown to propose a racing programme for 1953 and the result was the decision to run in most rounds of the Sports Car World Championship. Perhaps more important was 'Willie' Watson's plan for a more compact and lighter version of the DB3 to become the DB3S, which was taken on board by both John Wyer and David Brown and was to lead to the departure of von Eberhorst.

During 1952 the DB3 was announced as being available as a production car at a price, inclusive of purchase tax, of £3700, and a number were ordered for the 1953 season by private entrants who were of course unaware of the projected DB3S. DB3/2 became a works car, while Aston Martin completed DB3/6 for Tom Dickson, DB3/7 (with a distinctive coupé body) was sold to Tom Meyer, DB3/8 to former Connaught driver Ken Downing, DB3/9 to New Zealand driver Tony Gaze and DB3/10 to Graham Whitehead, the most successful of this largely unsuccessful band of privateers. More details of these cars are contained in Appendix 3.

1953

Because of Aston Martin's preoccupation with the DB3S, there were no major changes to the DB3 for the 1953 season. There were few changes in team drivers, although Roy Salvadori was invited to join the team before Le Mans and Abecassis left to drive his own HWM team's Jaguar-powered sports-racing car. Geoff Duke again made a couple

of appearances early in the year, but soon left to concentrate on motorcycle racing. Two cars plus a spare were taken to the Sebring 12 Hours race, the first round in the newly inaugurated Sports Car World Championship. DB3/5 was entered for Parnell/Abecassis and DB3/4 for Collins/Duke. Collins soon built up a good lead ahead of John Fitch (Chrysler-powered Cunningham) and Parnell. Parnell had made a poor start and, trying too hard to make up ground, slid on a patch of oil, hit a marker barrel and wrecked the nearside headlamp. More time was lost in the pits whilst the headlamp was changed. Collins stopped to hand over to Duke, who collided with a Jaguar XK120 and the damage was so bad that DB3/4 had to be withdrawn. Collins was thoroughly disgusted by what he regarded as his team-mate's inept performance. Parnell/Abecassis dogged the wheel-tracks of the Cunningham for the remainder of this race, but were never able to get in front and had to settle for second place, a lap in arrears.

At the end of April, Aston Martin made a serious attempt at winning the Mille Miglia with

The team of DB3 cars being loaded at the docks for shipping to the 1953 Sebring 12 Hours race. *(Geoffrey Goddard)*

Peter Collins with DB3/4 in the 1953 Mille Miglia; he finished 16th. *(Geoffrey Goddard)*

a three-car entry for Parnell (DB3/3), Collins (DB3/4) and Abecassis (DB3/5). John Wyer criticized himself for concentrating the team's efforts on learning the more difficult, slower parts of the circuit at the expense of the faster, but Aston Martin lacked the time and resources for a full-scale attack on the race and after ten days' practice came closer to winning this, the greatest of all road races, than any other British team. A supercharged DB3 was used during practice. Reg Parnell, partnered by photographer Louis Klementaski, finished a magnificent fifth, despite a broken mounting for the Panhard rod which, at Florence, seemed sufficiently bad for Wyer to want to withdraw the car. Later the throttle cable broke and he rewired it so that he could drive the car on full throttle with control only through the ignition switch. It was probably the best drive in

Parnell's long career. *Autosport* commented: 'This effort on Reg's part puts him well up in the class of the world's best drivers, particularly in view of the fact that it is accepted in Italy that a driver needs to cover the course under racing conditions at least three times before getting in the first ten places.' Peter Collins was partnered by Mike Keen and finished 17th with a very battered car. Abecassis was never in contention and crashed near Florence because of a loose steering rack.

At the International Trophy meeting at Silverstone the following month Aston Martin contested as usual the Production Sports Car race with entries for Duke (DB3/2), Parnell (DB3/3), and Collins (DB3/4). The wide latitude of interpretation of 'production' is indicated by the fact that accepted entries included Ferrari 340 MM, Kieft and Cooper. Moss was off form with his works C-type Jaguar after a practice crash and the race was won by Mike Hawthorn with a Vignale-bodied Ferrari 340 MM 4.1-litre works entry. Parnell (whose horn was operating from time to time without the driver's intervention) and Collins finished second and third and took the first two places in the 3000cc class. Geoff Duke retired with clutch failure and it was to be his last race appearance with a car until he raced a Gemini Formula Junior car some six years later.

Although this was the last works outing with DB3s, two of the cars were loaned by the works to Dennis Poore (DB3/3) and Eric Thompson (DB3/1) to drive at the Bristol MC & LCC meeting at Thruxton on Whit Monday. Poore finished third behind Jimmy Stewart and Ian Stewart (both with Ecurie Ecosse C-type Jaguars) in a 10-lap unlimited capacity sports car race. Poore and Thompson (followed across the line by Downing's DB3) took the first two places in a race for sports cars up to 3000cc and Poore also finished third in an unlimited capacity racing car event. Already, however, the DB3S had made its début at Charterhall the previous Saturday and the DB3 was yesterday's car.

3   DB3S: 1953

Although Aston Martin continued to race the DB3 in the early part of 1953, over the winter of 1952–3 designer W. G. Watson had been working on a new car that was to prove lighter, smaller, with better aerodynamics and much neater than the DB3 and was to pave the way for the team's first international successes. Watson carried out all the preliminary work on his own initiative and when he presented his proposals for the new car to John Wyer, he by-passed von Eberhorst. Wyer was enthusiastic about the new project; he persuaded von Eberhorst that the team needed a lighter car, that it should not be regarded as a criticism of the original DB3 design and, for a short while won von Eberhorst round to supporting the new project with guarded enthusiasm. Because so much of the new car was based on the DB3, the design – and the construction – moved swiftly by Aston Martin standards and the team was able to use the DB3 in most of 1953's races.

Watson had evolved a completely new and lighter chassis frame, with wheelbase reduced from 7ft 9in. to 7ft 3in. (and this resulted in a degree of 'skittishness' in the handling of the DB3S), and based on two 16-gauge chrome molybdenum steel tubular side members of 4in. diameter (instead of the 14-gauge of the DB3). There were three tubular cross-members in 14-gauge steel (instead of 12-gauge), with those at the front and rear of 5in. diameter and the centre member of 4in. diameter. The track was reduced to 4ft 1in. front and rear. In side view the main members of the chassis were cranked upwards towards the front, which had the effect of reducing the overall height. Attached to the outsides of the front cross-member were flanges which formed the attachment points for the housings carrying the lower arms of the front suspension, and platforms welded to the top of the front cross-member formed the attachment points for the front suspension dampers (the arms of these formed the top suspension links).

At the front the suspension was the same as that of the DB3, by trailing links and torsion bars, but there was a new layout at the rear. On the de Dion rear suspension of the DB3 von Eberhorst had used a Panhard rod to provide transverse location of the wheels. On bumpy roads, especially, this had caused snaking at high speeds and so Watson had devised a system whereby transverse location was provided by a central sliding block operating in mild steel guide plates bolted to the light alloy final drive casing. The basic suspension, by transverse torsion bars and parallel trailing links, was unchanged.

The rack-and-pinion steering was as on the DB3, as were the Girling drum brakes, initially outboard at the front and inboard at the rear, with 13in. Al-fin drums at the front and 11in. at the rear. The engine, developing 182 bhp at 5500 rpm, and the 4-speed David Brown S430/12 gearbox were exactly as used in the DB3. However, the very heavy Salisbury hypoid bevel final drive had been replaced by a David Brown spiral bevel final drive with light alloy casing.

Likewise the cooling system was unchanged, save that the header tank had been moved to the right-hand side of the bulkhead, the pipe from the cylinder head ran to this (instead of to the radiator in the nose as on the DB3) and a further pipe from the header tank ran to the top of the radiator.

The most dramatic and obvious change was the adoption on the DB3S of the superbly stylish bodywork with very rounded lines, dominated by an enormous 'egg-box' intake, and designed by Frank Feeley. Superb though this bodywork was, it failed to achieve the classic status of the rival D-type Jaguar, simply because over the years there were many detailed styling changes that transformed the impact of the lines, albeit without altering the basic shape.

DB3S was tested at Chalgrove airfield, the usual testing venue used by the team, and after the Mille Miglia the team travelled on to Monza, where the DB3S was driven by Peter Collins. Wyer was well satisfied with the Monza tests, for lap speeds were comfortably faster than those achieved there with the DB3 the previous December.

Wyer chose a quiet début for the new car and entered DB3S/1 (already registered YMY 307) with Reg Parnell at the wheel at Charterhall, an airfield circuit near Berwick-on-Tweed on 23 May. In the unlimited capacity sports car race Parnell chased hard after Ninian Sanderson's Ecurie Ecosse-entered C-type Jaguar and slipped into the lead on the 13th lap of this 15-lap race. The DB3S won by the narrowest of margins. It was later discovered that the Jaguar had a cracked brake drum.

By the Le Mans 24 Hours race, Aston Martin had ready a team of three newly built, but largely untested, DB3S cars, which were entered as follows:

R. Parnell/P. J. Collins (DB3S/2) with red-painted intake and red lights in the sides of the tail;
G. Abecassis/R. F. Salvadori (DB3S/3) with blue-painted intake and blue lights in the sides of the tail;
R. D. Poore/E. Thompson (DB3S/4) with yellow-painted intake and yellow lights in the sides of the tail.

All three cars were fitted with inspection panels so that fuel level could be monitored during refuelling and they ran without tonneaux and with twin spot lamps mounted on a bar across the nose. DB3S/1 was at the race, mainly to provide spare parts if needed. Pat Griffith was reserve driver. This was Salvadori's first race for Aston Martin in a career with the team that was to last until 1963. It was also the first year that the Aston Martin team stayed at the Hotel de France at La Chartre-sur-le-Loir to the south of Le Mans. It was a hotel that Wyer used throughout the remainder of his racing career. The writer stayed at the hotel with the Gulf-Porsche team for the 1970 Le Mans race; the hotel provided every facility for the team, with plenty of working space in the adjoining garage, excellent cuisine in a special dining area and, after night practice, an exceptional meal to the best 'Michelin' standards, despite the lateness of the hour.

1953 was the year when the entries at Le Mans were at their strongest. In addition to the works C-type Jaguars that finished first, second and fourth, there were strong teams from Alfa Romeo (with three of the 3.6-litre Colli-bodies coupés), Ferrari (two 4.1-litre coupés and a 4.5-litre), Lancia (a trio of 2.6-litre supercharged D20 coupés), Cunningham (one of whose cars finished third), Nash-Healey and Allard.

The Astons were outclassed so far as outright victory was concerned, and the best that the team could hope for was a class win. Despite the instructions of John Wyer, Abecassis and Parnell roared away from the start, trying to beat each other and mix it with the leaders. It was all pretty stupid and the result was that Parnell crashed at Tertre Rouge on lap 17 and Abecassis cooked the

rather weak single-plate clutch of his car so badly that co-driver Salvadori completed only a few laps before retiring because of bad clutch slip. The more reasonably driven DB3S of Poore/Thompson, holding 14th place, was eliminated on the Sunday morning by valve trouble.

All in all, a very disappointing outing for the new cars, but Aston Martin won every race entered during the remainder of the year.

John Wyer has written that Parnell was so upset after his crash at Le Mans that he asked if he could race the spare DB3S/1 in the British Empire Trophy to be held on the Douglas, Isle of Man, circuit the following Thursday with practice on the Tuesday and Wednesday. Unfortunately, John Wyer's memory was at fault, for in Autosport for 12 June, 1953 (published before the Le Mans race), Parnell and an Aston Martin are listed as entries in the Manx race.

In any event Parnell left La Chartre very early on the Monday morning and, after the Channel crossing, collected mechanic Eric Hind at the Feltham works and carried on with DB3S/1 to Liverpool, where they caught the Isle of Man ferry. Apart from Moss with a works C-type Jaguar, the opposition in the Unlimited class (cars over 2600cc) included Hans Ruesch (author of the motor racing novel, The Racers) with his private 4.1-litre Ferrari and Jimmy Stewart and Ninian Sanderson with Ecurie Ecosse C-types.

On both the Tuesday and Wednesday Parnell set fastest lap, but while the car was being driven back to the team's garage on the Wednesday by Eric Hind a drive-shaft broke. John Wyer, who had arrived on the Island that day, was unable to contact anyone at Feltham to bring over a spare and it was not until his wife telephoned him late in the evening that anything could be done. Mechanic Richard Green went to the works, removed a drive-shaft from one of the Le Mans cars, drove to Liverpool and then flew to the Isle of Man, where the car was repaired in time to start the race. Parnell convincingly won his 8-lap heat from Moss, Ruesch, Sanderson and Stewart and set fastest lap.

In the 16-lap final there were 28 starters, with the smallest cars having a three-minute start, the cars up to 2600cc a minute's start and the larger-capacity cars on scratch. The grid was, of course, arranged with the slowest cars at the front, and Parnell started from the ninth row. Over this appallingly difficult and dangerous 3.897-mile circuit he handled the DB3S with élan and took

Reg Parnell on his way to victory with DB3S/1 in the 1953 British Empire Trophy race in the Isle of Man.

the lead from Ken Wharton's Frazer Nash on lap 12. Wharton finished second, Ruesch third (after a stirring drive with a difficult car) and Moss was fourth. Parnell's average of 73.96 mph was 3.43 mph faster than the lap record set by Geoff Duke with a DB3 in 1952 and he raised the lap record to 75.48 mph. Interestingly, at this race, Parnell covered several demonstration laps with the V16 BRM, but they were all slower than his lap record with the DB3S.

Twice a year the Astons and the Jaguars (the latter sometimes with works entries, sometimes only with Ecurie Ecosse cars) would meet in confrontation at Silverstone, in May at the International Trophy meeting and in July at the British Grand Prix meeting. In July 1953 Aston Martin entered Reg Parnell (DB3S/4), Roy Salvadori (DB3S/3) and Peter Collins (DB3S/2). Salvadori was surprised, as the most junior member of the 'club', to be asked to drive at Silverstone in the place of more experienced team members. Wyer had recognized the fire in his belly and his sheer determination and when Salvadori queried his selection, he merely commented that

he had offered him the drive and that it was up to him whether or not he accepted it. In this race the main opposition came from Tony Rolt with XKC 052 (the fourth-place car at Le Mans), the Ecurie Ecosse C-types of Ian and Jimmy Stewart and Sanderson, the Cunninghams of Cunningham himself and Walters and Bill Spear with a Cunningham-entered Ferrari.

Parnell was fastest in practice and, at the Le Mans start, led away from Rolt. After three hard-fought laps Rolt went into the lead at Copse, Parnell went ahead again on lap 8 and Rolt, reconciled to second place, was forced to retire on lap 21 because of piston failure. Salvadori slipped ahead of Collins at Stowe and the Aston Martins took the first three places in this 102-mile race ahead of Bill Spear with Cunningham's 4.1-litre Ferrari and the C-type Jaguars of Ian and Jimmy Stewart. It was a fine victory for the David Brown team, whose DB3S cars handled much better than their Coventry rivals, but Jaguar had made their habitual mistake of not taking the race seriously enough and entering only one works car.

Reg Parnell at the wheel of the winning car (DB3S/2), which he drove to victory with Eric Thompson in the Goodwood 9 Hours race in 1953. *(Autocar)*

On 15 August Reg Parnell was again entered with DB3S/1 at Charterhall. The day proved wet and at the Le Mans start of the 20-lap unlimited sports car race Parnell was last away as the door of the DB3S would not open. Parnell fought his way through to take the lead and win at 72.07 mph, with the Ecurie Ecosse Jaguars of Ian and Jimmy

Parnell with DB3S/1 fought his way though the field to win the unlimited capacity sports car race at Charterhall in August from the C-type Jaguars of Ian and Jimmy Stewart. *(LAT)*

Stewart in second and third places. The Aston Martin driver also set fastest lap at 73.77 mph.

The 9 Hours race was held at Goodwood for the second time in 1953 and the team fielded cars for Parnell/Thompson (DB3S/2), Salvadori/Poore (DB3S/3) and Collins/Griffith (DB3S/4). As at Le Mans the cars had spotlights mounted on a bar across the air intake and they were now fitted with metal tonneau covers.

The main opposition came from a full team of Jaguars, the disc-braked Le Mans cars, driven by Moss/Walker, Rolt/Hamilton and Peter Whitehead/ Ian Stewart.

The initial order in the race was Jaguar (Moss) – Jaguar (Rolt) – HWM (Abecassis) – Jaguar (Stewart) – Aston Martin (Collins). Salvadori made an early stop because he was unhappy with the steering of his DBS, and he retired before 4.30 pm because of a holed crankcase. The 2.4-mile Goodwood circuit was notoriously hard on tyres and brakes and the Jaguars (on Dunlop tyres) and the Astons (on Avon tyres) averaged only 55 miles between wheel changes. As the race progressed, the Moss/Walker and Rolt/Hamilton C-types seemed firmly entrenched in the lead with Parnell/Thompson third and Collins/Griffith fourth. Both Parnell and Griffith suffered burst tyres, at the front and rear respectively, and Collins/Griffith fell back to fifth place behind the Jaguar of Whitehead/Stewart.

During the hours of darkness the disc brakes of

To advertise in the motoring 'weeklies' was the standard practice of both Aston Martin and Jaguar as a means of publicizing their competition successes. This advertisement was placed by Mintex, suppliers of brake linings to the David Brown team, to celebrate their success at the July Silverstone meeting. Advertising space had to be booked well before races and this led to some ludicrous advertising when the cars failed.

The start of the sports car race at Silverstone in July 1953 with the DB3S of Reg Parnell leading the C-type Jaguars of Tony Rolt (works car) and Ian Stewart (Ecurie Ecosse). *(Geoffrey Goddard)*

the works C-types were glowing cherry red and, with one hour to go, disaster struck the seemingly invincible Coventry team. At 10.57 Hamilton stopped at the pits to top up with oil, a few minutes later Walker brought the leading Jaguar into the pits to retire because of a broken con-rod and a bare minute later Hamilton was back in the pits to retire with no oil pressure. During the last hour of the race Eric Thompson cruised to victory and Pat Griffith was sped up by the Aston pit to take second place ahead of Whitehead/Stewart, whose C-type was suffering from overheated brakes and plummeting oil pressure. It was a fine victory for the David Brown team, albeit against purely British opposition.

Only a fortnight later Aston Martin and Jaguar met up again in the 823-mile Tourist Trophy in the Dundrod circuit. Although the race was a round in the newly inaugurated Sports Car World Championship, the only foreign entries were the two 745cc DBs entered by Ecurie Jeudy-Bonnet. Aston Martin entered cars for Parnell/Thompson (DB3S/2), Salvadori/Poore (DB3S/3) and Collins/Griffith (DB3S/4). The Parnell/Thompson entry was fitted with outboard rear brakes. From Jaguar there were three disc-braked C-types, driven by Rolt/Hamilton, Moss/Walker and Peter Whitehead/Ian Stewart.

Dundrod consisted of 7 miles 732 yards of undulating, winding and narrow public roads closed for the race, and its difficulties were worsened by a recently laid and very abrasive surface. As a result the Jaguars managed only about 50 miles on a set of tyres and the Astons fared little better. Salvadori freely conceded that he hated the circuit, and on his three appearances there performed well below his usual standard. In contrast Collins and co-driver Griffith loved Dundrod and revelled in its twists and turns and bumps.

In practice Collins and Moss both lapped in 5 min 2 sec and, unless Moss had speed in hand, which seemed unlikely, the outcome was almost a foregone conclusion. The race was run on a handicap basis, with the Jaguars having to cover one more lap than the Astons, and as the C-types were consuming tyres at an even higher rate than their Feltham rivals, it seemed highly improbable that they could make up the extra lap. In this race the Jaguars were to be beaten fair and square by their smaller-capacity rivals, but it was a circuit that suited the Astons' handling characteristics and gave no advantage to Jaguar's extra power.

The start was postponed from 9 am until 10.30 because of mist on the course. Early in the race the Jaguar team was reduced to a single car, for the C-types of Rolt/Hamilton and Whitehead/Stewart were both eliminated by gearbox trouble. On lap 38 Poore crashed his DB3S heavily, cutting an eye, at Tornagrough, about three-quarters of

Pit stop for Reg Parnell with DB3S/2 in the Goodwood 9 Hours race. *(Geoffrey Goddard)*

Pat Griffith at the wheel of the winning DB3S/4, which he shared with Peter Collins in the 1953 Tourist Trophy. *(Geoffrey Goddard)*

In the Tourist Trophy on the Dundrod circuit in Northern Ireland Aston Martin defeated the Jaguar team and took the first two places. This is the second-place DB3S/2 driven by Parnell/Thompson, seen in the thick mist that enveloped the circuit in the early stages of the race. *(Geoffrey Goddard)*

the way round the circuit. Poore, whose eyesight was not the best, was trying to pass Wharton (Frazer Nash), but Ken Wharton, a relentless, absolutely determined and ungiving driver, was a contender for the lead on handicap and was not prepared to yield an inch of road; there was nowhere for Poore to go, except into the bank.

Moss and Walker were leading on the road, but only gaining marginally on handicap. By 4.30 pm, after six hours' racing, Parnell/Thompson led Moss/Walker and Collins/Griffith with the Frazer Nash of Wharton/Robb in fourth place. Two hours later Collins/Griffith led on handicap and on the road, Collins lapped Moss and when the Aston and the Jaguar made their last pit stops, eight laps before the finish, Collins quickly rejoined the race, while Moss was very slow away. After only four more laps Moss stopped just short of the finishing line to await the chequered flag – the problem was the same gearbox trouble that had eliminated the other two Coventry entries. Collins/Griffith and Parnell/Thompson took the first two places and both had covered 111 laps, while Wharton/Robb were third with 110 laps completed and Moss/Walker with 107 laps were classified fourth.

Reg Parnell with DB3S/1 on his way to a win at Castle Combe in October 1953. *(LAT)*

DUNDROD

This map and gradient diagram reveal the difficulties of the Dundrod road circuit.

The following Saturday the Aston Martin Owners' Club organized a race meeting at Snetterton and as was David Brown's practice at AMOC meetings, Aston Martin sent along a works DB3S, the prototype car. What was unusual was that the driver was not a member of the works team, but a young Scotsman, Ron Flockhart, usually seen at the wheel of his ex-Raymond Mays 2-litre supercharged ERA, R4D, and to join the BRM team in 1954. Flockhart finished second overall to Abecassis' HWM-Jaguar in the unlimited sports car race (and first in the 3000cc class). He also drove in a Sports Car handicap, but his handicap was too great a burden for him to figure in the results.

In *Autosport* for 26 March, 1954, Flockhart wrote in an article, *The Cars I Drove in 1953*, of his impressions of the DB3S, 'My first impression in taking the car out in practice was that, despite the fact that the DB3S is light, small and powerful as sports cars go, it did not have the same sharp "zip" as a racing single-seater. This impression did not wear off either – perhaps I have become too familiar with the 350–400 bhp/ton performance of the D Type ERA. However, I was very impressed, indeed, by the cornering ability and the ease with which the car could be drifted. Handling and steering generally were completely free from vices. The engine revved smoothly up to its maximum 6000 rpm and gave that solid feeling of being unburstable. The gearbox was quite easy to manipulate, but I felt that brake pressure was too high to enable a heel-and-toe change to be done with any finesse. John Wyer, the Aston Martin team manager and development engineer, explained, however, that experience had show that the only way to achieve braking in long-distance events was to select a hard lining with a lower coefficient of friction, but requiring high pedal pressures. My only other criticisms of the car were that the cockpit became unduly warm, and – a purely personal point – there wasn't enough room for my legs!'

'. . . The Aston Martin is a very fine motor car and, like the ERA, gives a feeling of breeding, which, of course, it should.'

DB3S/1 made further appearance in 1953, at the National meeting at the 1.84-mile Castle Combe circuit on October. The driver was Reg Parnell and he won the 10-lap race for sports cars over 1500cc from Salvadori (Maserati A6GCS 2-litre) and Graham Whitehead (Aston Martin DB3), as well as setting a class lap record of 83.01 mph.

For the David Brown team, 1953 marked an important transitional year. The DB3S was a significant improvement on its predecessor and likely to prove a serious contender in the 3000cc class. Except on the more tortuous circuits it was not a serious challenger for outright victory in endurance racing. In the main the team had concentrated on British events throughout the year and after a poor start achieved a good measure of success. The following year a vastly over-ambitious racing programme was to result in almost complete failure.

4 DB3S and Lagonda: 1954

The first Championship race was the Buenos Aires 1000 Kms, a round in the Sports Car World Championship held on 24 January on a circuit that combined one of the circuits at the Autodrome with a section of the *Autostrada* ringing Buenos Aires. Because the fuel used in this race was 100/130 octane 'Avgas', the DB3S entries ran on a higher compression ratio of 9.4:1 and developed 194 bhp at 5500 rpm. Outboard rear brakes had been adopted on all the team cars and the brakes were fitted with automatic adjusters intended to compensate for lining wear and drum expansion. The three cars were driven by Parnell/Salvadori (DB3S/2), Collins/Griffith (DB3S/4) and local drivers Roberto Mieres/Tomasi (DBS/3). In addition the team brought along DB3/1, which had been sold to British resident Eric Forrest Greene and was to be driven by him and Stabile. The opposition included a works 4.5-litre Ferrari (Farina/Maglioli), a 2.5-litre Gordoni (Behra/Bayol) and Ecurie Ecosse's full team of 1953 ex-works C-type Jaguars. At this stage in its development the DB3S was barely a match for the previous year's Jaguars. One of the Wyer's worries about the DB3S was the weakness of the distributor drive-shaft, and during wet practice Salvadori flogged round and round the circuit as a test of the reliability of this component.

Ferraris took the first two places, with the 4.5-litre of Farina/Maglioli winning from the 3-litre

Reg Parnell with DB3S/2 passes the pits in the 1954 Sebring 12 Hours race. He retired after 22 laps because of a broken con-rod. *(Geoffrey Goddard)*

private car of de Portago/Schell. After a race characterized by steady lap times and efficient pit work, Collins/Griffith finished third ahead of the C-type Jaguar of Scott-Douglas/Sanderson. The Mieres/Tomasi car retired early in the race because of final drive failure and the distributor drive-shaft that had not broken during extended practice broke in the race on the Parnell/Salvadori car. Forrest Greene overturned his DB3 and suffered burns from which he died the following day. A remarkable performance was that of Carroll Shelby, who drove solo and finished tenth with his Allard-Cadillac. It was this drive that persuaded Wyer to include him in the Aston Martin team at Sebring.

It had been decided not to return to Feltham before the Sebring 12 Hours race in March and the cars were shipped direct to Florida. They were reverted to 'standard' 182 bhp form for this race, and whilst the driver pairings for two of the cars were as at Buenos Aires, DB3S/3 was driven by Shelby/Chuck Wallace. Lancia had entered a strong team of their D24 V6 3.3-litre cars and Briggs Cunningham entered both a 5.4-litre Cunningham and a 4.5-litre Ferrari. The Aston Martin team was never able to challenge for the lead and was soon out of contention. On lap 22 a con-rod broke on Parnell's car out on the circuit and Reg pushed the DB3S all the way back to the pits. For this he was awarded 'Man of the Race', but as Salvadori has pointed out, Parnell had greater mechanical knowledge than any other Aston Martin driver and so he should have known that the car could not be repaired. Sebring was notoriously hard on both tyres and brakes and on both the remaining DB3S entries the

Here, after his retirement, a far from happy Collins has been looking at the faulty brakes of the DB3S.

automatic adjusters, which had worked well at Buenos Aires, stripped the linings from the brake shoes and overheated the hub assemblies. The Lancias dominated much of the race, but they too had major problems and the race was won by Briggs Cunningham's 1500cc Osca driven by Moss/Lloyd from the Lancia of Rubirosa/Valenzano and the disc-braked Austin-Healey of Macklin/Huntoon (believed to be the only car left in the race with effective brakes).

Aston Martin returned to Feltham to prepare two entries for the Mille Miglia, DB3S/2 for Parnell/Klementaski and DB3S/4 for Collins/Griffith. Following their performance in 1953, the team believed that it had a very strong chance of winning. John Wyer has commented that the cars were fitted with the best single-plug engines ever built by Aston Martin (said to develop 190 bhp, were very carefully prepared, and the details

Peter Collins at the wheel of DB3S/4 in the early stages of the Sebring 12 Hours race.

included full-width perspex screens). The cars were fitted with tyres of sufficiently hard compound to run through the race without change, and although Wyer accepted these from Avon without complaint at the time, he always believed that it was because of Avon that the team failed to win. Using two of the lightweight DB2 coupés, Aston Martin spent three weeks training for the race and the drivers started with a good knowledge of the circuit. As usual there was an immensely strong Ferrari entry and Lancia fielded four of the 3.3-litre D24s.

Throughout the race the roads were in poor condition after a hard winter and the weather conditions were constantly changing from rain, fog and overcast conditions to hot sunshine. In these conditions the large-capacity Ferraris proved complete handfuls and several crashed. Collins moved up to fifth place with Parnell not far behind, but at Popoli (south-west of Pescara), Parnell spun on loose gravel deposited on the road after an earlier crash and wrecked the DB3S thoroughly. In *Motor Sport* Denis Jenkinson wrote, 'Parnell . . . smashed his Aston Martin completely when he ran off the road on a fast bend near Popoli. Neither he, nor his passenger, Klementaski, were hurt, but the left front wheel and suspension were torn from the chassis, engine crankcase and gearbox shells were split and the chassis broken; in fact, a write-off.' Collins dropped back to seventh, went off the road and damaged the car thoroughly. He limped into Florence to retire with only the prop-shaft resting on a cross-member keeping the engine in place. The race was won by Alberto Ascari (Lancia), who was able to cruise to the finish from Vittorio Marzotto (Ferrari *Mondial* 2-litre) and Luigi Musso (Maserati A6GCS). It seems that Wyer was disillusioned with the Mille Miglia after this race and it was never tackled seriously by Aston Martin again.

Two weeks later the team was out in force at the *Daily Express*-sponsored International Trophy meeting at Silverstone with four entries in the sports car race, three of which were new cars, intended to lead the Aston Martin attack at Le Mans.

Since 'Willie' Watson had joined David Brown in 1952 his main task had been the design of a new V12 engine which it was hoped would be capable of beating the Ferrari opposition and could also be used to power a new range of luxury cars. His brief also included following closely the general design features of the existing LB6 engine. Accordingly the new engine featured a similar barrel-type (aluminium instead of cast iron) crankcase and diaphragm main bearings (but seven instead of four bearings). The usual 60-degree cylinder layout was adopted, there were twin overhead camshafts per bank of cylinders, capacity was 4486cc (82.5 x 69.8mm), there were hemispherical combustion chambers, twin-plug ignition, dry sump lubrication and four Weber IF4C four-choke carburettors. Because of the use of wet liners, engine capacity could be increased to 5 litres. On an 8.5:1 compression ratio initial power output was 280 bhp at 6000 rpm. Although it was hoped that 350 bhp at 7500 rpm would eventually be achieved, the maximum ever developed was 312 bhp (as installed in the car raced by Parnell at Silverstone in July 1954). By comparison the 1953 V12 4.5-litre Tipo 375 MM Ferrari was said to develop 340 bhp at 6500 rpm.

Apart from the power deficiency problem, the Lagonda engine suffered from a fundamental design fault. Because the crankcase and the diaphragms carrying the main bearings were in the same metal, they expanded at the same rate, with the result that clearances remained constant throughout the engine heat range, the engine failed to seal and oil pressure dropped rapidly. This problem was bodged by building the engines with minimum bearing clearance, which meant that the engines refused to fire on cold days. Accordingly it became the practice to fill the radiator with hot water before firing up. The tragedy was that the team could not afford a redesign and a very real opportunity to develop a world beating range of competition and high-performance road cars was lost.

Although the Lagonda was bigger than the DB3S, the chassis was substantially the same. The wheelbase was increased to 8ft 4in., the chassis side-members had a diameter of 5in. and the cross-members of 4in. Suspension at the front was by trailing links and torsion bars. Transmission was initially by the same S430/12 4-speed gearbox used in the DB3S, but by Le Mans the S532 5-speed gearbox with overdrive top gear had been substituted. There was a David Brown spiral bevel final drive with open articulated drive-shafts. The body looked like a larger version of the DB3S, but with three separate air intakes. By Le Mans a one-piece grille had been substituted. Weight with oil and water was 2513 lb.

At the May Silverstone meeting the team ran the new fixed head coupés for the first time. This is DB3S/6 driven by Roy Salvadori. *(Geoffrey Goddard)*

As if a portent for the future, when the first car, DP115/1, was tested at Chalgrove shortly before Silverstone it caught fire whilst David Brown was at the wheel. The damage was not serious and was quickly repaired. The team soon realized that the Lagonda was a lost cause, but it was not abandoned until after Le Mans in 1955.

Three other new developments were seen at Silverstone. Aston Martin now had ready the A1. 60-degree twin-plug cylinder head and with three Weber 45 DCO carburettors power output was now 225 bhp at 6000 rpm, enough to make the cars really competitive. In late 1953 DB3S/5 had been completed as a road car for David Brown and at Silverstone the team ran two new cars, DB3S/6 and DB3S/7, both fitted with gloriously styled fixed head coupé bodies, incorporating vestigial tail fins in the rear wings and developed using Vickers wind-tunnel facilities. Unfortunately the

cars had not been adequately high-speed tested on the road. In addition the team entered DB3S/1 at Silverstone, fitted experimentally with Lockheed disc brakes at the front.

The Silverstone race was run in the wet. Gonzalez with the 4.9-litre Ferrari scored an easy win and the David Brown team was trounced. Behind the Argentinian the order was George Abecassis (HWM-Jaguar), Peter Walker (Ecurie Ecosse C-type Jaguar), Jimmy Stewart (Ecurie Ecosse C-type Jaguar), and the rumbling, ill-handling Lagonda. 'Lots of work to be done before Le Mans,' commented Reg as he climbed out of the cockpit. Sixth place was taken by Duncan Hamilton (Jaguar C-type) ahead of Salvadori (DB3S/6) and Collins (DB3S/1) with Graham Whitehead (DB3S/7) back in 12th place. Aston Martin's only consolation was that they had taken first three places in the 3000cc class.

The sports car race at Silverstone was run in torrential rain and Graham Whitehead seen here with DB3S/7 finished 12th. *(T. C. March)*

A magnificent view of the Lagonda that gives a superb impression of its sheer bulk. *(Geoffrey Goddard)*

The V12 Lagonda made its début at Silverstone in May.
Reg Parnell drove DP115/1 into fifth place.
(Geoffrey Goddard)

At Sebring Wyer and Carroll Shelby had struck a deal whereby the Aston Martin works would prepare a DB3S for the Texan to drive at certain races during the European season. Aston Martin prepared DB3S/3 with single-plug head in American white and blue colours. Shelby's first race with the car was at the inaugural event at Aintree (when an anti-clockwise circuit was adopted), and in a close race run in the wet Shelby finished second behind the C-type Jaguar of Duncan Hamilton.

For Le Mans, Aston Martin had made an entry of five cars, which was extending their resources beyond all sensible limits. There were to be two Lagondas, the DB3S coupés and a supercharged DB3S. Only one Lagonda could be made ready in time and the organizers agreed to accept Shelby's DB3S as a substitute. It was said at the time that the blown DB3S was the substitute, but John Wyer has indicated that this was not the case. Of the Lagonda, Denis Jenkinson wrote in *Motor Sport*,

On the first lap at Le Mans the DB3S coupé of Whitehead/Stewart leads the private DB2/4 of Colas/da Silva Ramos, a Maserati A6GCS, the Lagonda and a Gordini. *(Geoffrey Goddard)*

'There is usually some fashion in engine design that a new engine *must* contain, such as two plugs per cylinder, or two overhead camshafts, or one carburettor choke to each cylinder, but never has anyone gone the whole gamut as thoroughly as the Lagonda engineers in producing the new 4½-litre engine. It has everything that current design considers essential, and the resultant bonnet-full of machinery was a sight to please the most hardened motor-racing eyes.' The Lagonda was driven by Thompson/Poore.

The supercharged DB3S/1 was fitted with a Wade supercharger (necessitating a small bulge in the bonnet), a single-plug head, a single Weber 52 DCO carburettor and developed 240 bhp at 6000 rpm on a 7.0:1 compression ratio. Under the supercharged equivalency formula this DB3S was treated as having a capacity of 4091cc. Reg Parnell elected to drive this car, a choice endorsed by John Wyer, because of Parnell's mechanical sympathy, and he was partnered by Roy Salvadori. Of the coupés, DBS3/6 was driven by Peter Collins/'B. Bira' (his only drive with a post-war Aston Martin) and DB3S/7 by Graham Whitehead/Jimmy Stewart. Carroll Shelby was partnered in his white and blue, single-plug DB3S/3 by Paul Frère. At Le Mans all the cars ran with the top part of the air intake blanked off.

The race was won by the 4.9-litre Ferrari 375 *Plus* of Gonzalez/Trintignant by a narrow margin from the new D-type Jaguar of Rolt/Hamilton. For David Brown the race proved a complete disaster. After just two hours' racing Thompson, in ninth place, spun the Lagonda in the Esses in heavy rain, smashing the tail and nearside rear wing, which was pushed on to the tyre. With other cars passing only inches away (the Lagonda was facing against the traffic), Thompson struggled to lever back the panelling from the tyre with the jack handle and a hammer. Eventually he cleared the wing from wheel and toured back to the pits, where the car was retired because of damaged rear lights. Afterwards a sheared steering arm key was discovered, but whether this caused the accident or was caused by it was never established beyond doubt (although the former seems more likely).

Early in the race it had become clear that the DB3S coupés were aerodynamically unstable at speed as well as proving unexpectedly slow. The rear ends were lifting at high speed and the cars were becoming airborne over the hump on the

The Lagonda at the 1954 Le Mans race. The damage was the result of Thompson losing control at the Esses, bouncing from one side of the road to the other and damaging the tail so badly that the car had to be withdrawn. The car may have had a suspension defect. *(Geoffrey Goddard)*

Disastrously unsafe because of their aerodynamic shortcomings, both DB3S coupés crashed badly at Le Mans. This was DB3S/7 driven by Whitehead/Stewart. *(Geoffrey Goddard)*

approach to White House Corner. At 9.30 pm in heavy rain, DB3S/7 with Stewart at the wheel went out of control, slid wildly down the right-hand side of the road, struck a marker stone, bounced on its roof and ricocheted across the track. Stewart was thrown out of the wreckage and suffered bruises and a badly fractured elbow, which was to lead to his retirement from racing. Very close to the same spot on the Sunday morning, 'B. Bira', in fourth place, crashed DB3S/6 and was lucky to escape with minor injuries. As the photographs show, the cars were complete write-offs. The Shelby/Frère DB3S was withdrawn

The wreck of DB3S/6 driven by Collins/'B. Bira' is passed by the Talbot of Blanc/Nercessian. *(Geoffrey Goddard)*

because of a broken stub axle, probably the result of an off-course excursion by Shelby earlier in the race. The longest surviving entry was the supercharged DB3S, which raced on to a little after midday on the Sunday, despite Salvadori ramming a slower car (which he pushed off the road) and necessitating a pit stop for the headlamps to be straightened (they were pointing almost skywards after the accident). The blown Aston Martin was in sixth place when it retired.

On 27 June Shelby ran DB3S/3 with Graham Whitehead as co-driver in the Supercortemaggiore Grand Prix, a race for sports cars up to 3000cc at Monza. The race was Ferrari-dominated, and whilst Ferraris took five out of the first six places, Shelby/Whitehead moved up to finish fifth after the retirement of the 6-cylinder Maserati 250S entered by the works for Fangio/Marimon.

After the carnage of Le Mans, John Wyer considered that the team should withdraw for the remainder of the year, but David Brown disagreed strongly and decided to press on with a full entry in the over 1500cc sports car race at the British Grand Prix meeting at Silverstone in July. The entry consisted of Lagonda DP115/2 (Reg Parnell), DB3S/1 (now restored to normal twin-plug form and driven by Collins), DB3S/5, brought into the works team for Salvadori to drive, and Shelby drove his usual single-plug DB3S/3. Fortunately the opposition was not strong and, in the main, consisted of the Ecurie Ecosse team of C-type Jaguars driven by Rolt, Titterington and Sanderson. Although Rolt led away from the Le Mans start, the race soon settled into a pattern of David Brown domination and the finishing order was Collins, Salvadori, Shelby and Parnell with Archie Scott-Brown's 2-litre Lister-Bristol in fifth position ahead of all the Jaguar opposition. A minor, poorly supported race it may have been, but the team had regained its *amour propre*.

On the Saturday after the British Grand Prix the Aston Martin Owners' Club held its St John Horsfall Trophy meeting at Silverstone and

Longest-surviving David Brown entry at Le Mans was the supercharged DB3S/1 of Parnell/Salvadori, which survived until the Sunday morning before succumbing to a blown gasket. *(Geoffrey Goddard)*

Shelby at Silverstone in July with DB3S/3, sandwiched between the C-type Jaguar of Dunham and the Tojeiro-Bristol of Cliff Davis. Shelby finished third. *(T. C. March)*

David Brown lent his support by entering Shelby's DB3S/3 with Reg Parnell at the wheel. Parnell won the St John Horsfall Trophy race, a scratch event for Aston Martins, and was a member of the winning Aston Martin team in the handicap David Brown Challenge Cup, in which each of the three cars of the team had to complete five laps.

In September Aston Martin competed in the Tourist Trophy on the Dundrod circuit in Northern Ireland, a round in the Sports Car World Championship, but run on a handicap basis. Aston Martin entered DB3S/1 (Parnell/Salvadori), DB3S/2 (Collins/Griffith) and DB3S/3, now restored to a light green colour finish (Poore/Graham Whitehead), all in largely unchanged form. The main opposition on scratch came from Hawthorn/Trintignant (works Ferrari *Monza* 3-litre), a team of D-type Jaguars with roadholding unsuited for this difficult circuit, the usual 3.4-litre car for Rolt/Hamilton and 2482cc cars for Peter Whitehead/Wharton and Moss/Walker, and a team of four Lancias, two of which were the previously unraced 3.8-litre D25 cars. The favourites on handicap were a pair of French 745cc DB cars. Neither Parnell nor Salvadori liked the Dundrod circuit, so they could be disregarded as serious runners, and the team's hopes were pinned on Collins/Griffith.

Throughout the race, and despite the dreadful handling of the *Monza*, Hawthorn/Trintignant led on scratch. On lap 24 Collins retired his DB3S/2 with final drive failure. Parnell/Salvadori kept going, but well out of contention, until lap 63, when Salvadori, on the last lap before handing back to Parnell, misjudged the bend over the railway bridge at Leathemstown, failed to break off his drift early enough and clouted the wall on the inside of the circuit and, when he reached the pits, it was obvious that the car was too badly

At Silverstone Reg Parnell drove the second Lagonda, DP115/2, into fourth place. *(T. C. March)*

damaged to continue. It was something of a blow to Aston Martin, because it had been intended that Collins would take over this DB3S. The surviving car of Poore/Whitehead was plagued by minor problems and finished 13th. On handicap the winner was the DB-Panhard of Laureau/Armagnac from Hawthorn/Trintignant (the winners on scratch), Musso/Mantovani (Maserati A6GCS) and Taruffi/Piodi/Fangio (Lancia D24).

The fastest laps and highest speeds over the flying kilometre of the main contenders make interesting comparison and it was only too clear that the DB3S still needed further development:

	Fastest lap	Highest speed over the flying kilometre
Ferrari *Monza* 3-litre (Hawthorn/Trintignant)	92.39 mph	140.1 mph
Lancia D25 3.8-litre (Ascari/Villoresi)	92.06 mph	144.6 mph
Lancia D24 3.3-litre (Taruffi/Piodi/Fangio)	90.50 mph	141.8 mph
Jaguar D-type 3.4-litre (Rolt/Hamilton)	88.70 mph	137.9 mph
Aston Martin DB3S (Collins/Griffith)	88.70 mph	134.3 mph
Jaguar D-type 2.5-litre (Moss/Walker)	88.40 mph	133.4 mph

The following weekend the Bugatti Owners' Club organized its International hill climb at Prescott in Gloucestershire and both Aston Martin and Jaguar sent along entries. Just before rain began to fall, Poore with DB3S/5 set the best time for sports cars in 47.63 sec (but, after all,

Poore was a former RAC Hill Climb Champion with his Alfa Romeo 8C-308) and equalled the outright sports car record that stood to the credit of Sydney Allard. He would have beaten Allard's record but for a slight misfire as he left the line. Rain had begun to fall by the time Peter Walker went off the line with a works D-type, and with this unsuitable car on an unsuitable course the time is best forgotten.

On 2 October Aston Martin entered a team of three cars in the 17-lap (51-mile) sports car race at Aintree. Masten Gregory won the race with his private white and blue 375 MM 4.5-litre Ferrari, but Collins (DB3S/2) and Parnell (DB3S/1) finished second and third with Salvadori fifth (DB3S/5). Although there were no more works entries in 1954, the team was still active. For the Penya Rhin Grand Prix, the supporting sports car race to the Spanish Grand Prix in October, Graham Whitehead was loaned DB3S/1 and finished sixth.

At the 1954 London Motor Show Aston Martin announced the DB3S as a production car with a price tag of £2600 basic (£3694 9s. 2d. including purchase tax). The company's entry in the Show catalogue was very coy, not mentioning the make of carburettor fitted or any power output. It featured the 'Gothic Arch' body lines to be adopted on the 1955 works cars, but with single-plug cast-iron cylinder head, three twin-choke Solex carburettors, a power output of 180 bhp at 5500 rpm and drum brakes it looked very poor value compared to D-type Jaguar, also announced as a production car, with 250 bhp, disc brakes and a price of £1895 basic (£2685 14s. 2d. including purchase tax).

Although 1954 was probably the least successful year in post-war Aston Martin racing history there is little doubt that the DB3S was a much better car at the end of the year than it had been at the beginning and the team's prospects for 1955 looked good.

5 DB3S and Lagonda, 1955

Before describing Aston Martin's 1955 season, it would be worthwhile reviewing the state of play in sports car racing. The dominant make was to prove Daimler-Benz with the 3-litre straight-eight 300SLR, a direct development of Stuttgart's Formula 1 W.196 car, very complex, with the best all-round performance and superbly prepared with quite outstanding team organization under Alfred Neubauer. Jaguar concentrated on Le Mans and Reims (the latter a non-Championship race) with the D-type, superbly aerodynamic due to the work of Malcolm Sayer, plenty of power from the punchy 6-cylinder engine and the perfect Le Mans contender. Jaguar were well aware of the D-type's limitations and although the team competed at other circuits during the year, very often only a single car was entered and the reliability of these single entries indicated less than the highest standard of preparation and less than the highest level of commitment. In 1955 Ferrari raced very fast but very unreliable 4.4-litre 6-cylinder cars, and it was not to be Ferrari's year.

These were the main contenders for outright victory, but there was a second division of sports-racing cars running in the 3-litre class. Ferrari fielded the 4-cylinder Tipo 750 *Monza* in some events and these 260 bhp ill-handling brutes were also raced by many private entrants. The second Italian factory, Maserati at Modena, raced the 6-cylinder Tipo 300S, developing around 250 bhp at 6500 rpm. These cars were entered by both the works and private owners, but the Maserati competition department was hopelessly overloaded with both experimental work and the preparation of privately owned cars and so the works cars were frequently ill-prepared and unreliable.

It was against these second-division runners that Aston Martin competed in international endurance events, and the team did not achieve its real breakthrough until a 3000cc capacity limit was imposed in the Sports Car World Championship. During 1955–6 Wyer was struggling to achieve increased performance without loss of reliability from a design that was rapidly becoming outdated and at the same time the team was developing its successor, the DBR1 that would not be raced until Le Mans, 1956. During 1955 John Wyer was appointed Technical

Director of Aston Martin and Lagonda with full responsibility for engineering policy.

For 1955 the two coupés, DB3S/6 (now registered 62 EMU) and DB3S/7 (now registered 63 EMU), were rebuilt with open bodywork designed by Frank Feeley and featuring pronounced peaks to the wing line and running down the centre of the body (the so-called 'Gothic Arch' style) and with simple, smaller air intakes with wire-mesh grilles. The lines were very similar to those of the production DB3S. Both DB3S/6 and DB3S/7 were also fitted with ZF differentials, larger Lagonda spiral bevel final drives, Girling 11.5in. disc brakes front and rear and, to accommodate these brakes, Borrani wheels with offset rims. DB3S/5 was retained by the team with its original body, but was fitted with disc brakes.

Both DB3S/1 and DB3S/2 were also rebuilt with new bodies, but with higher rear wings like the 1954 coupés, giving a slight 'tail fin' effect. From the front they could be distinguished by the absence of wire mesh and the prominence of the vertical struts within the air intake openings. These cars retained drum brakes. DB3S/1 was sold to Roy Salvadori (for whom it was entered by Gilby Engineering) and DB3S/2 to Peter Collins, in both cases at very favourable prices. These cars were maintained, so far as major work was concerned, at Feltham and borrowed back by the works when the team was short of cars.

Development work on Lagonda had continued, but plans to run two of the V12 cars in the Mille Miglia were abandoned. It seems that these would have been the 1954 cars, running with modified bodywork. The only Lagonda entry during the year was at Le Mans.

Jocelyn Stevens bought DB3S/3 from the works and raced it along with P.A. Everard (DB3/10) under the banner of 'The Vermin Stable'. Graham Whitehead acquired DB3S/4, sold it quickly and took delivery of production car DB3S/105, but was very disappointed with the performance, and Berwyn Baxter acquired DB3S/101 (it was originally delivered to Ken Wharton, but after racing the car twice he returned it to the works because it was not competitive). Other production cars were supplied to the Australian Kangaroo Stable consisting of David McKay (DB3S/102),

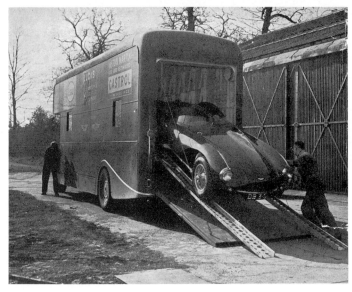

Three views of the AEC Regent III bus chassis with body by Markhams used as a transporter from 1955 onwards by the David Brown team. It could accommodate three cars on two decks. In the lower left photograph a production DB3S is being loaded prior to the Geneva Salon. In the photograph above Peter Collins is at the wheel.

Tom Sulman (DB3S/103) and Les Cosh (DB3S/104) and this team was planning a full European season with the cars.

In January Aston Martin entered three production DB2/4 coupés in the Monte Carlo Rally, at that time the most prestigious of all rallies, attracting an enormous entry and supported by works teams from many British manufacturers. The beautifully prepared Astons were driven by Reg Parnell/Louis Klementaski, Peter Collins/Graham Whitehead and Maurice Gatsonides/Marcel Becquart. The Astons suffered from two handicaps: as runners in the *Grande Tourisme* category they were subject to an 8 per cent handicap, but an even greater handicap were Parnell and Collins, who pressed on without regard to secret controls and amassed a vast number of penalty points. Whilst victory in the

Monte was very much of a lottery, Becquart threw away the chances of a win for himself and Gatsonides by firmly asserting that there would be no control at Annecy, his home town and where he was president of the automobile club. There was a secret control and they were caught by it.

Gatsonides/Becquart finished the road section in 17th place, Collins/Whitehead were way down in 79th place and Parnell/Klementaski were not amongst the top 100 eligible to run in the Speed/Performance test over the Monaco Grand Prix circuit. As a result of their performance in this final test Gatsonides/Becquart clawed their way back to seventh place and won their class. Interestingly, private Aston Martin entrant Hermanos da Silva Ramos set the fastest lap of the rally over the Monaco circuit. In addition, Aston Martin also won the team prize in the

Concours (this meant dragging private owner Van Zijil into the team) and Gatsonides was awarded the RAC Challenge Trophy (Road Safety, Comfort and Overall Rally Performance). The rally itself was won by the privately entered Sunbeam Mk III of Norwegians Malling/Fadum.

To enter the Monte Carlo Rally was something of a distraction from the team's main purpose, but, nevertheless, despite a lack of team discipline, the results were good enough to give a worthwhile boost to the production cars.

On 27 February Graham Whitehead raced DB3S/4 at Agadir, a seaside resort in Morocco, but retired because of final drive problems. The race was won by Mike Sparken (Ferrari). Whitehead also ran at Dakar in Sénégal on 13 March, but without success.

At the British Empire Trophy at Oulton park on 2 April, Aston Martin entered a single car, DB3S/5, for Reg Parnell. This was powered by a twin-plug 2493cc (83 x 76.8mm) engine with 8.4:1

compression ratio, three Weber 42 DCO carburettors and a power output of 214 bhp at 7000 rpm. In addition Salvadori and Collins drove their private cars, Graham Whitehead made a final appearance with DB3S/4 and Wharton drove his production car.

The race was run in three heats and a final, and in the heat for cars up to 2700cc Parnell won from Archie Scott-Brown with the Lister-Bristol. The 3-litre cars did not fare so well in the unlimited capacity heat. This was won by Mike Sparken (Ferrari) from Duncan Hamilton (ex-works Jaguar D-type) with Collins third, Wharton fourth and Whitehead seventh. Salvadori retired on the first lap with throttle problems.

The unlimited heat had been run in heavy rain and it was still raining heavily when the final was run. With the big cars on scratch, the 1500cc cars had a handicap advantage of two laps less 1 min 40 sec and the cars up to 2700cc one lap less 1 min 40 sec. It was obvious that the unlimited

Reg Parnell in the final of the British Empire Trophy race at Oulton Park in April 1955 with the misfiring 2.5-litre DB3S/5. Note the offset rims used with the disc brakes. DB3S/5 was taxed for the road and driven to the circuit – the taxation disc is on the left of the bodywork. *(LAT)*

Peter Collins, driving solo with DB3S/5 in the 1955 Mille Miglia. After delays caused by a puncture, he retired because of a broken con-rod bolt. *(Publifoto)*

The start of the sports car race at Silverstone in May with, left to right, Hawthorn (Jaguar D-type), Collins (DB3S) and Sparken (Ferrari *Monza*). *(T. C. March)*

Parnell won the Silverstone race after the radiator hose blew on Hawthorn's D-type. This photograph shows off the superb 'Gothic arch' lines of the 1955 DB3S. *(T. C. March)*

capacity cars would be right out of the picture, and it was all a question of whether Parnell and Scott-Brown could catch the 1500s. Scott-Brown headed the chase, while Parnell lost ground because of a misfiring engine. On lap 22 of this 25-lap race Scott-Brown passed McAlpine's Connaught, the leading 1500cc car, and Parnell had to settle for third place. Collins finished eighth, Wharton 11th and Whitehead 12th.

Peter Collins raced his DB3S very little during the 1955 season, but Salvadori's car proved a great asset to the Gilby team. Gilby were entering their Maserati 250F Formula 1 car for Salvadori for the second season and were to achieve a good measure of success. However, they were in trouble in sports car racing, for the Maserati A6GCS that they had raced in late 1953 and throughout 1954 had not proved suitable for British short circuit events; for 1955 they transferred the Maserati engine and gearbox to a Cooper chassis and the result was an understeering, ill-handling brute that achieved little success. In contrast DB3S/1 won race after race in British events during the year and brought Salvadori and Gilby good starting and prize money and good bonuses from the team's trade sponsors.

At Goodwood on Easter Monday Salvadori was unable to match the pace of Mike Sparken (Ferrari *Monza*) and Duncan Hamilton (Jaguar D-type), but both these drivers were penalized for jumping the start and Salvadori, third on the road, was promoted winner; Collins finished fifth. Shortly afterwards, Salvadori won the unlimited capacity sports car race at the Dorset Ibsley circuit from Scott-Brown (Lister-Bristol) and Peter Blond (ex-works, ex-Ecurie Ecosse Jaguar C-type).

The Mille Miglia was dominated by the Mercedes-Benz 300SLRs, and Stirling Moss (partnered by Denis Jenkinson) scored a magnificent victory, with another 300SLR driven solo by Juan Fangio in second place. Conscious that prospects of success were slim indeed, Wyer had contented himself with entering DB3S/5 for

Old-style DB3S. With DB3S/3, now registered HNR 1, Tony Everard set fastest time by a sports car at the May Prescott hill climb. *(T. C. March)*

Peter Collins driving solo and two of the Monte Carlo DB2/4s for Paul Frère/Louis Klementaski and Tommy Wisdom/Peter Bolton. Collins was delayed by a puncture and, driving in a furious temper, later blew up the engine. Neither of the DB2/4s were able to make much of their potential in the GT category, as both were eliminated by faulty clutches supplied by Borg & Beck.

At the International Trophy meeting at Silverstone both Aston Martin and Jaguar were out in force for the 117-mile sports car race. The David Brown team entered Parnell and Salvadori with DB3S/6 and DB3S/7 respectively, while Collins drove his own car, DB3S/2, and DB3S/1 was borrowed back from Salvadori for Peter Walker to drive. Walker, a farmer in daily life, had raced ERAs, driven works BRMs and had been a stalwart of the Jaguar team (including winning at Le Mans in 1951), before switching to Aston Martin. He was a fast, reliable driver who stayed with the David Brown team for two years. Later he fell on hard times and lived in very impoverished circumstances.

Jaguar borrowed back one of the 1954 D-types, OKV 1, and entered it for its new owner Duncan Hamilton, and entered OKV 2 for Tony Rolt (this car was delivered after the race to Johnny Broadhead for Bob Berry to drive) and OKV 3 for Mike Hawthorn (Hamilton also bought this car).

Hawthorn took pole position in the line-up for

the Le Mans start, but at the end of the first lap Rolt led from Titterington (Ecurie Ecosse D-type), Collins, Parnell and with Hawthorn fifth. By lap 3 Hawthorn was in front, but as the race progressed Parnell and Salvadori moved up into second and third places ahead of Rolt, with Walker fifth, Hamilton sixth and Collins trailing in eighth place. The Farnham driver seemed invincible, setting a new sports car lap record of 96.67 mph, but with only four laps to go, the top radiator hose blew on the D-type and Hawthorn quickly dropped back. Parnell went on to win the race at 93.58 mph with the drum-braked DB3S entries of Collins and Walker back in sixth and seventh places.

The following day at the Belgian Spa-Francorchamps circuit Aston Martin fielded a single car for Paul Frère in the 175-mile Spa Grand Prix for production sports cars, which, in reality, meant sports-racing cars in the trim that they were sold to private entrants. The Aston entered was new works chassis DB3S/8, but for this race only fitted with single-plug ignition and drum brakes. By this time the production DB3S was fitted with three Weber 40 DCO carburettors and John Wyer has indicated the power output was 200 bhp at 6000 rpm. Aston Martin *claimed* 210 bhp for the production cars on Webers, but this figure looks suspect. Frère took the lead on the first lap and stayed in front for the remainder of this 175-mile race, soundly thrashing the newly delivered Ferraris of Équipe Nationale Belge. It was not a trouble-free race, for on one lap Frère spun wildly in front of the pits as he lost the DB3S on the exit from La Source hairpin and for much of the race the car was overheating and soaking his feet with hot water.

On the following day Frère demonstrated the DB3S to King Baudouin, taking the car up to 125 mph on the *Autoroute* when there was a suitable gap between two lorries. For Baudouin it was a very draughty ride, for the passenger seat was over the battery and so the passenger's head was right in the airstream. Baudouin drove the car back to his château and as Frère departed is said to have commented, 'It must be rather gay to motor race.'

On 29 May private owners were out in force in the Hyères 12 Hours race held on the Île d'Or circuit on the French Riviera. There were only ten finishers out of 34 starters, and although the Whitehead half-brothers retired Graham's DB3S, the other Aston entries all finished. Tony

Gaze/David McKay (DB3S/102) finished second (almost catching the leading Ferrari of Canonica/Munaron), Cosh/Cobden (DB3S/104) were third and Sulman/Brabham (DB3S/103) fourth, with the DB3 coupé (DB3/5) of Mann/Morris-Goodall sixth despite an engine fire during the race.

At Snetterton on Whit Saturday both Collins and Salvadori were entered with their cars, but 'Salvo' non-started and Peter was beaten into second place by Scott-Brown with the 2-litre Lister-Bristol. Salvadori did, however, run at the Crystal Palace on the Monday, but he too had to give best to Archie and finished second in the Norbury Trophy race. Salvadori's DB3S was always driven on the road to meetings and the writer remembers, after the meeting, a Gilby mechanic edging this immaculate light green car through the Bank Holiday traffic, blipping the throttle to avoid oiling the plugs.

Once again Aston Martin had a formidable entry at Le Mans, three DB3S cars together with a Lagonda, but their performance was overshadowed by the battle of the titans – and by tragedy. Initially the race was led by the fantastically quick 4.4-litre Ferrari of Castellotti/Marzotto, followed by Hawthorn/Bueb (Jaguar) and Fangio/Moss (Mercedes-Benz 300SLR). As the race progressed, the Ferrari dropped behind Hawthorn and Fangio, who were battling furiously for the lead. At 6.30 pm there occurred the horrific accident that changed the face of motor racing. Levegh's Mercedes-Benz collided with Macklin's Austin-Healey in front of the pits and was launched into the spectator enclosure. More than 80 spectators were killed. The race went on whilst the Mercedes team consulted the directors at Stuttgart. By 9 pm the Fangio/Moss Mercedes led the 'long-nose' D-type Jaguar of Hawthorn/Bueb by two laps. Three and three-quarter hours later the Mercedes, now in first and third positions, were withdrawn and the D-type carried on to score a well-deserved, but unhappy, victory. The performances of the David Brown entries are set out below:

Salvadori (DB3S/7) and Collins (DB3/6) playing games through the Esses at Le Mans out of sight of John Wyer. *(T. C. March)*

No 1 Lagonda DP166/1 driven by R. Parnell/R. D. Poore

For 1955 the team had developed a new chassis for the Lagonda with a narrow multi-tubular space-frame to form a rigid central backbone structure and with the driver and passenger sitting outside the frame. Girling disc brakes were fitted front and rear. The car looked, and was, bulky, with low nose and the whole of the bonnet hinging forward as on the old DB2. Because of continuing engine problems, one of the two V12 entries was scratched. The sole starter was never in contention and retired after 93 laps. The reason was the failure of the *plombeur* to properly attach the fuel filler; the fuel splashed out and the Lagonda spluttered to a halt out on the circuit. The Lagonda's fastest lap was 4 min 21 sec.

No 23 Aston Martin DB3S/6 driven by P. J. Collins/P. Frère

For much of the early part of the race Collins and Salvadori (at the wheel of DB3S/7) enjoyed a furious dice all round the circuit out of sight of Wyer. Even after Levegh's crash these two drivers still battled furiously and full of fun – when Salvadori spun, Collins waited for him to catch up – but then slowing off in accordance with Wyer's instructions to pass the pits at 50 mph. DB3S/6 lasted the course to finish second and win the 3000cc class at 104.46 mph, some 60 miles behind the winning Jaguar. The fastest DB3S lap was 4

On their way to second place, DB3S/6 and Paul Frère on the Sunday morning at Arnage. *(T. C. March)*

min 23 sec and it was timed at 155.60 mph on the Mulsanne straight (compared with 181.57 mph for the Mercedes-Benz 300SLR and 173.94 mph for the Jaguar D-type).

No 24 Aston Martin DB3S/7 driven by R. F. Salvadori/P. D. C. Walker

By quarter-distance DB3S/7 was in 12th place, five places behind DB3S/6 and it retired after 106 laps because of a broken crankshaft.

No 25 Aston Martin DB3S/8 driven by C. A. S. Brooks/J. Riseley-Prichard

Tony Brooks was a driver of immense potential who had turned in some fine drives with Hely's Frazer Nash and Riseley-Prichard's ex-Rob Walker Formula 2 Connaught. Before the year ended, he was to become a regular member of the team. Riseley-Prichard was a keen amateur, a director of Willis Faber, the insurance brokers, and it was his only drive for the team. By quarter-distance DB3S/8 was in 16th place and it retired after 83 laps because of a flat battery caused by dynamo failure. DB3S/8 was now to full 1955 team specification with 220 bhp engine and disc brakes.

The new Lagonda V12, DP166/1, was driven at Le Mans in 1955 by Parnell/Poore, but retired because of a fuel leak. *(Geoffrey Goddard)*

Peter Collins with DB3S/6 on his way to second place in the Aintree race. *(T. C. March)*

By this race the wire-mesh grilles had been removed from the DB3S works cars, there were carburettor air intakes mounted on the bonnet tops and brake cooling ducts at the sides of the radiator intakes.

Second place was Aston Martin's best result to date at Le Mans and was cause for celebration, despite the withdrawal of the Mercedes-Benz team and the retirement of two of the Jaguars.

Roy Salvadori at Aintree after winning the sports car race. Eric Hind congratulates him. *(T. C. March)*

On 25 June Roy Salvadori and DB3S/1 were late entrants in the Eastern Counties '100' race at Snetterton. Salvadori had been entered with the Maserati 250F at Rouen, but this race had been cancelled following the Le Mans disaster. The Snetterton race was run on a handicap basis, but all cars from 2 litres upwards were on scratch and Salvadori soon moved into the lead to win from Archie Scott-Brown (Lister-Bristol) and Bill Smith (Jaguar C-type).

The following day the Kangaroo Stable was in action in the sports car Portuguese Grand Prix at Oporto with two cars driven by Gaze (DB3S/102) and Cosh (DB3S/104). The opposition was strong, the circuit fast and the private Astons were completely outclassed. Jean Behra with a works Maserati 300S won this 253-mile race at 91.65 mph from Masten Gregory (Ferrari *Monza*) and Duncan Hamilton (Jaguar D-type). Gaze was classified eighth and Cosh ninth.

In 1955 the British Grand Prix was held at Aintree and the David Brown team was out in force with four entries for Parnell (DB3S/5, now rebodied in 1955 style), Collins (DB3S/6), Salvadori (DB3S/7) and Walker (DB3S/8). The main opposition came from Mike Hawthorn with a solitary Jaguar D-type. Hawthorn led initially, but fell back because of a leaking fuel union and the Astons came through to take the first four places in the order Salvadori, Collins, Parnell and

The start of the sports car race at the Grand Prix meeting at Aintree in July with the four works DB3S entries leading away from Hawthorn's D-type Jaguar. *(Geoffrey Goddard)*

Walker. This was the day when Mercedes-Benz took the first four places in the British Grand Prix and Mercedes engineer Rudolf Uhlenhaut is reputed to have told Wyer that if Stuttgart had entered the 300SLRs in the sports car race, the Astons would have beaten them – a statement inspired, surely, by only the desire to please.

David Brown once again supported the Aston Martin Owners' Club St John Horsfall meeting at Silverstone on 23 July, with Parnell at the wheel of DB3S/5 and Salvadori driving DB3S/1. They took first and second places in that order in a 5-lap race for sports cars over 1500cc, were unable to beat their handicap in the St John Horsfall Trophy for Aston Martins and, as a team running with Jocelyn Stevens (DB3S/3), were out of the picture in the David Brown Challenge Cup Relay race.

On 24 July production DB3S cars were out again in the 186-mile Lisbon Grand Prix on the Monsanto circuit. Masten Gregory (Ferrari *Monza*) was the winner from de Graffenried (Maserati 300S) with the DB3S entries of Whitehead, Cosh (DB3S/104) and Sulman

(DB3S/103) finishing down the field in eighth, tenth and 11th places, respectively. Tony Gaze retired his DB3S because of a locking front brake.

At the Crystal Palace on August Bank Holiday Saturday the works team entered Salvadori with DB3S/5 in the sports car race. The inducement was that the race was being televised and there were prospects of good publicity if Salvadori won; the risk was that Scott-Brown with the Lister-Bristol had already beaten Salvadori with DB3S/1 at the Crystal Palace at Whitsun and could well repeat his success on this very tight circuit. At the fall of the flag Salvadori ensured that the DB3S was quick off the mark and, thanks to the disc brakes, was able to score a convincing win. Salvadori also set a new sports car lap record. On the Monday Graham Whitehead ran his production DB3S at Brands Hatch and finished fifth in the Kingsland Trophy – one place behind Salvadori with the ill-handling 2-litre Cooper-Maserati.

On Saturday, 6 August, the works entered Reg Parnell with DB3S/5 in the 20-lap *Newcastle*

Journal Trophy race at Charterhall. Parnell should and would have been able to beat the opposition, but was plagued by gear-selector problems and finished a poor sixth behind Titterington (Ecurie Ecosse Jaguar D-type), Rosier (Ferrari *Monza*), Scott-Brown (Lister-Bristol), Sanderson (Ecurie Ecosse Jaguar D-type) and Smith (Jaguar C-type).

When Aston Martin were competing at Le Mans, Prince Bertil of Sweden extended a personal invitation to David Brown for the team to compete in the Swedish Grand Prix at Kristianstâd on 7 August. It was neither a race of international importance, nor had the publicity potential of the longer British events, and the fact that Mercedes-Benz were entering meant that there was little chance of success. Prince Bertil was a good friend of David Brown, but as Salvadori has commented, if he had been a *real* friend, he would have persuaded Mercedes not to enter. Accordingly the team made a token effort and dispatched Collins and Salvadori to run their own cars as private entrants. Collins's DB3S/2 broke a con-rod in practice and could not be repaired in time for the start. In the 130-mile race Fangio and Moss took the first two places for Mercedes ahead of Castellotti (Ferrari) and Salvadori, not driving at his best, finished seventh.

In 1955 the Goodwood 9 Hours race was held for the third and last time. The problem was simply that the race attracted insufficient spectators to make it an economic proposition. Aston Martin entered three cars, DB3S/8 (Parnell/Salvadori), DB3S/6 (Collins/Brooks) and DB3S/7 (Walker/Poore). All three cars were fitted with the wider, 12.5in. disc brakes from the Lagonda and DB3S/8 was fitted with new camshafts that boosted power output to 246 bhp at 6000 rpm. By this stage the block had been strengthened to cope with the extra power and weight rose by about 60 lb. The team had set up a radio link so that observers at the chicane could report tyre wear back to the pits. In addition the Kangaroo Stable car, DB3S/102, was driven by Gaze/McKay.

The opposition came from Ferrari and Jaguar. Ferrari *Monzas* were driven by Hawthorn/de Portago (a works entry), Jonneret/Wharton and Schell/Lucas. Hamilton-entered D-type Jaguars were driven by Hamilton/Rolt and Peter Whitehead/Michael Head, the Broadhead car was driven by Berry/Dewis (Norman Dewis was Jaguar's Chief Tester) and there was an Ecurie

Ecosse entry for Titterington/Sanderson.

Hawthorn led away from the Le Mans start followed by Walker, Collins, Parnell and Sanderson. After only three laps Parnell was in the pits to retire DB3S/8; at that start he had let the clutch in too fiercely and overstrained a rear hub, causing bearing failure. Rolt retired his D-type early in the race and Hawthorn lost a vast amount of time in the pits because of gear-selector problems. So Collins/Brooks and Walker/Poore led from the D-type of Titterington/Sanderson. After two hours Collins/Brooks still led, but Schell/Lucas were in second place, followed by Titterington/Sanderson, and Walker/Poore had dropped to fourth. As the race progressed, the Ecurie Ecosse D-type pressed the leader more and more closely and by 6 pm the Jaguar led. Collins/Brooks were back in front by 6.30 pm, but only seconds separated the two cars.

Baulked by a slower car, Titterington ploughed through several marker posts, smashing a headlamp. This was to slow the Ecurie Ecosse drivers during the night hours and help ensure an Aston Martin victory. By this time Walker/Poore had lost the use of second gear. Collins/Brooks were delayed in the pits by an electrical problem and at 10 pm the Ecurie Ecosse Jaguar was again in the lead. When the Jaguar made its final pit stop, the Aston of Walker/Poore went back in front and with Walker at the wheel was able to run through to the midnight finish without a further stop. Because of the loss of second gear Walker was entering the chicane in third, slipping the clutch and selecting first at the exit. At the finish he was a lap ahead of the Jaguar with Collins/Brooks in third place.

In the 1950s there was just as much competition between newspapers as now and one of the most popular means of promotion was to sponsor a motor race. It had begun when the *Daily Express* sponsored the May Silverstone meeting and it soon spread. For the sponsor a major spin-off was that the race meeting would usually be televised. In August 1955 the *Daily Herald* sponsored an international 221-mile sports car race at Oulton Park and it attracted a strong entry.

After his bad mistake at Goodwood, Reg Parnell persuaded John Wyer that he should be a late entrant at Oulton Park and he drove DB3S/8 alongside Collins and Salvadori, who were driving their private cars. Facing the Astons was a strong entry of Ferrari *Monzas*, headed by Mike

Hawthorn (with a works car) and with other entries from Masten Gregory, Louis Rosier, Jean Lucas, Herbert Mackay Fraser and Gunnar Carlsson. Carroll Shelby started from the back of the grid with the first 6-cylinder Ferrari in private ownership, a 4.4-litre car entered by American Tony Parravano's Scuderia Parravano. Ecurie Ecosse and Ducan Hamilton missed the race and the only D-type entered was Broadhead's car driven by Bob Berry.

Oulton Park proved a two-car race. The extra power of the *Monza* Ferrari was balanced by the superb handling of the DB3S on this tortuous course. Parnell rocketed away from the start and led throughout the 80 laps, despite all Hawthorn's brave efforts with the thunderous red Ferrari. Hawthorn was, however, handicapped by running on a mixture of Pirelli and Dunlop tyres that materially affected the handling. The Aston averaged 81.16 mph, Parnell set a new sports car

lap record of 82.97 mph and at the finish he was over 30 seconds ahead. It was one of the finest drives in Parnell's long career and, when the champagne flowed after the race, he commented, 'It's in the race that you need it most!' Collins finished third with DB3S/2 ahead of Gregory, Berry, Harry Schell (HWM-Jaguar) and Moss with Peter Bell's 1500cc Connaught. Poor Salvadori lost the use of third gear early in the race – the gear most needed at Oulton – and was hit up the back by Scott-Brown's Lister, and trailed round to finish eighth. Cosh was 13th with his Kangaroo Stable entry, DB3S/104.

The following weekend there was a 51-mile unlimited sports car race at the *Daily Telegraph* meeting at Aintree. Salvadori drove DB3S/1 and the main opposition came from the Ecurie Ecosse D-type Jaguars of Titterington and Sanderson. Salvadori was well aware that he had to lead into the first corner with the DB3S or else the sheer

At the start of the Goodwood 9 Hours race Hawthorn (Ferrari *Monza*) leads away from Peter Walker and Peter Collins. *(Geoffrey Goddard)*

power of the D-types would prove unassailable. On this occasion 'Salvo' was not quick enough off the mark, and throughout the race his car seemed down on power. Titterington led away from the Aston, Sanderson barged past Salvadori on the second lap and this was the finishing order, with Harry Schell (Ferrari) fourth, Whitehead (Cooper-Jaguar) fifth and Jenny (Maserati 300S) sixth.

On 17 September, the Tourist Trophy, the penultimate round of the Sports Car World Championship, was held on the Dundrod circuit in Northern Ireland and was now run as a scratch race. Mercedes-Benz were out in force with three 300SLRs for Moss/Fitch, Fangio/Kling and von Trips/Simon. For reasons that are far from clear Jaguar contented themselves with entering a single 'long-nose' D-type driven by Hawthorn/Titterington, backed up by Broadhead's private car driven by Berry/Sanderson. Scuderia Ferrari fielded two *Monzas* for Castellotti/Taruffi and Maglioli/Trintignant, while from Officine Alfieri Maserati there were two 300S cars for Behra/Bordoni and Musso/Musy. Aston Martin entered the usual DB3S cars for Collins/Brooks (DB3S/6),

Parnell/Salvadori (DB3S/8) and Walker/Poore (DB3S/7). DB3S/6 ran with an increased bore of 84mm (giving a capacity of 2992cc) and developed 240 bhp at 6000 rpm. There was a very large entry of smaller-capacity cars.

Without doubt the 1955 Tourist Trophy had attracted the best ever entry seen at a British sports car race, but it was to be a race marred by tragedy, and, to the relief of many drivers, the circuit was condemned as dangerous and never again used.

Berry and Hawthorn headed the line-up for the Le Mans start (the line-up was based on engine capacity and not practice times) and they led away. By the end of the first lap Moss led from Hawthorn and Berry, Walker was the leading Aston driver in fifth place, with Parnell ninth and Collins, whose car had refused to fire until the mechanics had by-passed the starter, was back in 15th place. On lap 2 Berry retired out on the circuit because of a puncture.

On only the next lap tragedy occurred. Although what happened did not directly affect the Aston Martin team, it is relevant to the racing

Peter Collins at the wheel of DB3S/6 which, with Brooks, he drove to third place in the Goodwood 9 Hours race.
(Geoffrey Goddard)

of the period. It was common in the 1950s for inexperienced drivers to be admitted to major races and such a driver at the Tourist Trophy was the Vicomte de Barry entered under the banner of Écurie Côte d'Azure at the wheel of a road-going Mercedes-Benz 300SL. De Barry's fastest lap with his 3-litre car was 5 min 38 sec, 32 seconds slower than the best lap of the 1100cc Bueb/MacDowell Cooper and only five seconds faster than the best lap of the 745cc DB of Armagnac/Laureau. Admittedly, there were other slow cars in the race, but de Barry was making life difficult for other drivers by not keeping to the edge of the road and thereby causing overtaking problems on this narrow circuit. On a stretch of road at Cochranstown, Wharton (Frazer Nash) tried to pass the Mercedes, pulled back in again and Jim Mayers (Cooper-Climax) shot through on the right and hit a massive gate-post at the side of the road. The Cooper disintegrated in flames and Mayers was killed instantly. Young Bill Smith (Connaught) ploughed into the wreckage of the Cooper and died in the inferno, Macklin drove his Austin-Healey into the ditch to avoid the wreckage, Wharton crashed and was dragged from the wreckage by marshals and Peter Jopp deliberately crashed his Lotus to avoid plunging into the debris. The truth was that de Barry should not have been allowed to take part in the race and the great tragedy was the death of young Bill Smith, who would undoubtedly have been a works Jaguar driver in 1956.

In the meantime Moss was increasing his lead, Hawthorn was second, Fangio was closing rapidly on the Jaguar and Collins had come through to sixth place; he passed Behra's Maserati and then set about von Trips's Mercedes. As Hawthorn, setting a new circuit record of 94.67 mph, began to pull away from the third-place Mercedes of Fangio, so Moss pulled further into the lead, and Collins was all over the fourth-place Mercedes, but unable to get by. After the first round of pit stops Titterington led, Fitch was in second place (Moss had brought the 300SLR into the pits with the rear offside tyre in ribbons and the thin bodywork badly damaged), Kling was third and Collins was in fourth place ahead of Simon. While Titterington extended his lead, Collins passed Kling and then lost more than five minutes in the pits whilst an oil-soaked distributor was changed. Heavy rain began to fall, Brooks took over from Collins, but left the pits with a badly misfiring engine and on lap 43 retired because of a broken

con-rod bolt.

As the race progressed, so Moss clawed back the Jaguar's lead, Fangio/Kling held third place, von Trips/Simon were fourth, the Walker/Poore DB3S was fifth and Parnell/Salvadori were still running steadily in sixth place, despite both drivers' dislike of the course and despite time lost in the pits because of a sticking throttle. On lap 56 Moss went ahead of Hawthorn, and although the Jaguar seemed set to take second place, two laps from the finish the engine seized and the D-type spun out of the race.

The Mercedes-Benz 300SLRs finished in the first three places with Walker/Poore fourth (three laps behind the winner), Musso/Bordoni/Behra (Maserati) fifth, Castellotti/Taruffi (Ferrari) sixth and the DB3S of Parnell/Salvadori in seventh place. It had been a very commendable effort by Aston Martin and the undoubted star had been Peter Collins, who had brought his car through from last to fourth place in one of the most brilliant drives in his career. It was to lead directly to a drive with the Mercedes-Benz team in the Targa Florio.

The best lap times and speeds of the leading contenders form an interesting comparison:

	Best lap	Speed over flying kilometre
Jaguar (Hawthorn/ Titterington)	4 min 42 sec (94.67 mph)	148.50 mph
Ferrari (Maglioli/ Trintignant)	5 min 00 sec (88.99 mph)	138.20 mph
Mercedes-Benz (Moss/Fitch)	4 min 43 sec (94.34 mph)	147.70 mph
Mercedes-Benz (Fangio/Kling)	4 min 44 sec (94.00 mph)	148.90 mph
Mercedes-Benz (von Trips/Simon)	4 min 38 sec (92.70 mph)	148.10 mph
Maserati (Behra/Bordoni)	4 min 50 sec (92.06 mph)	138.90 mph
Aston Martin (Collins/Brooks)	4 min 45 sec (93.67 mph)	142.10 mph

| Aston Martin (Walker/Poore) | 4 min 54 sec (90.81 mph) | 138.20 mph |
| Aston Martin (Parnell/ Salvadori) | 4 min 57 sec (89.89 mph) | 138.90 mph |

To complete the story of the DB3S in 1955, it is necessary to mention one other minor race meeting, at Castle Combe on 1 October, where Salvadori drove DB3S/1 in the RedEx International Trophy race for unlimited capacity sports cars. He built up a substantial lead over Abecassis's HWM-Jaguar, only to retire when the final drive failed.

For Aston Martin 1955 had proved a year of steady development of the DB3S, coupled with the reluctant abandonment of the V12 Lagonda after the failure at Le Mans, and it was the most successful year since David Brown entered racing. To celebrate the year's successes Aston Martin published an illustrated booklet, *Background To Victory* by Tom Wisdom some pages of which are illustrated here. Although the DB3S was now outdated and the appearance of its successor still some way in the future, the team embarked on its 1956 programme with a high degree of optimism.

Reg Parnell was very keen to participate in the Tasman races in early 1956. These New Zealand Formule Libre races had attracted a fair European following because the starting and prize money were so good. Aston Martin built up for Parnell a single-seater chassis, DP155, with

Peter Collins, seen here power-sliding DB3S/6, drove one of the finest races of his career in the Tourist Trophy, but the DB3S was eliminated by con-rod bolt failure. *(Geoffrey Goddard)*

An excellent example of the Le Mans type start as

With a roar of exhausts and a scream of tyres, the field ge

Running a motor-racing team is one of the most difficult problems in the sphere of sport ; there are to-day but four top ranking racing managers and 45-year-old John Wyer is one of them. A director of Aston Martin and a qualified engineer responsible for the present basic design of Aston Martin and Lagonda cars, he has a job which would make most big industrialists flinch.

Wyer's first responsibility is that he must initiate the design, then build, maintain, and race a car which is, in essentials, the car of the future, in fact, a car which his firm will eventually produce for use by the public. The Aston Martin team, wisely, has adopted the policy of racing to test new devices which, if successful, are destined for eventual full-scale production and sale to the public.

But what a problem ! First of all there is the basic design of the car involving also decisions as to the best types of innumerable accessories ; the programme of races for the season must be considered and laid down ; the recruitment of " back-room " boys—designers, draughtsmen, mechanics and liaison with experts from the various outside accessory manufacturers. All that is—comparatively—simple ; then comes the selection of drivers for the team. This is probably the team manager's biggest headache ; for one thing top-ranking drivers are few and far between.

GOODWOOD 9-HOUR.
(*Left*) *Walker makes a hasty exit as the two mechanics set to work.*
(*Right*) *Brooks reports to Wyer as Collins waits anxiously to take over while the car is re-fuelled and tyres changed.*

The really top-class racing motorist is a prima donna—far more temperamental than any film star, and if they weren't they wouldn't be any good. The driver, a man who is prepared to " have a go " must obviously be imaginative and highly   As Wyer puts it himself :
" The driver who is pr   ever make
an attempt to get out   and he should know s   sometimes in the guise   martinet, for many ye

The 9-hours race at Goodw
strenuous and exacting of the
year's race was of even greater
Martin point of view, since the
on the two previous occasions
against strong opposition from
" works " cars, the team manage
a thorough appraisal of the prob
One of the chief fears was tyre
innumerable fast turns and a s
this was a serious matter if the
their maximum for nine hours.
unnecessary lap on worn tyres an
at the Chicane turn just before
by radio-telephone with the team
first sign of tyre wear the driver co
" come-in " signal. The scheme
It was an exciting race from
one hour the two Aston Martins
positions, and a lap ahead of the
end of the seventh hour Peter Co
brilliant young newcomer to the te
with the Peter Walker-Dennis Poo
With little more than two hou
into the pits for examination of
was causing his headlights to fli
just over nine minutes, a delay wh
the race, for he finished seven min
but the Wyer strategy had worked —
was there to fill the breach and win
Three times the winner of a race
it has been held is a remarkable re
It is of interest to examine the in
performance in these three events
speed was 75.42 m.p.h., the follow
78.94 m.p.h., while this year the
same—up to 82.24 m.p.h.

Background to Victory, the illustrated booklet published by David Brown to publicize Aston Martin's 1955 successes.

cars at the start of the 1955 Goodwood 9-Hour Race.

...rtin DB3S—the eventual winner—makes a good start.

BACKGROUND TO VICTORY

by T. H. WISDOM

...'s team is "the tops." The drivers do ...since the cars are race winners. Even ...his year his " boys " have been little

..., of this season, which was to be one ...ssful in Aston Martin's long history, ...of a sports car that could beat the best ...chassis, gearbox, ...stem was

...most ...this ...Aston ...race ...Up ...alian ...made

...with ...asive, ...near ...an ...oned ...nked ...t the ...ssary

...After ...ond ...the ...s, a ...ead ...nd. ...lled ...nich ...sted ...lins ...r ; ...rtin

...ons

...tin ...ng ...to ...he

GOODWOOD

OULTON PARK

The 221 miles sports car race at Oulton Park on August 27th proved once again a personal triumph for the " Pathfinder ", as veteran Reg Parnell is affectionately known in the Aston Martin team.

Driving at his brilliant best he defeated, and quite inevitably, a strong international field. Not only was he driving a lone works DB3S model against Italian and British cars, but, in fact, among the thirty starters were most of the leading drivers from seven countries.

Parnell made a dazzling start and went straight into the lead and never loosened his grip of the race. Hawthorn's Ferrari in second place, driven at the limit, never looked like catching the Derby flyer. And just to show that he had the race fully under control, in the final laps Parnell went on to a new lap record at 82.97 m.p.h.

which they had been experimenting. It was in effect a narrower version of the DB3S with the driver seated over the prop-shaft and was originally intended to be powered by a supercharged 3-litre DB3S engine. Unfortunately this engine blew up during testing, so as a 2.5-litre engine, similar to that used in the works DB3S in the British Empire Trophy race, was substituted. Parnell non-started in the New Zealand Grand Prix at Ardmore, finished a poor fourth in the Lady Wigram Trophy race at Christchurch, took second place at Dunedin and finished third at Invercargill. The chassis/body were subsequently sold to inveterate special-builder Geoff Richardson, who fitted a Jaguar engine to form the second of his RRA Specials when Aston Martin declined to sell him the twin-plug engine used by Parnell.

A note on the fate of the Lagondas would be appropriate at this point. During 1955 the two 1954 cars, DP115/1 (with, it seems, a new body) and DP115/2 were hired by The Rank Organisation for use in the film *Checkpoint*, in which they appeared as 'Warren Ingrams'. For this film the intake grilles were removed, replaced by a simple squarish opening in the nose and with large bonnet top carburettor intakes fitted. Later the two cars were sold, one through HW Motors in July 1957, by when it was registered 4 DPC. Both 1954 cars are now owned by that great Lagonda enthusiast Maurice Leo. The 1955 DP166 chassis were retained for use with the DBR2 (see Chapter 7).

6   DB3S: 1956

John Wyer has commented that Aston Martin made far less progress in 1956 than the previous year, but it proved a year of consolidation and gradual development. Above all, the season was planned carefully and in the majority of races entered the team had good prospects of success. Stirling Moss had now joined Aston Martin, the price for his services was high and stimulated the whole organization into justifying his presence. Tony Brooks was also now a regular member of the team. Dennis Poore had retired from racing and Peter Collins, now living in Modena, had to divide his efforts between Formula 1 (and some sports car racing) for Scuderia Ferrari and sports car racing with Aston Martin. There were no technical changes to the cars at the beginning of the year.

Early in 1956 Graham Whitehead (now with the ex-Salvadori DB3S/1) and Kerguen with a new production DB3S, DB3S/117, ran in the Agadir and Dakar races in North Africa. At Agadir, Kerguen finished sixth and Whitehead tenth. By Dakar Whitehead was at the wheel of one of Duncan Hamilton's D-type Jaguars, a car more suited to what was at that time the world's fastest sports car race and he finished fifth, but Kerguen and his DB3S failed to figure in the result.

After an interval of two years Aston Martin returned to compete in the Sebring race. Three DB3S cars were entered for Moss/Collins (DB3S/6), Salvadori/Carroll Shelby (DB3S/7) and Parnell/Brooks (DB3S/8). Facing the Astons were a strong team of Tipo 860 3.4-litre 4-cylinder Ferraris, works 300S Maseratis and works-prepared D-type Jaguars entered by the Briggs Cunningham team.

Moss held second place in the opening laps and, after three hours, DB3S/6, now with Collins at the wheel, was in fourth place when the engine seized because of failure of the oil pump drive. The same problem eliminated the Parnell/Brooks entry, which was in third place, after nine hours' racing. Despite losing second and third gears, Salvadori and Shelby staggered on to the finish, taking fourth place overall behind the Ferraris of Fangio/Castellotti and Musso/Schell and the Jaguar of Sweikert/Ensley and winning the 3-litre class. In fifth place came the Maserati 300S of Behra/Taruffi.

Roy Salvadori had persuaded John Wyer to sell him a car again in 1956 and he bought DB3S/5, regarded by the team as something of a 'lemon'. At the Easter Goodwood meeting Salvadori offered his drive to Stirling Moss, who ran away with the over 1500cc sports car race to win by more than 20 seconds from George Abecassis (HWM-Jaguar).

Because the works cars were still in transit from Sebring, Salvadori loaned DB3S/5 back to the works for the British Empire Trophy race at Oulton Park. It was driven by Reg Parnell, with the 2493cc engine developing the slightly increased power output of 217 bhp. At this meeting Salvadori drove a works Cooper-Climax. Parnell won the heat for cars up to 2700cc from Archie Scott-Brown with the new, but misfiring, Lister-Maserati, a car that was to prove a failure because of persistent engine problems.

In the unlimited capacity heat DB3S Astons were driven by Whitehead, Berwyn Baxter (DB3S/101) and Lt. Col. Arthur Bryant of the US Navy with his white and blue-painted DB3S/114. For much of the heat Bryant battled with the similarly painted Ferrari *Monza* of Herbert McKay Fraser, eventually got ahead and then, sadly, crashed at Druid's with fatal results. Bryant was a great Aston Martin enthusiast who had previously raced a DB2/4.

The final was dominated by the faster 1500cc cars and Parnell was right out of the picture. He finished 11th at 81.07 mph. The 1500cc cars were given a 25 seconds handicap advantage, but by 1956 were faster than the larger-capacity cars on this tight circuit. Stirling Moss, with a 1500cc Cooper-Climax borrowed from the works, was the winner at an average of 83.72 mph. The first of the unlimited cars was the D-type Jaguar of Ron Flockhart in seventh place at 82.77 mph.

On 21 April at Aintree, Salvadori with DB3S/5, now back in 3-litre form, won the 10-lap unlimited sports car race from the Ecurie Ecosse D-type Jaguars of Titterington and Sanderson and set a new sports car lap record of 84.38 mph.

In 1956 Aston Martin missed the Mille Miglia and next appeared at the International Trophy meeting at Silverstone on 5 May. The team also brought along two of the new DB3S fixed-head coupés, based on the production chassis and with,

Aston Martin's advertisement after the 1956 class win.

in effect, a hardtop grafted on to the existing body and lacking the air-flowed lines of the ill-fated 1954 coupés. These new cars were not raced and were intended primarily for the use of David Brown and his family, but listed at a basis price of £3200. Four cars were entered at Silverstone, Salvadori at the wheel of his own car, DB3S/5, Collins with DB3S/6, Parnell with DB3S/7 and Moss with DB3S/8. Jaguar entered D-types for Mike Hawthorn, Desmond Titterington and Jack Fairman. Ecurie Ecosse D-types were driven by Ron Flockhart, Ninian Sanderson and Alan Brown and another potent contender was Bob Berry with Johnny Broadhead's D-type.

There was dissension in the Aston Martin camp in practice because Moss wanted to take over Salvadori's car, which he thought was faster – Wyer refused because DB3S/5 was Salvadori's own property and so the team was not at its happiest even before the start. Salvadori, Hawthorn and Titterington all lapped in under 1 min 50 sec in practice and Moss was fractionally slower.

At the Le Mans start of this 73-mile race Moss was first across the track and led away in a power slide, Salvadori passed him on the approach to Stowe corner, at Club corner Titterington tried to overtake Salvadori on the inside, but Roy firmly

closed the door. Titterington lost control, spinning wildly in a cloud of tyre smoke and was rammed by Collins; in taking avoiding action Parnell ended up in the ditch and Sanderson mounted the bank. Salvadori now had a comfortable lead over Hawthorn, with Moss third and Alan Brown fourth. At the end of lap 15 Hawthorn pulled into the pits, restarted fourth and retired two laps later because he was unhappy with his D-type's steering. At the end of this 25-lap race Salvadori led Moss by 28 seconds and third place went to Berry's D-type. Interestingly Salvadori's race average of 94.79 mph was slower than the 95.13 mph at which he won the 1500cc sports race with a works Cooper-Climax.

During the afternoon the Aston Martin team held an enquiry into the accident and Moss firmly expressed the view that Salvadori was to blame for pushing too hard and starting off the accident. Poor Salvadori was not there to defend himself, as he had crashed the Gilby Maserati 250F in the International Trophy race and was taken to hospital unconscious, and quite badly burned by the hot exhaust. Neither Aston Martin's enquiry, nor one held later by the organizers, the British Racing Drivers' Club, came to any firm conclusion about the cause of the accident.

Reg Parnell at the wheel of DB3S/5 in 2493cc form in his heat of the British Empire Trophy at Oulton Park in April. Parnell won his heat, but could only finish 11th in the final. *(T. C. March)*

Lt. Col. Bryant with production DB3S/114 chases Herbert Mackay Fraser (Ferrari *Monza*) in his heat of the British Empire Trophy. Bryant managed to pass the Ferrari, but then crashed with fatal results. *(T. C. March)*

The following weekend there was again a Production sports car race on the Spa circuit in Belgium. The regulations were now rather more relaxed and Reg Parnell was entered with Salvadori's DB3S/5, complete with twin-plug head and disc brakes. The 105-mile race was led by the Ecurie Ecosse D-types of Sanderson and Titterington (these D-types were near enough genuine *production* cars), but Titterington retired and Sanderson won from Parnell and Dutch driver Hans David (formerly a C-type Jaguar) with his orange-painted production DB3S/118.

There was a meeting at the Snetterton airfield circuit in Norfolk on the Saturday. Salvadori was still not fit following his Silverstone accident and non-started, but Tom Kyffin raced DB3S/2, which we had bought from Peter Collins. He retired in a cloud of steam when a radiator hose burst.

On the Saturday the Grand Prix des Frontières was held at Chimay in Belgium over a distance of 149 miles. It was a favourite race for British drivers and Graham Whitehead drove DB3S/1 into third place behind Benôit Musy (Maserati 300S) and Duncan Hamilton (Jaguar D-type).

In 1956 the 1000 Kms race on the tortuous, winding, 14.7-mile Nürburgring circuit was revived after an interval of three years. In 1953 Roy Salvadori had finished second with Ian Stewart (but with Salvadori doing most of the driving) at the wheel of an Ecurie Ecosse C-type Jaguar and the race gave the sweet-handling, but admittedly four-year-old, DB3S reasonable prospects of success. Aston Martin entered DB3S/5 for Collins/Brooks and DB3S/8 for Salvadori/Walker. Stirling Moss had an arrangement with Aston Martin that he could drive for Maserati when needed and in the German race he was in the Maserati team. Reg Parnell had crashed badly with Rob Walker's Formula 1 Connaught at the Crystal Palace on Whit Monday and as a result Aston Martin was desperately short of drivers. Accordingly there was no alternative but to bring Salvadori back into the team, even though he was still in considerable pain and could barely walk following his crash at Silverstone. The one advantage enjoyed by Aston Martin was that they had visited the circuit earlier in May for testing and the cars were properly set up when practice started.

Ferrari had entered four cars, a pair of Tipo 860 4-cylinder *Monzas* for Fangio/Castellotti and de Portago/Gendebien and a pair of Tipo 290 MM V12 3.5-litre cars for Musso/Trintignant and Phil Hill/Wharton. From Maserati came a trio of 3-litre Tipo 300S cars for Moss/Behra, Taruffi/Schell and Perdisa/Manzon. Even Jaguar supported the race with a brace of D-types for Hawthorn/Titterington and Frère/Hamilton.

Two views of the very handsome 'production' DB3S fixed-head coupés that first appeared at Silverstone in May. This is DB3S/120. *(T. C. March)*

Roy Salvadori with DB3S/5 on his way to his controversial victory in the sports car race at Silverstone in May. (T. C. March)

Moss set the pace, and when the rear transverse leaf spring of his 300S broke, the Moss/Behra pairing took over from Taruffi/Schell and went on to win the race at 80.59 mph. Ferraris took second and third places, a Porsche was fourth and Collins/Brooks brought their DB3S across the line in fifth place, a lap in arrears. Salvadori/Walker should have finished fourth, but the de Dion tube broke a lap and a half before the finish of this 44-lap race, and the DB3S shed a rear wheel and brake drum. Of the works Jaguars, totally unsuitable for this circuit, the Frère/Hamilton car broke its gearbox early in the race, while Hawthorn and Titterington drove their D-type with great verve, holding fourth place for some while, but were delayed by a fuel leak and eventually eliminated by a broken half-shaft. For Aston Martin the lessons learned would pay a good dividend in the future.

On 23 June there was a race meeting at Aintree and Salvadori was entered in the sports car race with DB3S/5. He was fastest in practice, led away at the start and at the chequered flag he was over ten seconds ahead of Titterington (Ecurie Ecosse D-type).

One of the more interesting races in 1956 was the 203-mile Rouen Grand Prix run on the picturesque Circuit des Essarts and limited to cars of 3000cc. Aston Martin entered a team of four cars. Peter Collins had formed the view that the fitting of disc brakes, which increased the unsprung weight of the DB3S, impaired its handling. At his request DB3S/6 was prepared for him with drum brakes. DB3S/7 was entered for Tony Brooks. There were two brand-new cars, DB3S/9 and DB3S/10, for Moss and Salvadori. The new cars had much smoother frontal treatment, with the headlamps under perspex covers and a large streamlined headrest. Ferrari entered a 3-litre *Monza* for Castellotti and a V12 car for de Portago. There were works 300S Maseratis for Behra and Perdisa and Ecurie Ecosse entered a Jaguar D-type with 3-litre engine devised by 'Wilkie' Wilkinson for Desmond Titterington.

In practice Moss tried Collins's drum-braked DB3S and lapped marginally faster with this car. Naturally he wanted it for the race, but Wyer told him that as it had been specially prepared for Collins, he could only have it if Collins himself asked Wyer. So Stirling set to work on Collins and in due course Collins asked Wyer if Moss could have DB3S/6. In truth, Collins was far from happy about the proposal and his feelings were clearly revealed by his driving in the race. Practice was dominated by the Maseratis of Behra and Perdisa and they sandwiched Castellotti's Ferrari on the front row of the gird, with Collins and Moss on the second row.

At the start Perdisa led away and Collins and Moss accelerated through from the second row to hold second and third places. Collins was in a high dudgeon and, driving at his hardest, had forced his way into the lead by the end of lap 6, with Moss pushed back to fourth place behind Behra and Perdisa. Two laps later Behra was in front of Collins and steadily built up a good lead. Roy Salvadori was already in trouble after his brakes had jammed at the hairpin and would not release. After bending back part of the scuttle to free the pedal, Salvadori rejoined the race to fight his way back from 13th place.

Collins pulled into the pits to retire at the end of lap 16 with his tachometer 'tell-tale' at 7300 rpm and the whole car glowing red hot. John Wyer was not amused. A little after half-distance Castellotti passed Moss and then the Maserati domination evaporated. On lap 37 Perdisa coasted into the pits to retire with transmission failure. Castellotti began to close on Behra, who had slowed after a stone thrown up by a rear wheel had damaged a rear shock absorber and resulted in the loss of all the fluid. First Castellotti and then, a lap later, Moss passed the Maserati. With five laps to go to the chequered

In the sports car race at Silverstone in July Salvadori finished second with DB3S/8 to Stirling Moss with a works Maserati 3000S. *(T. C. March)*

flag Moss was ten seconds behind Castellotti and the Aston Martin pit showed their number one driver the 'faster' signal. The gap was too great, the DB3S was insufficiently powerful and at the flag Moss was 3.9 seconds in arrears. Behra finished third and Brooks and Salvadori took fourth and fifth places. It had been a fine effort by the Aston Martin team and with a little more power under his right foot Moss would have won.

At the British Grand Prix meeting at Silverstone Aston Martin entered only a single car, DB3S/8, powered by 2992cc engine developing 237 bhp at 5800 rpm. Salvadori was also entered by Gilby Engineering with DB3S/5. Originally DB3S/8 was to be driven by Reg Parnell, but when it became evident that the Derbyshire driver was still not fit after his Crystal Palace crash, it was decided that Tony Brooks should take his place. Brooks crashed in the Grand Prix when the throttle of his BRM jammed open, so Salvadori switched from DB3S/5 to the works car. This 25-lap race was dominated by Stirling Moss with a works Maserati 300S and, within a few seconds of being lapped by the leader, Salvadori finished a comfortable second ahead of Titterington (Ecurie

Ecosse Jaguar D-type) and Protheroe (Tojeiro-Jaguar). Kyffin entered DB3S/2 in this race, but retired after three laps.

As a direct result of the 1955 disaster, substantial modifications were made to the Sarthe circuit, especially in the pits area, and these resulted in the postponement of the race until 28–29 July. For the 1956 race there were also substantial changes to the regulations, as a result of which it was not a round in that year's Sports Car World Championship. These changes can be summarized as follows:

Engine capacity limit of 2500cc for 'Experimental' cars.

Full-width windscreen and tonneau of flexible material compulsory.

No refuelling before 34 laps had been completed and subsequent refuelling at intervals of not less than 34 laps.

130 litres (approximately 29 Imperial gallons) maximum fuel capacity and not more than 120 litres (approximately 26½ gallons) to be taken on at refuelling stops.

The line up of works cars at Le Mans in 1956 with, from left to right, the new DBR1 driven by Brooks/Parnell, DB3S/10 (Walker/Salvadori) and DB3S/9 (Moss/Collins). The fourth car is a Superleggera Touring-bodied DB2/4. *(Geoffrey Goddard)*

Production cars were allowed to run with optional extras as shown in the maker's catalogue and this was interpreted to mean that Jaguar could run their long-nose fuel-injection D-types and Aston Martin were able to field their latest DB3S cars with the new bodywork, 12-plug cylinder heads and disc brakes. The team entered DB3S/9 for Moss/Collins and DB3S/10 for Walker/ Salvadori, while in the Prototype class there was the brand-new DBR1 with 2493cc engine for Brooks/Parnell. The DBR1 is discussed in the next chapter. Jaguar entered three D-types for Hawthorn/Bueb, Frère/Titterington and Fairman/ Wharton and there were private D-types from Ecurie Ecosse for Flockhart/Sanderson and from Equipe Nationale Belge for Swaters/Rousselle. Ferrari fielded three *Testa Rossa* cars (the then production 2-litre model) with bodywork by Carrozzeria Touring and 2490cc 4-cylinder engines (very similar to the engines used in the 1955 Tipo 625 Formula 1 cars). Although there were also entries from Gordini and Talbot (the latter with Maserati-powered cars), neither of these teams could be considered serious contenders for victory. Aston Martin were worried

about fuel consumption and this was to inhibit the performance of the DB3S during the race.

At the start of the race light rain was falling and Hawthorn led away from the start. By the end of the second lap the order was Hawthorn–Flockhart–Walker–Moss. Already two of the works Jaguars were out of the race. Frère had lost control on the slippery surface through the Esses and spun into the bank, Fairman had spun to avoid him and just as he was restarting he was rammed by de Portago's Ferrari. After only four laps Hawthorn was in the pits because of a misfiring engine and a total of 24 laps was lost before the problem was traced to a split fuel injector pipe. Although Hawthorn/Bueb were to fight back to make up some of the lost ground, Jaguar honours were now carried by the Ecurie Ecosse D-type of Flockhart/Sanderson, which led from Moss/Collins. Collins went ahead during the third hour and he and Moss built up a good advantage on the streaming wet and treacherous track. Once the rain ceased and the track started to dry out, Flockhart/Sanderson forged ahead again and both Moss and Collins were struggling to conserve fuel by selecting neutral and coasting

At Le Mans in 1956 Moss, seen here at the wheel, with Collins, took second place, narrowly beaten by the Jaguar D-type of Flockhart/Sanderson. *(Geoffrey Goddard)*

well before the end of the Mulsanne straight and slip-streaming the 1500cc Porsche entries.

By midnight Walker/Salvadori, driving a restrained race, were fifth and Brooks/Parnell seventh. Moss/Collins were back in the lead by 4 am, 19.3 seconds ahead of the Jaguar, but then the Jaguar went back in front. At about 7.30 am Peter Walker crashed badly in heavy rain at the Dunlop bridge, rebounding off the bank and coming to rest with the DB3S upside down in the road. Moss/Collins lost second gear and with it their chances of staying with the Ecurie Ecosse Jaguar, and the blue D-type pulled out an ever-increasing lead. All the while the DBR1, one of the noisiest cars on the circuit, had been thundering round, but with four hours to go to the finish it ran its bearings. At the 4 pm finish Flockhart/Sanderson were seven laps ahead of Moss/Collins; Trintignant/Gendebien took third place for Ferrari, the Belgian-entered Jaguar of Laurent/Rousselle was fourth, the 1500cc Porsche of von Frankenberg/von Trips fifth and the D-type of Hawthorn/Bueb had climbed back to sixth place. Moss/Collins had driven a fine race, but apart from the loss of second gear, the lack of sufficient power, inadequate aerodynamics and poor fuel consumption had reduced the prospects of an Aston Martin victory. Because of the exceptionally wet weather the second-place DB3S completed the race on one set of tyres.

On August Bank Holiday Monday Salvadori was due to drive DB3S/5 in the over 1900cc sports car race at Brands Hatch, but instead he was taken to hospital after crashing his sports Cooper-Climax in an earlier race. With DB3S/1, Graham Whitehead finished second to Archie Scott-Brown's Lister-Maserati.

Aston Martin missed the Swedish Grand Prix, now a round in the Sports Car World Championship, but following the success of Parnell in 1955 at Oulton Park, entered a team of cars in the *Daily Herald* International Trophy race. The race was marred by heavy rain that had flooded the circuit and, although after a great deal of pumping and sweeping the circuit was considered safe for racing, David Murray did not agree and withdrew the Ecurie Ecosse Jaguars. The decision was much criticized at the time (but Roy Salvadori was one of many to agree with Murray) and it meant a virtual walk-over for Aston Martin. Moss (DB3S/9) won at 76.99 mph from Brooks (DB3S/8), Parnell (DB3S/7) and Salvadori (DB3S/6), whose performance reflected his unease about the state of the circuit. They

The Aston Martin advertisement following the team's win at Oulton Park. Interestingly, the advertisement shows a production DB3S.

were followed by Scott-Brown (Lister-Maserati), Peter Blond (Jaguar D-type) and Graham Whitehead (DB3S/1).

At the autumn Goodwood meeting on 8 September Aston Martin entered two cars in the 21-lap Goodwood Trophy race for sports cars over 1500cc. Inevitably the race proved an Aston Martin benefit. Tony Brooks won with DB3S/7 and for all Salvadori's efforts with the newer DB3S/9 he had to settle for second place. Ron Flockhart (Ecurie Ecosse D-type) was third and Noel Cunningham-Reid (HWM-Jaguar) fourth.

In September at the Radio Show a pit stop competition with change of wheels was staged between Aston Martin and Jaguar – Feltham was narrowly beaten by Coventry. Also in September Whitehead with DB3S/1 won a 10-lap sports car race at a British Automobile Racing Club Members' meeting at Goodwood.

Although Aston Martin had achieved some notable performances in 1956, especially at Rouen and Le Mans, it had been a year of marking time until the new DBR1 was ready and carefully selected events in which the team stood a serious chance of success. The Aston Martin star was in the ascendant and 1957 would bring better results.

7 DBR1 and DBR2: 1957

Following the appointment in late 1956 of John Wyer as General Manager of what was now known as Aston Martin-Lagonda Limited, Reg Parnell became Racing Manager. Parnell was a canny and able driver of vast experience, but since his bad crash with Rob Walker's Formula 1 Connaught at the Crystal Palace in 1956, he had never achieved his former level of fitness.

For the time being Aston Martin retained DB3S/9 and DB3S/10, and a new car, DB3S/11, with wishbone front suspension was completed from unsold production car DB3S/109. Although the new car was never raced and sold to an American customer, the team did run DB3S/10, with technical changes to which reference is made later, in a couple of events. DB3S/6 and DB3S/7 were rebodied in 1956-style and sold, respectively to Graham Whitehead and Peter Whitehead, whilst DB3S/8 had also been rebodied and sold to a United States consortium that included Joe Lubin and Carroll Shelby. Salvadori sold DB3S/5 to 'Tommy' Atkins, for whom it was raced by Graham Hill in 1957.

The team's main effort was concentrated on the DBR1, first seen in 2493cc form at Le Mans in 1956. The new car was largely the work of designer Ted Cutting and featured a multi-tubular space-frame constructed from small-diameter chrome molybdenum tubing and, at a weight of around 116 lb complete with bulkhead, scaled around 50 lb less than the chassis of the DB3S. The wheelbase was increased to 7ft 6in., which did much to improve the handling, and the track was increased to 4ft 3.5in. The suspension was derived from that of the DB3S with trailing links and torsion bars at the front and, at the rear, a de Dion axle passing behind the gearbox assembly; the de Dion tube was located by a Watts linkage (retaining the sliding guide of the DB3S) and there were longitudinal torsion bars. Steering was by rack-and-pinion. There were dished Borrani wire wheels to accommodate Girling single-caliper disc brakes without servo assistance, although off-set Borrani wheels as on the DB3S were fitted in 1956.

Although the 1957 DBR1 RB6 engine retained the cylinder dimensions of the DB3S (83 x 90mm) and the 60-degree twin-plug cylinder head, it featured gear-driven (instead of chain-driven) overhead camshafts, dry sump lubrication and, initially, a four-bearing crankshaft. The most significant change was the adoption of an aluminium-alloy cylinder block that successfully obviated the problems suffered with the V12 Lagonda. In this form, with three Weber 45 DCO carburettors, power output was 240 bhp at 6250 rpm.

The greatest weakness of the DBR1 was the new David Brown CG537 gearbox, mounted transversely at the rear of the car. The aim was to concentrate the masses of the engine and transmission at the front and rear of the car respectively, and this layout did much to improve the handling compared with the DB3S. From the 7.5in. triple-plate Borg & Beck clutch at the rear of the engine, the drive was taken through a Hardy Spicer propeller shaft to a pair of helical gears on the front of the gearbox. These gears were separately detachable for changes of final drive ratio. The second of these gears drove a bevel pinion meshing with a crown wheel on the primary shaft laid across the car. The five forward gears and reverse were all of the straight-toothed constant-mesh type, engaged by dogs, with the central pinion gear on the secondary shaft driving the ZF differential mounted above the gearbox. There was dry-sump lubrication for the gearbox with oil supplied to loaded gears through valves in the selector rods. Drive to the rear wheel was by Hardy Spicer drive-shafts.

The layout of the gearbox was inspired to a certain extent by the design of the Maserati 250F gearbox/final drive, an example of which was loaned to Aston Martin by the Gilby team at the request of Roy Salvadori. In early races there was a marked tendency for the 'box to stick in gear and even when the trouble had been sorted, drivers had difficult in changing down and frequently grated and crashed the gears in their efforts to find the right ratios. It was ironical that such an unsatisfactory gearbox should have been the product of David Brown's own company that was supposed to be a specialist in the field.

The body of the DBR1 was panelled in 20-gauge magnesium alloy, only 0.03in. thick and very much prone to damage of a minor nature in the paddock or workshop, and this in itself made the DBR1 unsuitable for private owners. The car

The experimental 2490cc DBR1 on its début at Le Mans in 1956. *(Geoffrey Goddard)*

scaled dry 1760 lb., 301 lb. lighter than the DB3S in its final form and much the same as the contemporary Ferrari *Testa Rossa* V12 3-litre.

When the engine development was fully completed, the DBR1 would prove to be as fast as any of the 3-litre cars, but in the meanwhile its improved roadholding would do much enhance

An interesting photograph taken in the Racing Department at Feltham in early 1957. DBR1/1 is seen with the less rounded 1957 nose, but with the longer 1956 headrest and DB3S off-set wheels.

Aston Martin's chances of success. To have produced a new car that was so nearly right from the moment it was first raced was a magnificent achievement for a small company – the team's limitations were only too obviously exposed by the fact that only the original DBR1 with 2493cc engine was ready to race at the beginning of 1957.

For 1957 Roy Salvadori and Tony Brooks remained with the team, but Moss was now fully committed to Maserati in sports car racing and Peter Collins to Ferrari. Noel Cunningham-Reid, a promising young driver who had handled Lister-Bristols and HWM-Jaguars with success, joined the team and other drivers were brought in for various races.

Aston Martin were not ready in time to compete in the Sebring 12 Hours race in 1957 and so their first event was in the British Empire Trophy at Oulton Park in April. Because of the fuel restrictions following the Suez crisis, the organizers ran the event as three separate races, for cars up to 1200cc, up to 2000cc and over 2000cc. The team fielded DBR/1, still in 2493cc, 223 bhp form, for Roy Salvadori and DB3S/10 for Cunningham-Reid. The DBR1 featured the less

In 1957 Roy Salvadori sold DB3S/5 to 'Tommy' Atkins. Here the car is being tested at Goodwood by Graham Hill before the start of the racing season.

rounded nose and smaller headrest adopted in 1957 and the offset wheels. The DB3S was fitted experimentally with CAV fuel injection and in this form had a power output of 236 bhp at 6250 rpm. At one stage Wyer was considering using CAV fuel injection on the DBR1, but rejected the idea for the usual reasons associated with early fuel injection, a poor power curve and unsatisfactory throttle response.

In practice Archie Scott-Brown with the new

Roy Salvadori waits to move out on to the grid with DBR1/1 for the Unlimited Capacity race at the 1957 British Empire Trophy meeting at Oulton Park.
(T. C. March)

Lister-Jaguar was two seconds faster than Salvadori. He made a poor start in the race, but was leading at the end of the first lap with the works Astons in second and third places. At the finish of this 25-lap race Salvadori was beaten into second place by ten seconds and Cunningham-Reid in third place was nearly a minute behind Salvadori. Aston Martin were not disappointed with the results, for, after all, the Lister-Jaguar was a lightweight 'sprint' car. A portent of the future troubles was the jamming gearbox suffered by Salvadori in the closing laps and about which he complained vociferously to Reg Parnell in the paddock after the race. Although Parnell and Salvadori were good 'mates' and Roy drove for Parnell long after Aston Martin had retired from racing, there was always an 'edge' between them. In this race Graham Whitehead finished fourth with DB3S/6.

Sixteen days later Aston Martin were in action again at the Easter Goodwood meeting with the 2493cc DBR1/1 driven by Salvadori and DB3S/9 driven by Tony Brooks. At Goodwood DB3S/9 was fitted with a 2992cc engine developing 224 bhp at 6000 rpm. As at Oulton Park, the principal opposition in the 50-mile Sussex Trophy came from Archie Scott-Brown with the Lister-Jaguar and he won by a margin of 21.2 seconds from Salvadori with Brooks third. Behind the leaders came Duncan Hamilton (Jaguar D-type), Peter Blond (HWM-Jaguar) and Graham Whitehead (DB3S/6), and Graham Hill (DB3S/5) finished tenth.

For their next outing the Aston team chose the Belgian Sports Car Grand Prix at Spa-Francorchamps on 12 May. The DBR1s ran for the first time with full 2922cc engines with DBR1/1 driven by Salvadori and DBR1/2 driven by Brooks. The opposition was not of the strongest (the last Mille Miglia road race was run the same weekend) and, apart from Jacques Swaters with a 3.4-litre V12 Ferrari, consisted of a total of six Jaguar D-types, plus the private DB3S entries of Peter and Graham Whitehead.

At the start of the race Brooks shot into the lead, heading Salvadori, Hamilton (Jaguar D-type), Henry Taylor (D-type entered by Jaguar dealer Murkett Brothers) and Rousselle (Equipe Nationale Belge-entered D-type). Brooks revelled in the high speeds and fast curves of the Spa circuit which, Salvadori freely admitted, intimidated him, and led throughout to win at 103.97 mph and set fastest lap of 109.37 mph. Salvadori had a less happy race, for, in torrential

Salvadori on the grid at Oulton Park in conversation with Aston Martin tester Roy Parnell and Reg Parnell. (T. C. March)

rain, he was passed by both Taylor and Rousselle, but as the rain eased he was able to fight his way back to finish second, 1 min 52 sec behind his team-mate. Behind the Aston Martins came a quartet of D-types, the 1500cc Lotus of Herbert Mackay Fraser and the private DB3S entries of Peter and Graham Whitehead. Both DBR1s were slowed because of rain entering the cockpits and getting under the drivers' visors, a fault rectified before the cars were next raced.

On 19 May Graham Hill drove DB3S/5 in a 10-lap unlimited capacity sports car at Brands Hatch. Right from the start he fought a furious duel with Peter Blond (HWM-Jaguar), he was second on the last lap, came out of Druids in the lead and spun at Clearways, rejoining the race to finish third behind Blond and Maurice Charles (Jaguar D-type).

The same day Peter and Graham Whitehead drove their DB3S cars at Snetterton. In the unlimited sports car race Graham retired because of clutch problems, but Peter finished third behind Scott-Brown (Lister-Jaguar) and Protheroe (Tojeiro-Jaguar). The last race of the day was a Formule Libre event and Peter Whitehead was again third behind Scott-Brown and Jim Russell with the now obsolescent Gilby Maserati 250F.

Salvadori finished second at Oulton Park to Scott-Brown's Lister-Jaguar. This photograph shows off the superb lines of the DBR1. (T. C. March)

At Oulton Park Noel Cunningham-Reid finished third with DB3S/10 fitted with CAV fuel injection. *(T. C. March)*

Another DB3S driver in the 1957 British Empire Trophy, Graham Whitehead with DB3S/6 which he drove into sixth place in the over 2000cc race *(T.C. March)*

The first important race entered by Aston Martin in 1957 was the Nürburgring 1000 Kms event on 26 June, a round in the Sports Car World Championship and an event, on paper at least, in which the team's prospects of success were not of the greatest. Aston Martin entered DBR1s for Salvadori/Les Leston (DBR1/1) and C. A. S. Brooks/Noel Cunningham-Reid (DBR1/2), together with DB3S/10 for Peter and Graham Whitehead. DB3S/10 ran with a 2992cc engine developing 231 bhp at 6000 rpm and experimental wishbone front suspension. The team also brought DB3S/9 as a spare.

Maserati entered a total of four cars, two V8 4.5-litre 450S models, a V12 3.5-litre and a 6-cylinder 300S driven by Fangio, Moss, Schell, Herrmann, Bonnier, Scarlatti, Godia-Sales and Gould in various – and confusing – permutations. From Ferrari came a V12 4.1-litre (Collins/Gendebien), a V12 3.8-litre (Hawthorn/Trintignant) and the V12 3-litre *Testa Rossa* prototype (Gregory/Morolli). Scuderia Ferrari had also entered a 3-litre *Europa* Grand Touring coupé, but Trintignant crashed heavily with this in practice and it non-started. There were also three Jaguar D-types entered by Ecurie Ecosse

and the Murkett Brothers' D-type for Henry Taylor/Scott-Brown.

In practice in the wet on the Thursday Brooks was fastest, he was second fastest only to Fangio on the Friday and Aston Martin did not practice on the Saturday. Denis Jenkinson wrote in *Motor Sport*, July 1957, 'The whole Aston Martin team were put very severely in their place by the unbelievable Brooks, and no one was more embarrassed about it than Brooks himself, but he just cannot help being a superb driver and even when not trying he is faster than most, so that when he does "have a go" he shakes the very top of the tree, and it will not be long before some of the accepted stars will have to come tumbling down.'

The Le Mans start was headed by two Maseratis, one to be driven by Fangio and one to be driven by Moss, but Fangio had set the times for both. Brooks was first away, but his initial lead soon evaporated and by the end of lap 8 Moss was heading the field. On only the next lap, however, Moss's 450S shed a wheel and Brooks went back in font. While Cunningham-Reid was at the wheel, the DBR1 stayed ahead and by lap 22, half-distance, Brooks/Cunningham-Reid led by four minutes with Salvadori/Leston and the

Tony Brooks with DBR1/2 on his way to a win in the Spa race in May 1957. This was the first time that the DBR1 was raced with a 3-litre engine. *(Geoffrey Goddard)*

Whiteheads holding fifth and sixth places. The Maseratis were out of the picture because of mechanical problems and the Ferraris lacked the steam to close the gap on the leader.

As the race drew to a close, the tension in the Aston Martin pit was immense. To quote *Autosport*, 'Half an hour and three laps to go … a daily newspaper correspondent was confident enough of the result to round off his story and reach for the phone to London. Two laps and 20 mins … nobody in the Aston Martin pit spoke a word, nor hardly dared mention the leading car. One lap, 14 miles, less than 10 mins … surely nothing could go wrong now, not *now* … Then, as on that first lap seven and a half hours earlier, the clear note of the Aston's engine could be heard two miles down the road. The note grew in volume like the approach of an angry hornet, and as suddenly as before the car crested the rise beneath the bridge and plummeted past the chequered flag to the sound of German cheers, seldom so freely awarded to a foreign winner.'

By the finish Salvadori/Leston, slowed by the DBR1 gearbox jamming in fourth and by a broken chassis, had dropped back to sixth place and the Whiteheads were classified ninth. For Aston Martin it was a magnificent triumph, scored in the face of immensely strong opposition, but opposition that had not proved as fast or as reliable as form would have indicated. Behind the winning Aston the order was Collins/Gendebien (Ferrari 4.1-litre), Hawthorn/Trintignant (Ferrari 3.8-litre), the 1.5-litre Porsche of Maglioli/Barth fourth and with the Maserati 300S taken over by Fangio/Moss fifth.

On 30 May the Fôrez 'Six Hours' meeting was held at St. Étienne. The circuit was the 3.5-mile Terrenoire composed of closed public roads and including both sides of a dual carriageway *Autoroute*. Despite the billing of 'six hours' the races for sports cars up to 1500cc and over 1500cc lasted only 1½ and 2 hours, respectively. It was a perfect meeting for private owners and the Unlimited race was dominated by Jaguar D-types with the Ecurie Ecosse entries of Ron Flockhart and John Lawrence finishing first and second and with Duncan Hamilton third. Aston Martin was represented by the Whiteheads; Graham finished a sound fourth, whilst Peter finished back in ninth place.

At Le Mans the 3670cc DBR2 made its début driven by Peter and Graham Whitehead and ran exceptionally well until eliminated by gearbox problems. *(Geoffrey Goddard)*

DBR2

The Aston Martin team had been developing a new car, primarily intended for short British races, the DBR2. The power unit was the Tadek Marek-designed 3670cc (92 x 92mm) 6-cylinder twin overhead camshaft engine with single-plug ignition, the valves set in the head at 80 degrees, the inlet ports on the right-hand side of the engine and the exhaust ports on the left (the opposite to the DBR1), that was being developed for the production DB4 to be announced at the 1958 Earls Court Show. Compression ratio was 9.25:1, there were six Weber 48 DOE single-choke carburettors and power output was claimed as 287 bhp at 5750 rpm. Transmission was by the SC532 5-speed gearbox, similar to that of the Lagonda.

When David Brown sold the V12 Lagondas, they were based on the 1954 chassis. The 1955 chassis were retained and now used for the DBR2. These chassis, with a wheelbase of 7ft 9in and front and rear track of 4ft 5in, were of multi-tubular construction, but of the backbone type so that the driver sat outside the chassis proper. Suspension followed that of the DBR1, with trailing links and torsion bars at the front and a similar de Dion rear axle. The body, ostensibly similar to that of the DBR1 was carried on light tubes with supporting points at the front, scuttle and rear.

For the Le Mans race Aston Martin prepared a team of three cars, DBR1/1 for Salvadori/Leston and DBR1/2 for Brooks/Cunningham-Reid, while the new DBR2/1 was entrusted to the Whitehead brothers. For Aston Martin the race proved an unmitigated disaster, just as it did for Ferrari and Maserati, while Jaguar, whose cars were now entered only by private owners but with works support, enjoyed an immense triumph. In the opening hours the Ferraris and the Maseratis battled for the lead and the DBR1s and the D-types kept a watching brief. Soon the race settled into a repetition of 1956, with the Ecurie Ecosse D-type of Flockhart/Bueb leading the DBR1 of Brooks/Cunningham-Reid, and by midnight the gap was still only 2 min 24 sec.

By 2 am, when Cunningham-Reid handed over to Brooks, the DBR1 was two laps in arrears and plagued by the gearbox jamming in fourth. Not long after he had taken over, Brooks lost control at Tertre Rouge whilst trying to find another ratio, hit the bank and was rammed by Maglioli's Porsche. He suffered quite bad injuries, but was just about fit enough to race again for Vanwall in the European Grand Prix at Aintree three weeks later. By this time both of the other Aston Martins were out of the race. Although very much down on power because of fuel starvation and misfiring, the DBR2 ran well and surprisingly swiftly until the gearbox breather became blocked and the gearbox pumped out all its oil. After the race it was found that because of the complicated fuel system necessitated by the six carburettors, the engine was over 50 bhp down compared with the maximum achieved in bench tests and that this system was also causing misfiring above 5000 rpm. The Salvadori/Leston DBR1 was another victim of a jammed gearbox and limped round in fourth until an oil pipe broke on lap 113.

The D-type Jaguars of Flockhart/Bueb, Sanderson/Lawrence, Lucas/'Jean Marie' and Frère/Rousselle took the first four places, with the Ferrari of Lewis-Evans/Severi fifth and another D-type, that of Hamilton/Gregory, sixth. One Aston Martin did survive the race, the privately entered production DB3S of Colas/Kerguen, which finished 11th overall, was the sole survivor in the 3000cc class and thus the class winner.

Only DBR1/1 was entered for Salvadori in the sports car race at the British Grand Prix meeting at Aintree on 20 July, but Peter and Graham Whitehead entered their private DB3S cars. Archie Scott-Brown at the wheel of the Lister-Jaguar was fastest in practice by a margin of ⅕th of a second and 'Salvo' knew that his prospects of beating the Lister were slim indeed. The race was run in drizzle falling on to a streaming wet track and at the finish the Aston was well behind in second place. Duncan Hamilton took third place with his D-type Jaguar.

On August Bank Holiday Monday Graham Whitehead drove DB3S/6 in the Kingsdown Trophy race at Brands Hatch, finishing third behind Scott-Brown (Lister-Jaguar) and Graham Hill (Tojeiro-Jaguar), but beating Peter Blond (HWM-Jaguar) after a stiff fight.

Although Aston Martin had originally planned to compete in the Swedish Grand Prix in August, they did not enter and next ran in the Grand Prix of the Royal Automobile Club of Belgium held at Spa-Francorchamps over three hours on 25 August. DBR1/1 was driven by Salvadori, while Brooks was at the wheel of DBR1/2, fitted for the first time with the new 95-degree cylinder head

Although the works cars failed at Le Mans, the production DB3S of Colas/Kerguen finished 11th overall and won the 3000cc class. *(Geoffrey Goddard)*

stop at the pits for a wheel-change. In all, Genebien stopped at the pits three times, while Brooks lapped steadily to win at 118.56 mph. Masten Gregory (Ferrari 3.8-litre) finished second ahead of Gendebien, Salvadori with his gearbox jammed in fourth and a lap in arrears took fourth place and Brian Naylor with the Murkett Brothers' D-type Jaguar finished fifth ahead of the private DB3S cars of Graham and Peter Whitehead.

Another minor success followed at Snetterton on 1 September, when Peter Whitehead drove DB3S/7 into second place behind Scott-Brown's Lister-Jaguar in the very wet over 2700cc sports car race.

The Suez crisis in late 1956 had resulted in the 1957 International Trophy meeting being postponed from its usual date in May to September. David Brown made a very determined effort at this meeting with an entry of four cars in the race for sports cars over 1500cc. Salvadori drove the newly completed DBR2/2, while DBR2/1 was entrusted to Cunningham-Reid; Tony Brooks was at the wheel of DBR1/2 with the new 95-degree cylinder head and Stuart Lewis-Evans, by now a regular member of the Vanwall team and being given a trial drive by Aston Martin, was at the wheel of DBR1/1 with the original 60-degree cylinder head.

The team was determined to make a show of strength, but there was very real hope that Salvadori with the extra power of his DBR2 might be able to beat Scott-Brown with the Lister-Jaguar. The Lister had dominated British sports car races throughout the year and had defeated the DBR1 twice. Although the DBR2 was a very undeveloped car, Salvadori like it, found it easier to drive than the DBR1 and was much happier with the gearbox in unit with the engine. In practice he was 0.6 seconds faster than Scott-Brown.

In the race Salvadori led initially from Brooks, but Scott-Brown had made a very poor start. By the fourth lap Scott-Brown had thrust the Lister into the lead, Salvadori choosing to use only third and fourth gears on this circuit fought back, passed Scott-Brown on the approach to Stowe corner on lap 5 and went on to win the race, despite all Archie's desperate efforts to stay with the DBR2. Salvadori's average of 96.08 mph was the fastest ever in a British sports car race and he set a new sports car lap record of 98.48 mph. Cunningham-Reid finished third, Brooks fourth and Lewis-Evans sixth.

which, with a compression ratio of 9.25:1, boosted power output to 252 bhp at 6000 rpm. In addition the team fielded DBR2/1, now running on three Weber twin-choke 50 DCO carburettors and with a power output of 279 bhp at 5750 rpm, for Noel Cunningham-Reid. It was an odd decision that the fastest car should be entrusted to the most junior member of the team.

From Aston Martin's point of view practice was not encouraging. Cunningham-Reid crashed heavily, and although he was unhurt, the car was too badly damaged for him to run in the race. Olivier Gendebien was fastest in practice with his 4.1-litre Ferrari in 4 min 11.7 sec and Brooks, who thoroughly enjoyed Spa, could only respond with 4 min 15.8 sec before his engine lost all its oil pressure. Throughout practice and the race Salvadori was plagued by gearbox trouble. Brooks was only able to start the race because David Brown's de Havilland Dove aircraft flew out a replacement crankshaft.

At the start Brooks was first away, but throughout the race he had to closely monitor his oil pressure. Fortunately for Aston Martin Gendebien made a very poor start and each time he closed up on the leading DBR1, the shortcomings of his Englebert tyres caused him to

Roy Salvadori with DBR1/1 on his way to second place in the rain-soaked sports car race at the British Grand Prix meeting at Aintree in July. *(T. C. March)*

Shortly afterwards John Bolster tested the Lister-Jaguar for the motor sport weekly *Autosport*, and his test was headed 'A Weekend with Britain's Fastest Sports Car'. This, coupled with the success of the DBR2 at Silverstone led to some interesting correspondence in the magazine.

In the issue of 25 October there was published a letter from J. C. M. Barman of Poole, Dorset:

'Much as I admire the magnificent efforts of the "small concern" in producing really fast cars, I feel that your contributor John Bolster seldom does credit to the "bigger boys".

'He writes in headlines on page 498 of the 18th October issue, that he had tested "Britain's Fastest Sports Car" – one can only assume that Mr David Brown has not yet lent him a DBR2.

'I, and a few of my friends, watched – with bated breath – the whole of that magnificent race at Silverstone. A. S. B. (more power to his elbow) needed *all* the road on *all* the corners in his vain effort to keep up with a car that appeared to be going on rails.

'Britain's *second* fastest sports car – Please!'

This drew support for Lister-Jaguar and there

was a post-script to Gilbert R. Mann's letter in the issue for 8 November:

'Can any of the Aston Martins compare favourably, taking into consideration the difference in engine size, with 0–100 mph in 11.2 sec of the Lister-Jaguar?'

This attracted the 'big guns' and in the issue for 15 November there was published a letter from Alan Dakers, Public Relations Office of The David Brown Companies:

'It is a little unfortunate that certain of your readers seem unable to discuss this subject without becoming emotional about the driving ability of Archie Scott-Brown [many of us still feel *very* emotional about the driving ability of Archie – *Author*] or the extent of Brian Lister's resources, neither of which is in question and neither of which is relevant.

'The simple facts are that on the only occasion that the Lister-Jaguar and the 3.7-litre Aston Martin have met, the Aston Martin won. The only inference to be drawn is that on that day on that circuit either the Aston Martin was the fastest car or Salvadori was the faster driver. We leave it to the Lister-Jaguar–Scott-Brown supporters to

Aston Martin finally beat Scott-Brown and the Lister-Jaguar in the sports car race at the International Trophy meeting at Silverstone in September. Here is the winner, Roy Salvadori with DBR2/2. *(T. C. March)*

decide which they prefer.

'Mr Gilbert R. Mann asks if the fact that Salvadori's race average was 0.6 seconds faster makes the Lister-Jaguar the second fastest car. He appears to have answered his own question. Does he suggest that it makes the Aston Martin the second fastest car and by what inverted reasoning does he arrive at this conclusion? Incidentally, Salvadori's winning speed (96.08 mph) was the fastest sports car race ever won at Silverstone or anywhere in Britain.

'Mr Mann also poses the question, "Can any of the Aston Martins compare favourably taking into consideration the difference in engine size, with the 0–100 mph at 11.2 seconds of the Lister-Jaguar?" Mr Mann's generous allowance for the disparity in engine size is not necessary. The Aston Martin DBR1 (2922cc) was recently timed from 0–100 mph in 11.2 seconds, the mean of two consecutive runs in opposite directions carrying a passenger in addition to the driver. The Aston Martin DBR2 (3670cc) in identical conditions was timed in 11 seconds dead. The axle ratios in both cases were as raced at Silverstone and the speed was accurately recorded by a fifth wheel speedometer.'

The DBR1 had more than proved its worth during the year, especially as the result of its success at the Nürburgring and despite its transmission shortcomings. Once again, however, the team suffered as the result of a divided effort and it is ironical that despite the fact that only two DBR1s were available, the team embarked on yet another new project, the DBR2, which there was insufficient time to fully develop. In addition Aston Martin dissipated effort on minor races rather than concentrating on the rounds in the Sports Car World Championship.

8   DBR1 and DBR2: 1958

Late in 1957 the Fédération Internationale de l'Automobile determined that there would be a 3000cc capacity limit in Sports Car World Championship events from the 1958 season. It was a very late decision, but in many ways it was anticipating a trend. The first and immediate effect was that Maserati, already in financial trouble from trade debts in the Argentine following the collapse of the Péron government and with a hopelessly over-extended motor racing programme (including the vast cost of developing and racing the Tipo 450S sports cars), withdrew from both sports car racing and Formula 1. The main contenders were now Ferrari with the 3-litre V12 *Testa Rossa* cars and Aston Martin (although the British team still did not contest all the rounds in the Championship). Porsche, previously battling only for class success, was now in with a chance for outright victory when the 3-litre cars fell by the wayside. The Jaguar D-type was obsolescent, and following Jaguar's withdrawal of its works team at the end of 1956, there were little prospects of a successor. Coventry did, however, produce a 3-litre version of the famous XK120 engine for use in the D-type, as well as the 'spirit specials', the Listers and Tojeiros. The new engine proved lacking in stamina in endurance races. The DBR2 was restricted to non-Championship races, nothing much was done to develop it apart from increasing engine capacity and results soon showed that the 3.8-litre Lister-Jaguar *was* the faster car.

The remaining DB3S cars were sold by the works. Graham and Peter Whitehead retained DB3S/6 and DB3S/7, respectively, and achieved a notable international success. Barton Motors (Preston) Ltd were involved in some very interesting deals in DB3S Aston Martins at this time. It seems that they bought DB3S/10 off the works. DB3S/10 was quickly sold to John Dalton (and registered JFD 40) and he part-exchanged DB3S/2 (now registered UDV 609), which he had acquired late in 1957. Later in 1958 UDV 609 was bought by Roy Bloxam, who part-exchanged his HWM-Jaguar. Dalton achieved many success in minor events with DB3S/10, still fitted with wishbone front suspension.

On the championship trail Aston Martin entered the Sebring 12 Hours race on 22 March. Stirling Moss, who had rejoined the team following Maserati's withdrawal from racing, co-drove DBR1/2 with Tony Brooks – a convenient partnership as both drove for the Vanwall Formula 1 team again in 1957 – and Salvadori/Shelby were entered with DBR1/1. All DBR1s raced in 1958 had the new 95-degree cylinder head and they were fitted with the new seven-bearing crankshaft, together with Weber 50 DCO carburettors. The opposition at Sebring included a strong Ferrari team and two Lister-Jaguars entered by Briggs Cunningham.

Stirling Moss took the lead on the first lap, ahead of Hawthorn (Ferrari) and Salvadori, who were scrapping hard. Brooks relieved Moss in the third hour, still in the lead, and Shelby, who had taken over from Salvadori, was fourth. After 62 laps the Salvadori/Shelby car was retired because of a broken front cross-member (bolted on DBR1/1, but welded on DBR1/2 and subsequent DBR1s) and the leading DBR1 slowed because of the almost inevitable sticking gearbox. When Brooks came into the pits, 3 min 45 sec were lost while the mechanics battled with the gearbox, and then Moss started a frantic chase after the now leading Ferrari of Phil Hill/Peter Collins. Despite the bonnet flying off, breaking away part of the windscreen and chipping Moss's visor, Moss closed to within 15 seconds of the leader before the DBR1 finally succumbed to its gearbox malady. Hill/Collins won the race for Ferrari at 86.60 mph.

At the Easter Monday meeting on the Sussex circuit Aston Martin entered DBR2/1 for Stirling Moss in the 21-lap Sussex Trophy race for Sports cars over 1100cc. Since 1957 a number of modifications had been made to the DBR2s. Engine capacity was now 3910cc (95 x 92mm) and on compression ratio of 8.7:1 power output was 284 bhp at 5500 rpm. The engines fitted to the DBR2s remained the same throughout their racing careers despite modifications. The main opposition at Goodwood came from Archie Scott-Brown with the works 3.8-litre Lister-Jaguar, whilst perhaps the most interesting entry was a works Ferrari with 2-litre V6 engine driven by Peter Collins. Moss was first away from the Le Mans start, but the green and yellow Lister shot ahead on Lavant Straight, Moss was back in front

At Goodwood on Easter Monday Stirling Moss drove DBR2/1 to a win in the sports car race. *(Geoffrey Goddard)*

Moss in the paddock at Oulton Park talking to tester Roy Parnell with DBR2/1 before the 1958 British Empire Trophy race. *(T. C. March)*

on lap 8 and two laps later the duel came to an end when the Lister retired with steering problems. At the finish Moss was over 20 seconds ahead of Collins and Duncan Hamilton (Jaguar D-type) took third place.

Only a week later the team was in action again in the British Empire Trophy race at Oulton Park, once again run in three heats and a final. Aston Martin entered DBR2/1 for Stirling Moss and DBR2/2 for Tony Brooks. DBR2/2 was now developing 298 bhp at 5700 rpm on an increased compression ratio of 9.0:1. Scott-Brown was fastest in practice and again there were prospects of a great battle in the Unlimited capacity class. In practice Brooks's DBR2 broke its ZF final drive and for the race there was substituted a 3.9:1 axle ratio (all that was available) in place of the original 4.1:1 ratio and as a result Brooks was unable to get into top gear anywhere round the circuit.

Scott-Brown led away at the start of the Unlimited heat, but after a few laps he eased his pace (it later emerged that he was worried about rising oil temperature), Moss went into the lead on lap 10 and shortly afterwards Scott-Brown was forced to retire because of a broken steering arm. Moss won the heat with Brooks, well back, in second place. For the final Scott-Brown took

On the starting grid for the final of the 1958 British Empire Trophy race with, nearest the camera, Stirling Moss and DBR2/1. *(T. C. March)*

over Bruce Halford's private Lister-Jaguar. Moss soon settled into the lead in the final, Brooks moved up into second place after the retirement of Cliff Allison's 2-litre Lotus 15 and this was the finishing order with Scott-Brown third and Duncan Hamilton (Jaguar D-type) fourth. Moss, jointly with Graham Hill (Lotus 15), set a new circuit record of 89.70 mph.

So far, by default, the score was 2–0 in favour of the Astons, but only a week later the DBR2s and the works Lister-Jaguar were in action again at the International meeting at Aintree. In the 45-mile unlimited capacity sports car race Brooks was at the wheel of DBR2/1 and Salvadori drove DBR2/2. From the fall of the flag Scott-Brown led from Masten Gregory (Ecurie Ecosse-entered Lister-Jaguar). After only ten laps Brooks was out with final drive failure (a recurrent problem on the DBR2), Salvadori took second place when Gregory spun his dark blue Lister and in his pursuit of the leader set a new sports car lap record of 87.38 mph. Gregory recovered to finish third.

Next came the International Trophy meeting at Silverstone and Aston Martin fielded three

cars in the over 1500cc sports car race. Brooks drove DBR2/1, Salvadori DBR2/2 and Moss was at the wheel of the experimental DBR3/1; this was a DBR1 chassis with a modified Tadek Marek-designed DB4 engine with dry sump lubrication, very oversquare cylinder dimensions of 92 x 75mm (2992cc), six single-choke Weber 48 DOE carburettors and a claimed power output of 258 bhp at 7000 rpm on a 8.9:1 compression ratio. At this stage in its development the DBR3 had only marginally greater power than the DBR1, but there were hopes that power could be boosted to a much higher figure. At the front there was double wishbone and longitudinal torsion bar suspension (as on the already built, but as yet unraced, DBR4 Formula 1 car) and the DBR3 was distinguished by a bulge in the bonnet to clear the rather deeper engine.

Facing the Astons was a strong entry of Lister-Jaguars, but only two of these really counted, the works car of Archie Scott-Brown, which was fastest in practice in 1 min 43 sec, and the Ecurie Ecosse car of Masten Gregory, which was second fastest in 1 min 44.6 sec. Tony Brooks was the fastest of the

The experimental DBR3/1 driven by Stirling Moss at Silverstone in May 1958. Note the bulge in the bonnet necessary to clear the deeper engine. *(T. C. March)*

The DBR2s took the first two places in the final at Oulton Park. This is Brooks with DBR2/2, who finished second. *(T. C. March)*

Silverstone was dominated by the Lister-Jaguars, with Hawthorn's Ferrari third. The best Aston Martin performance was that of Roy Salvadori, who finished fourth with DBR2/2. *(T. C. March)*

Tony Brooks in practice for the Targa Florio with DBR1/3. *(Geoffrey Goddard)*

Aston drivers in 1 min 46.2 sec, but Moss was not much slower with the incredibly noisy DBR3. Another important entry was the works V6 3-litre Ferrari driven by Mike Hawthorn.

As usual there was a Le Mans start and Scott-Brown led away from Brooks and Salvadori. By the end of lap 5 Scott-Brown still led, Gregory had moved up into second place, then came the Astons and Hawthorn's Ferrari. At the end of the following lap Brooks stopped at the pits, losing two minutes. Brooks had been unhappy with the handling of his car and when Gregory pumped his brakes just after passing the Aston, Tony had mistaken his brake lights for a signal that there was something obviously wrong with the Aston. Reg Parnell was not best pleased.

Gregory now had the bit between his teeth, passed Scott-Brown at Copse on lap 7 and soon began to pull out a good lead. Salvadori, unhappy with the handling of his car, was holding off Hawthorn, whose Ferrari was very quick in a straight line but deficient in roadholding, and Moss was right up the Ferrari's exhausts. It was

an exciting race by any standards. Moss retired at the end of lap 14 when the DBR3's engine ran its bearings, Hawthorn passed Salvadori and at the finish the order was Gregory–Scott-Brown–Hawthorn–Salvadori–Brooks. Gregory's race average of 99.54 mph was higher than the previous sports car lap record and the DBR2s were simply not quick enough to beat the latest Listers. Everyone, including Archie himself, had been astounded by Gregory's performance and the ease with which he had been able to pull away from the works Lister. For no obvious or known reason John Wyer did not develop the DBR3 further and the chassis was used to form the basis of DBR1/4, raced in 1959.

Immediately after the Silverstone race the David Brown team flew in a chartered Avro York to Sicily, where the new DBR1/3 was to be driven in the Targa Florio by Moss/Brooks with DBR2/1 as a training car. The Targa Florio was a round in the Sports Car World Championship, held over the 44.7-mile Little Madonie circuit, the last of the great road races now that the Mille Miglia had

A superb shot of the Sicilian landscape with Moss powering past the pits in DBR1/3. *(Geoffrey Goddard)*

come to an end. It was to survive until 1973 and one of the highlights of the motor racing year was to watch a sports-racing car hurtling over the winding, narrow, badly surfaced Sicilian roads, parting the densely packed crowds as it approached and hearing its exhaust reverberating off the walls as it roared through the small villages.

It was at Moss's instigation and as a result of his pressure that the team entered the race, but it was sad that David Brown did not make a full team entry in the Sicilian race and get there in plenty of time for training and preparation. The principal opposition faced by Moss and Brooks was a quartet of Ferrari V12 *Testa Rossas* driven by Musso/Gendebien, Hawthorn/von Trips, Collins/ Phil Hill and Munaron/Seidel. If the big cars failed, then victory was likely to go to a 1500cc Porsche or Osca.

Brooks was forced to learn the circuit from scratch and reckoned that he lapped it in training 16 times (a greater distance than the actual race) in a variety of cars; Moss, familiar with the circuit from 1955, took his wife Katie for a lap in the DBR2 and turned in a time very close to his 1955 lap record with the Mercedes-Benz 300SLR.

The start was at 6.30 am and the race was to last 10½ hours, right through the heat of the day, and it was run in strong sunshine under a limpid blue sky. The slowest cars started first and the runners were released at intervals of 40 seconds. On the first lap Moss went off the road, buckling a wheel, and came round in tenth place after having the spare fitted at the Aston outpost in the mountains. When Moss arrived at the finishing line, he went straight into the pits. The problem was a serious vibration caused by fracturing of the crankshaft damper. Nearly half an hour was lost in the pits, during which the damper was removed and the wheels changed. Once he was back in the race Moss drove at a furious pace, and by the end of his fourth lap he had twice lowered the lap record, leaving it at 42 min 17.5 sec (63.33 mph) and had risen to eighth place. It was all to no avail, for on the fifth lap the gearbox broke and the DBR1 was out of the race without Brooks even getting a drive. Musso/Gendebien (Ferrari) won from Behra/Scarlatti (Porsche).

A week later the Aston Martin team was in action again in the Belgian Sports Car Grand Prix on the very fast Spa circuit. Ian Scott-Watson, who was accompanying Jim Clark, entered with the Border Reivers' ex-Murkett Brothers' D-type, reported the race for *Autosport*

and, as no mean driver himself, his comments make interesting reading:

'To the driver making his first appearance what a truly formidable circuit Spa appears! Up hill and down dale, sweeping though series after series of fast bends, many of them among the typical wooded Ardennes scenery, it is indeed a circuit which requires the most from a driver. The sweep down and up through Eau Rouge, the corner at Burnenville which tightens up, the long downhill sweep through the bend past Malmédy to Stavelot, where the houses seem to jut out into the road, that fast uphill stretch after Stavelot corner where one loses count of the bends and finally the hairpin at La Source before the pits – any one seems equally awe-inspiring!'

As this was not a Championship race, there was no capacity limit and the leading contenders were the Lister-Jaguars of Masten Gregory and Archie Scott-Brown and the Aston Martin DBR2s of Paul Frère (DBR2/2), included in the team because of his intimate knowledge of the circuit, and Carroll Shelby (DBR2/1). Moss, Brooks and Salvadori were all competing that weekend in the Monaco Grand Prix. The total entry included five Listers, four Ferrari *Testa Rossas* and three D-type Jaguars. In comparison with the fastest Listers, the Astons were disappointingly slow and it seemed that the team's only hope of victory was that the Listers should blow their engines.

The early laps of the race witnessed a frightening duel between Scott-Brown and Gregory, with the green and yellow and the dark blue constantly swapping the lead, Frère and Shelby third and fourth and Bueb fifth with an Ecurie Ecosse D-type. Scott-Brown was in the lead when he lost the Lister round Clubhouse Bend on a road freshly dampened by a rain shower. The Lister grazed the Clubhouse wall, hit a road sign which broke the right-hand track-rod and, out of control, the car careered down the slope at the edge of the road, rolled and caught fire; Scott-Brown was pulled from the wreckage terribly burned and he died the following day. Unchallenged, Gregory won the race by a very comfortable margin at 121.33 mph from Frère and Shelby.

After this race the DBR2s were not again raced by the works, but soon afterwards were exported on loan to the United States with the engines increased in capacity to 4164cc (98 x 92mm).

For the Nürburgring 1000 Kms race Aston Martin made a serious and determined effort with three cars for Moss/Jack Brabham (DBR1/3), Brooks/Lewis-Evans (DBR1/2) and Salvadori/Shelby (DBR1/1). In addition, as practice 'hacks', the team brought along a DBR2 and a DB2/4 coupé. Brabham was regarded by Reg Parnell as a very good prospect for inclusion in the Aston Martin team and Salvadori, who partnered Brabham at Cooper, encouraged the choice. Despite their somewhat strained relationship, Reg always took notice of what Roy had to say. As it was, Brabham had never settled down to driving the DBR1 with the same confidence and verve as he did with Coopers, and there is reason to suppose that once he had driven the rear-engined Coopers, he was never again really happy with a front-engined car. With Lewis-Evans in an Aston, this meant that the complete Vanwall team was driving for David Brown. Lewis-Evans was a superbly skilled, balanced driver, but he was so slight in frame and low in stamina that he suffered badly in endurance racing. The works entries were backed up by DB3S/6, driven by Peter and Graham Whitehead.

Once again the main opposition came from Ferrari with a team of four V12 *Testa Rossas* and these were driven by Hawthorn/Collins, Musso/Phil Hill, von Trips/Gendebien and Seidel/Munaron. Ecurie Ecosse entered a team of three Jaguar D-types, but they were uncompetitive, largely due to their primitive roadholding. Fastest in practice was Hawthorn in 9 min 43.4

sec, but, despite the fact that practice with the Aston Martin race cars was kept to a minimum to save them for the race, Moss was second fastest in 9 min 45.6 sec.

Moss led away from the start and on that first 14.17-mile lap built up an enormous lead from Hawthorn, Brooks, von Trips and Salvadori. At the end of the second lap Salvadori crawled into the pits to retire with the gearbox jammed in top. On the same lap Brooks spun off and as he accelerated away, there was a fuel blow-back and flames from the exhaust blistered the paintwork on the driver's door; he rejoined the race in 14th place. Moss stopped at the pits at the end of lap 10 to hand over to Brabham and the Australian joined the race with the difficult task of maintaining the lead at the wheel of a car that he had driven for only three laps in practice. Within two laps Hawthorn had caught and passed the Aston Martin and a lap later Brabham was back in the pits. After the DBR1 had been refuelled and four new tyres fitted, Moss rejoined the race in third place; he passed von Trips for second place and he took the lead again when Hawthorn's Ferrari punctured an Englebert tyre. By this stage Brooks was in fifth place and at the end of lap 15 he stopped for fuel and tyres and to hand over to Lewis-Evans. Poor Lewis-Evans felt sick because of the turns and bumps of the Nürburgring, he lost fifth place to Phil Hill, Hill had a rear tyre puncture, the leading Porsche

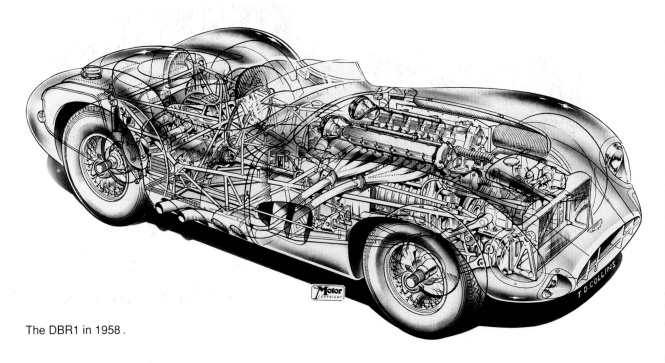

The DBR1 in 1958.

Partnered by Jack Brabham, Stirling Moss scored a magnificent victory with DBR1/3 in the Nürburgring 1000 Kms race. *(Geoffrey Goddard)*

retired and Lewis-Evans assumed fourth place.

Moss stopped again at the end of lap 24 to hand over to Brabham and the Aston's lead was so immense that there was little chance of Brabham losing it. Brabham handed back to Moss after five laps and there was excitement in the pits, for Collins had stopped to hand over to Hawthorn and both Aston Martin and Ferrari were on the same lap. The Aston pit work was slicker and Moss roared off to consolidate his lead. Two laps from the finish Brooks put the fourth-place car into the ditch when a slower car crossed his line. At the chequered flag Moss/Brabham were 3 min 44 sec ahead of the Ferrari of Hawthorn/Collins, with other Ferraris driven by von Trips/Gendebien, Musso/Phil Hill and Seidel/Munaron third, fourth and fifth. The Whiteheads brought their DB3S across the line in tenth place. It was a

When Brabham and Collins (Ferrari) stopped at the end of lap 29 at the Nürburgring, their positions in the pits represented their positions on the road. Reg Parnell on the pit counter blares final instructions, with Brabham to his left, as Moss takes off in DBR1/3 with full tanks and new rear tyres. Hawthorn spent another minute in the pits before joining the race. *(LAT)*

brilliant success for Aston Martin, but much of the credit was due to the superb driving of Stirling Moss.

Three weeks later the team was in action again at Le Mans and, now that the race was limited to cars of up to 3000cc, with their best chance of success to date. The line-up was DBR1/3 driven by Moss/Brabham, DBR1/2 driven by Brooks/Trintignant and DBR1/1 driven by Salvadori/Lewis-Evans. In addition the Whiteheads entered DB3S/6. The principal opposition came from the works Ferrari *Testa Rossas* and there were also Lister-Jaguar and Jaguar D-type entries.

Despite all the promise, it was a bad race for the team. The four Aston Martins led away from the start, by the end of the first lap Moss was four seconds in front of Hawthorn (Ferrari), Brooks, von Trips (Ferrari) and Salvadori, and gradually extended his lead. Moss was acting as 'Tiger' for the Aston Martin team, just as he had for Jaguar in years gone by. Within the first 30 minutes of the race both Ecurie Ecosse D-types were out

with engine trouble. With just over two hours' racing completed, Moss's DBR1 blew its engine because of a broken con-rod on the Mulsanne straight. The Moss/Brabham car was running with a lower axle ratio than the other team cars, but, certainly, Moss had not over-revved.

Shortly afterwards torrential rain began to fall and it fell for most of the remainder of the race. After four hours, Hill/Gendebien (Ferrari) led from von Trips/Seidel (Ferrari), Hamilton/Bueb (D-type), Brooks/Trintignant and Kessler/Gurney (Ferrari) with the Whiteheads seventh and Salvadori/Lewis-Evans eighth. Shortly afterwards Lewis-Evans collided with a spinning Panhard on the approach to Tertre Rouge, revolved into the bank and crawled back to the pits, where Reg Parnell decided that the car was too badly damaged to continue.

Brooks/Trintignant were still lapping steadily and by midnight the order was Hamilton/Bueb, Gendebien/Hill with the surviving works Aston Martin third, three laps in arrears, and the

The private DB3S/6 of the Whitehead brothers which finished tenth at the Nürburgring in 1958. *(Geoffrey Goddard)*

At Le Mans Aston Martin prestige was maintained by Peter Whitehead (seen here) and Graham Whitehead with DB3S/6, with which they finished second behind the Ferrari of Phil Hill/Olivier Gendebien. *(Edward Eves)*

private DB3S fourth. At 6 am Trintignant retired DBR1/2 at Mulsanne corner with gearbox failure and at 11.30 am Hamilton lost his D-type, then in second place, at Arnage and crashed heavily. Olivier Gendebien/Phil Hill went on to win the race for Ferrari and the Whiteheads did much to maintain Aston Martin prestige by finishing second, almost 100 miles behind the winner.

On 12 July Graham Whitehead drove DB3S/6 at the Aston Martin Owners' Club meeting at Silverstone, winning the 10-lap scratch race for sports cars over 1500cc from John Dalton's DB3S and finishing third in the Arthur Bryant Memorial Trophy handicap race behind Jean Bloxam (DB3S coupé) and John Dalton.

Aston Martin declined to enter the Sports car race at the Grand Prix meeting at Silverstone in July because the organizers refused to implement a 3000cc capacity limit. David Brown was not prepared to expose the team to yet another pasting from the Listers.

The Tourist Trophy was revived at the

The Le Mans start at the 1958 Tourist Trophy race at Goodwood. As usual Moss is quickest off the mark and leads away from team-mates Shelby and Salvadori. *(LAT)*

Pit stop for Moss with the winning DBR1/2 in the Tourist Trophy. *(LAT)*

Goodwood circuit in Sussex in 1958 and was held on 13 September with sponsorship from *The News of the World*. It was a round in the Sports Car World Championship, but counted only for half-points as it lasted a mere four hours. Ferrari had the Championship in the bag, so did not enter, the Listers failed to provide serious opposition and the DBR1s had an easy race. DBR1/2 was driven by Moss/Brooks, DBR1/3 by Shelby/Lewis-Evans and DBR1/1 by Salvadori/ Brabham. Both DBR1/2 and DRB1/3 had engines with the increased bore of 84mm, giving a capacity of 2992cc. Moss was fastest in practice in 1 min 32 sec, with both Brooks and Salvadori just a fifth of a second slower.

Moss led away from Shelby and Salvadori at the Le Mans start and the Astons held the first three places for most of the race. On lap 10 Salvadori collided with Greenall's Lotus and lost 24 seconds while his car was checked in the pits. When he rejoined the race, he had lost a couple of places, but

On his winning drive in the Tourist Trophy Moss was, for once, superbly partnered and Tony Brooks, seen here, also drove a fine race. *(Geoffrey Goddard)*

he was soon back in third position. Towards the end of the race Salvadori passed Lewis-Evans to take second place and Reg Parnell stage-managed an in-line finish with only four-fifths of a second covering the three DBR1s. Moss/Brooks averaged 88.33 mph and Moss set a new sports car lap record of 93.30 mph. Behind the Astons came Behra/Barth (Porsche), Gregory/Ireland (Jaguar D-type) and Blond/Hamilton (D-type).

In the Sports Car World Championship Aston Martin finished second with 18 points to the 32 of Ferrari, but it must be remembered that Porsche had in fact achieved the same number of points as Aston Martin (but lost out on the number of wins) and six of Aston's points had been gained by the Whiteheads with their private entry at Le Mans.

In October David Brown agreed to a request from Joe Lubin, a long-time Aston Martin supporter, to compete in the 203-mile Riverside Grand Prix at Riverside Raceway, California.

DBR1/1 was shipped out on the *Queen Mary* shortly after the Tourist Trophy and Salvadori flew across the drive the car. There was no capacity limit at Riverside and the entry list included Lance Reventlow's immensely successful, home-built 5.5-litre Scarabs and 4.1- and 4.9-litre Ferraris. The DBR1 was hopelessly outclassed and in the oppressively hot conditions on race day was plagued by fuel vaporisation. Salvadori was eighth fastest in practice and he finished sixth in the race after a spin. As a public relations exercise, the race proved a fiasco for Aston Martin.

Although the opposition was weaker than previous years, and despite the 3000cc capacity limit, Aston Martin was still not the dominant marque in sports car racing. The success had been pretty well balanced by the failures, but the best was yet to come.

9 DBR1: 1959

Aston Martin's two preoccupations for 1959 were the new Formula 1 programme and Le Mans, which was to be the only race in which the DBR1s were to be entered – although the latter decision was reversed early in the year. In all races the works DBR1s had 2992cc engines and Weber 50 DCO carburettors were adopted. In addition the team built up a fifth DBR1, DBR1/5, with 2922cc four-bearing engine for privateer Graham Whitehead, who had been racing Aston Martins since 1953. This was raced with more than a small degree of works support.

The first deviation from the original plans came when the organizers of the Sebring 12 Hours race pressured John Wyer to enter the 1959 event. Wyer was reluctant, but agreed when the organizers committed themselves to paying all the team's expenses (in the past 'proper' starting money had never been paid at Sebring, just a contribution such as meeting the cost of

hotel bills). As time was short, Team Manager Reg Parnell and the mechanics flew with DBR1/1 to New York, where they were met by a transporter which took the car to Sebring and back.

As raced at Sebring, DBR1/1 on a compression ratio of 9.1:1 developed 254 bhp at 6400 rpm. The drivers were Roy Salvadori and Carroll Shelby, both of whom drove the team's Formula 1 cars in 1959. Although Stirling Moss (Lister-Jaguar) and Lance Reventlow (Ferrari) were fastest in practice the main opposition came from a team of works *Testa Rossa* Ferraris. Salvadori led initially, but then slipped back to battle furiously for third place with Pedro Rodriguez (Ferrari). Salvadori stopped at the pits with a misfiring engine, the plugs were changed and he rejoined the race. Shortly after Shelby had taken the wheel, with 32 laps completed, the car retired because of what John Wyer has described as clutch trouble. However, according to Roy

In 1959 the British Empire Trophy was held as a Formula 2 race, but there was also a race for unlimited capacity sports cars. Graham Whitehead drove his private DBR1/5, but went off the road at Old Hall in the wet. *(T. C. March)*

Also running at Oulton Park was John Dalton with DB3S/10, but the results were dominated by Climax-powered cars and Dalton was unclassified. *(T. C. March)*

Salvadori's memory, the gear-lever broke and Gregor Grant in *Autosport* reported, 'He [Shelby] had not been driving long when the gear-lever came away in his hand. Furious, Shelby parked the car by the side of the track and walked back to the pits, where he threatened to hit Reg Parnell over the head with the broken lever. And so the lone Aston was out.' Ferraris took the first two places ahead of Porsche.

Graham Whitehead made his début with DBR1/5 in a 21-lap race at Goodwood on Easter Monday, finishing third behind the works Lister-Jaguars of Ivor Bueb and Peter Blond. Next for Whitehead came the British Empire Trophy meeting at Oulton Park (the Trophy race itself was now a Formula 2 event); in the 20-lap sports car race, held on a wet track, Whitehead went off at Old Hall after a slow drive. A week later Whitehead was in action at the Aintree '200'

The Aston Martin line-up in the paddock at the May Silverstone meeting. Note that there were two DBR1s for Stirling Moss. *(T. C. March)*

In the sports car race at Silverstone Stirling had to settle for second place behind Salvadori with Coombs's Cooper-Maserati. *(T. C. March)*

Jack Fairman at the wheel of the winning DBR1/1 in the Nürburgring 1000 Kms race. Unfortunately Fairman was not up to the job and this threw an immense burden on Stirling Moss, who did most of the driving. *(Edward Eves)*

Fairman out, Moss in, as Stirling almost fights his way back into the cockpit after Fairman's first spell at the Nürburgring. Fairman had spun off in avoiding a slower car, denting the tail of the DBR1, and Moss had to make up a 22-second deficit. *(LT)*

meeting and he finished fifth in the 17-lap race for sports cars over 1100cc. That the DBR1s and even the Listers were no match for the modern lightweight breed of Cooper Monacos and Lotus 15s was rubbed home in the 1100–3000cc sports car race at the International Trophy meeting at Silverstone in May. David Brown entered Stirling Moss with a choice of DBR1s, DBR1/1 and DBR1/2, and he chose the latter for the race. Again the team had diverted from its original plans, under pressure and special pleading from the organizers, the BRDC. Graham Whitehead also entered DBR1/5. Salvadori was the winner with John Coombs's 2.5-litre Cooper-Maserati (and Graham Hill had led with his 2-litre Lotus 15 until forced to retire' with final drive problems). Moss finished second and Whitehead again took fifth place.

Stirling Moss was very keen to drive a DBR1 in the Nürburgring 1000 Kms race and John Wyer eventually agreed, on the understanding that he used DBR1/1, the team's spare, and paid all the expenses himself. Aston Martin's only contribution was to provide two mechanics. Moss wanted a steady dependable co-driver and it was agreed that Jack Fairman would fit the bill perfectly. Graham Whitehead also entered DBR1/5 with Brian Naylor as co-driver. The opposition came from three works Ferrari *Testa Rossas* and the works Porsche team. Despite limited practice to conserve the car, Moss was fastest in 9 min 43.1 sec.

At the Le Mans start Moss was away first and as the race progressed he built up an ever-increasing lead. Whitehead was already in trouble, for the oil filler had not been properly closed and he was well smothered with oil before

At Le Mans Aston Martin scored the victory that the team had sought for so long. Here Roy Salvadori is at the wheel of the winning DBR1. This photograph reveals clearly the aerodynamic changes made for this race. *(Geoffrey Goddard)*

he could manage to close it. The private Aston Martin was in fourth place when it retired because of a broken gear-lever. When Moss made his stop for Fairman to take over on lap 17, he had a lead of almost 5½ minutes, after successively breaking the lap record. The Ferraris steadily closed on Fairman, but he seemed to have plenty of advantage in hand. On lap 23 Fairman was baulked by a slower car and spun off into a ditch tail first. While Fairman dug the car out with his bare hands, the minutes ticked by and Stirling started to pack his bag to go home. Eventually Fairman arrived at the pits, having pushed the car out with his back, 1 min 15 sec behind the now leading Ferrari, the tail of the Aston crumpled and his overalls covered in mud.

A quick check-over of the car, and Moss was away in fourth place and started a furious chase of the leaders. It was just the sort of race that Moss relished, as he calmly out-drove the opposition and clawed his way back to the front. On lap 24, he took third place from Maglioli's Porsche, on lap 28 he took second place from the Ferrari of Gendebien and a lap later he was back in the lead. When Moss stopped at the pits again at the end of lap 33, he had pulled out a lead of 2 min 43 sec. Fairman, with the car refuelled, left the pits with a lead of 1 min 47 sec and when he stopped again two laps later the Gendebien/Phil

Hill Ferrari was leading again narrowly. In the remaining nine laps Moss regained the lead and built up an advantage of 41 sec.

It had been one of the finest drives in Moss's career, matched only by his performances in the 1961 Monaco and German Grands Prix. It was a marvellous 'hat trick' for Aston Martin with the team's victories at the circuit in 1957, 1958 and 1959, and Moss was to make it a 'hat trick' for himself by winning the 1960 race with Dan Gurney at the wheel of the Camoradi 'Bird-cage' Maserati. As for Fairman, he was a sound, reliable 'journeyman' driver and his poor performance at the Nürburgring was out of character. Denis Jenkinson commented in *Motor Sport*, 'Admittedly the Aston Martin tactics paid off, as they did last year, but surely it would make winning more easy if they found Moss a co-driver of higher calibre. To run a single-handed race two years running is enough to take years off his life.'

For Le Mans a number of changes were made to the cars; apart from a great deal of development work, the DBR1s had modified higher and rounder rear bodywork with valances over the rear wheels, partially enclosed front wheels, long exhaust systems that ran under the cockpit and emerged at the tails of the cars and ducts under the nose for cooling the front brakes. The entry was made up as follows:

No. 4, Moss/Fairman (DBR1/3, four-bearing engine, 9.6:1 compression ratio, 255 bhp at 6000 rpm)

No. 5, Salvadori/Shelby (DBR1/2, seven-bearing engine, 9.3:1 compression ratio, 244 bhp at 6000 rpm)

No. 6, Trintignant/Frère (DBR1/4, seven-bearing engine, 9.3:1 compression ratio, 242 bhp at 6000 rpm)

Henry Taylor was reserve driver.

It was part of the team's strategy that Moss with the fastest car should be the pace-setter and the car was regarded as expendable. Graham Whitehead had entered DBR1/5 for himself and Brian Naylor. The car had been fitted with an engine rebuilt at the works, but this blew during practice (possibly because it had been over-revved before it had fully 'freed') and the team lent Whitehead its spare seven-bearing unit.

The only real opposition faced by the Aston Martins was a strong team of works Ferrari *Testa*

Rossas and, although a number of Jaguar-powered cars were entered, the D-type engine in 3-litre form lacked the reliability to last a 24-hour race. Moss was first away and in the early laps of the race he led from the howling pack of red V12s. Further back the other Astons were all running steadily with Salvadori eighth, Trintignant ninth and Whitehead 11th. Behra (Ferrari) snatched the lead from Moss, Moss went ahead again when the thirstier Ferrari made its first, rather disorganized pit stop, and when Fairman relieved Moss after 2 hours 35 min, No. 4 Aston Martin had a lead, after the pit stop, of a few seconds. Gurney, who relieved Behra, went ahead of the rather plodding Fairman, and Salvadori/Shelby and Trintignant/Frère were still running steadily in fifth and eighth places. Naylor flipped the Whitehead DBR1, in tenth place, at White House and was removed to hospital with arm injuries. Although the Moss/Fairman car dropped back to third place, it came to the front again only to retire because part of the head of a valve had broken away. Behra/Gurney dropped back with their

Another view of the winning DBR1 at Le Mans, this time with Carroll Shelby at the wheel. *(Geoffrey Goddard)*

The start of the 1959 Tourist Trophy with Shelby well on his way. Moss is already out of sight. No 29 is Graham Hill (Lotus 15). *(Geoffrey Goddard)*

works *Testa Rossas* because of falling oil pressure and retired later as a result of overheating and the Salvadori/Shelby DBR1 took the lead, followed by the surviving two works Ferraris.

During the night hours the leading DBR1 developed a bad rear-end vibration and Salvadori stopped at the pits for this to be investigated. The mechanics could not trace the problem, despite a second stop, and Salvadori was told to carry on until the routine pit stop. When the car was jacked up, it was discovered that the problem was a damaged rear tyre, probably the result of running over debris dropped by another car. Reg Parnell was very critical of Salvadori for not diagnosing the problem, but clearly the mechanics should have found it. Back into the race, Salvadori started to make up lost ground, for the Aston was now in second place, three laps in arrears. The Gendebien/Hill car retired

because of overheating on the Sunday morning and Salvadori/Shelby went on to score a fine victory ahead of Trintignant/Frère from the Ferrari 250GT of 'Beurlys'/Helde. Le Mans was the one victory that David Brown had sought and the victory in itself brought another goal, the Sports Car World Championship, in which Aston Martin trailed Ferrari by two points. Accordingly the decision was made to enter a full team of cars in the Tourist Trophy at Goodwood in September.

At Goodwood Aston Martin revealed a new single-car transporter based on a lengthened chassis intended for use with the production Lagonda V12 saloon that never proceeded. The team also brought along DBR1/1 as a spare, fitted with a Maserati 5-speed gearbox with right-hand change of which Stirling Moss commented, 'Throughout the DBR1's career we had soundly criticized its dreadful gearbox and in TT practice

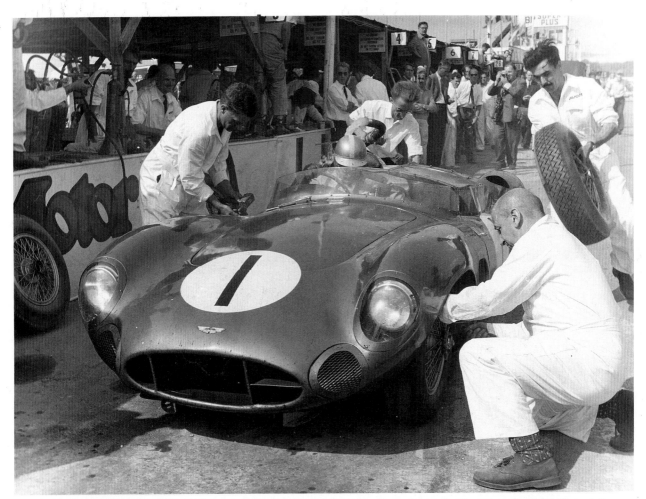

A classic photograph that is well worth reproducing again. Roy Salvadori has stopped at the pits with DBR1/3, Jack Sopp is at the nearside front wheel and fuel is gushing from the refuelling hose. Within moments the car was ablaze. *(LAT)*

The fire extended to the pits and to Avon's stock of tyres, but fortunately it was soon brought under control. *(Geoffrey Goddard)*

Reg Parnell helps push away the badly burnt DBR1. Among those looking on is radio commentator and journalist John Bolster, recognizable by his deerstalker. *(Geoffrey Goddard)*

Moss took over DBR1/2 from Shelby/Fairman and, as usual, driving superbly, went on to win the race and ensure Aston Martin's victory in the Sports Car World Championship. *(Geoffrey Goddard)*

I drove one fitted for the first time with a Maserati transaxle, which was superb. At last the DBR1 really had become a fabulous car, and I as pulling 6300 rpm in top and 6500 through the gears, and still – just – taking Fordwater flat.'

Changes to the team cars included reversion to the original exhausts, deletion of the rear wheel valances, ducts in the tops of the rear wings (to aid tyre cooling) and Jackall built-in jacks operated by compressed nitrogen. DBR1/3 (four main bearing engine developing 250 bhp at 6000 rpm on a 9.6:1 compression ratio) was entered for Moss/Salvadori, DBR1/2 (seven main bearing engine developing 240 bhp at 6000 rpm on a 9.3:1 compression ratio) for Shelby/Fairman and DBR1/4 (seven main bearing engine developing 242 bhp at 6000 rpm) for Trintignant/Frère. In addition Graham Whitehead entered DBR1/5 for himself and Henry Taylor.

There was strong Ferrari and Porsche opposition in this 6-hour race, but Moss was fastest in practice and soon built up a commanding lead, with Shelby second. Whitehead's car stopped out at Lavant because of an electrical fire; after an interval it reappeared in the pits covered with dried extinguisher foam and following a lengthy pit stop Henry Taylor took the wheel. Just after 2½ hours' racing Salvadori brought the leading Aston Martin into the pits. Salvadori was slow to get out of the car, as he fumbled to put it into first gear ready for Moss, but the mechanics were quick and as mechanic Bryan Clayton opened the filler cap, fuel was already gushing out of the hose, soaking Salvadori and the tail of the car, the hot exhaust ignited and within moments the DBR1 was ablaze. Salvadori jumped out of the car, his overalls burning, but a St Johns ambulanceman immediately removed his overcoat and wrapped it round Salvadori to extinguish the flames. The driver's gloved right hand was still burning and so he wrapped his cap round it. By this time the fire had spread to the Aston Martin pit and the 50-gallon fuel drum mounted on a steel tower collapsed on to the pit roof as the heat buckled the supports. Fortunately the fire was soon extinguished, but it was obvious that neither DBR1/3 nor Salvadori were going to race again that afternoon.

Reg Parnell called in Fairman and immediately Moss started another chase for victory. As the works pit had been destroyed, Graham Whitehead withdrew his DBR1 so that the team could use his pit. Moss caught the now-leading Porsche of Bonnier/von Trips, lost the lead when he stopped to refuel and at the chequered flag was 32.4 sec ahead of the Porsche with the Ferrari of Brooks/Hill/Allison/Gendebien only two seconds behind the Porsche. Aston Martin won the Championship with 24 points to the 22 of Ferrari and 21 of Porsche. If Brooks with the third-place Ferrari had caught and passed the Porsche – which he so nearly did – Aston Martin and Ferrari would have had equal points. At a victory dinner on 28 October to celebrate the win, David Brown announced the team's withdrawal from sports car racing. His statement is set out in Appendix 4.

10 Postscript to the DBR1: 1960–62

Following Aston Martin's withdrawal from sports car racing, the two DBR2s were returned from the United States, where they had been raced with some success by private owners (see Appendix 3), and they together with the DBR1s were overhauled. The following advertisement appeared in *Autosport* for 15 January, 1960:

DBR/1 was retained by the works. The two DBR2s were sold to private owners (who achieved little), DBR1/1 was not sold until 1961, but the other two DBR1s continued to enjoy a measure of international success. DBR1/2 was acquired by Major Ian Baillie (who had previously raced a D-type Jaguar) and DBR1/3 was bought by Jock McBain's The Border Reivers team for Jim Clark to drive (this team had previously raced D-type Jaguar and Lister-Jaguar cars). Graham Whitehead continued to race DBR1/5.

Clark made his début with the DBR1, newly painted dark blue and converted to Appendix 'C' with full width windscreen and the modifications to comply with International racing regulations, at the BARC meeting at Oulton Park on 2 April and finished third in the race for sports cars over 1500cc behind the Lotus 15s of Tom Dickson and Michael Taylor. This DBR1 was in action again over the Easter weekend at Goodwood, but Clark spun in practice, denting the tail and splitting the petrol tank, and retired with mechanical problems in the sports car race on the Bank Holiday Monday. At the International Trophy meeting at Silverstone in May, Clark was in sixth place in the over 1500cc sports car race when he retired because of broken throttle linkage.

DBR1/2, DBR1/3 and DBR1/5 were entered in the Nürburgring 1000 Km race. Salvadori was brought into The Border Reivers to co-drive

Jim Clark, later that year to become a member of the Lotus Formula 1 team, at the wheel of DBR1/3 in Group 'C' trim entered by The Border Reivers, in the sports car race at the May Silverstone meeting in 1960. *(T. C. March)*

At Le Mans in 1960 Roy Salvadori was invited to partner Jim Clark at the wheel of DBR1/3 and they finished third behind two Ferrari *Testa Rossas*. Note the high windscreen needed to comply with the latest regulations. *(Geoffrey Goddard)*

The start of the 1961 Le Mans race with Salvadori (No 4) leading away with DBR1/4 entered by John Ogier and co-driven by Tony Maggs from the DB4GT Zagato of Franc/Kerguen (No 1), the winning Ferrari (No 10), the Tipo 63 Maserati of Vaccarella/Scarfiotti (No 9) and the DB4GT Zagato of Fairman/Consten (No 22). *(Geoffrey Goddard)*

DBR1/3 with Clark, but Clark was in fourth place when he retired on lap 6 because of valve trouble and Salvadori never even had a turn at the wheel. Likewise Graham Whitehead retired his car early in the race because of a broken universal joint and his co-driver Henry Taylor was deprived of a drive. Major Ian Baillie and the Hon. Edward Greenall enjoyed an almost pedestrian race with DBR1/2; it was classified fifth in the class for sports cars, 2001–3000cc, but it was so far down the field that its finishing position overall is lost in the mists of time. Not long afterwards, on 12 June, Fairman drove Whitehead's car to an easy win in the Rouen Grand Prix, run as two two-hour heats, ahead of the Ferrari 250GTs of Schlesser and Seidel.

At Le Mans Graham Whitehead ran his Ferrari 250GT, so just the two DBR1s were entered and The Border Reivers car was supported by Reg Parnell and some of the mechanics from Feltham. Salvadori again co-drove with Clark; the DBR1 was a serious contender throughout the race and eventually finished third behind the two leading Ferraris, and Baillie, now partnered by Jack Fairman, took ninth place. There were few further opportunities for the DBR1s to be races in 1960, but one such race was the Angola Grand Prix held in September over a 4.6-kilometre circuit along the sea front and through a side street and the main shopping centre of Luanda. Fairman drove Whitehead's car and was in third place when he retired because of a broken valve spring.

For the Formula 1 team in 1960 Aston Martin had developed the RB6/250 engine with 80-degree cylinder head and transposed porting with the inlet on the right and the exhaust on the left. This engine appeared in a number of private DBR1s. In 1961 John Ogier's Essex Racing Stable acquired DBR1/1, The Border Reivers continued to race DBR1/3, but Baillie with DBR1/2 restricted his outings to minor British events. Graham Whitehead took DBR1/5 to Southern Rhodesia, to run in a couple of races and sell the car. He retired in both the Rhodesian Grand Prix at Salisbury and the Marlborough meeting, but

Early in the 1961 Le Mans race Salvadori (DBR1/4) leads Clark (DBR1/3). Note that DBR1/4 has the later engine with the exhaust on the left side. *(Geoffrey Goddard)*

Salvadori is seen here again with DBR1/4 in the twilight of the Saturday evening; DBR1/4 was eliminated by a fuel leak, after rising to fourth place. *(Geoffrey Goddard)*

the car was sold to G. Pfaff.

Jim Clark was too heavily engaged to drive with The Border Reivers often, but he appeared with Bruce McLaren at the wheel of the Essex car at the Nürburgring. Clark led initially and the car ran very well until lap 25, when, in fourth place, it retired because of a broken oil pipe. At Le Mans the Essex entry, DBR1/4, loaned by the works and fitted with the later engine, was driven by Salvadori and Tony Maggs and The Border Reivers car by Clark/Ron Flockhart. Both entries had full works support, but both retired. Salvadori/Maggs were eliminated by a split petrol tank when in fourth place and Clark/Flockhart by clutch failure when in sixth place. The DBR1s

were now slower in a straight line than some of the Ferrari 250GTs and *Autosport* commented that Moss (with a 250GT) 'caused great amusement by passing both DBR1 Aston Martins right in front of the pits, only to be overtaken again in the Esses'.

The Border Reivers only ran their car in a couple more 'home' events, while they were offering it for sale, and it was a considerable time before it was disposed of. The final serious International appearance of DBR1 was when the Essex car ran at the Nürburgring in 1962, taking a remarkable fifth place overall driven by McLaren/Maggs.

11 DBR4 and DBR5: 1959–60

With some projects Aston Martin devoted too much time and too much effort – far more than their resources would permit – on half-hearted efforts. By the time the project was tackled seriously, the opportunity was wasted. The worst example of this procrastination was the Grand Prix programme. Not long after the DB3 had made its début at Dundrod in 1951, Aston Martin toyed with a modified DB3 chassis powered by a 2-litre version of the LB6 engine. This would have complied with the 2-litre Formula 2 then current and adopted as the Grand Prix Formula of 1952–53, following the withdrawal from racing of Alfa Romeo and the failure of the V16 BRM to become a serious force. The project apparently was opposed by von Eberhorst and before long it was abandoned. It seems that John Heath wanted to buy the 2-litre engines for use in his Formula 2 HWMs, which were powered by what were basically pre-war Alta 4-cylinder twin-cam units, but Aston Martin refused. The problem would not have been the use of engines by HWM, but the constant demand for spares which would have diverted Feltham from more important pursuits.

Two years later Aston Martin projected a car for the 2500cc Grand Prix Formula of 1954 onwards based on a DB3S chassis reduced in width and to be powered by a 2493cc (83 x 76.8mm) version of the DB3S engine. John Wyer reckoned that an alcohol fuel power output was the same as for the 3-litre on pump fuel. In 1953 the DB3S developed around 180 bhp and this sort of power output would not even have made the car competitive with early 1954 Maserati 250Fs and Ferrari Tipo 625s, which developed 220/230 bhp. Once again the project was abandoned, following von Eberhorst's departure from Aston Martin in late 1953 (and in any event the German engineer had been against the plan), although the engine was used in twin-plug form in the British Empire Trophy at Oulton Park in 1955 and 1956.

In 1955 Wyer agreed with Reg Parnell that Aston Martin would build up a single-seater, known as the DP155, using the 1953 chassis. The car was to be entered in the New Zealand part of the Tasman series early in 1956, and as these were Formule Libre races it was intended to use a 3-litre supercharged engine, but this broke during testing at Chalgrove. A 2493cc engine was substituted and

this apparently was fitted with special camshafts, connecting rods and pistons, but how 'special' is far from clear. Parnell non-started in the New Zealand Grand Prix at Auckland on 7 January, 1956, because the engine put a con-rod through the block. Instead he drove Peter Whitehead's Cooper-Jaguar into fifth place. By the Lady Wigram Trophy at Christchurch a replacement, but less powerful 2.5-litre, engine had been fitted to DP155. The Aston Martin was uncompetitive and Parnell finished fourth behind the 3-litre Ferraris of Peter Whitehead and Tony Gaze and Leslie Marr's Jaguar D-type-powered Connaught. A week later Parnell finished second behind Gaze in the 75-mile Dunedin race, ahead of Jensen (Cooper-Norton) and Whitehead (Ferrari). Parnell rounded off the Aston's outings by finishing third in the Southern Centennial race at Invercargill. It had been a cheap learning curve.

Contemporaneously with the development of the DBR1 from mid-1955 Aston Martin put in hand work on a new Formula 1 car. Not only was this a fatal diversion of effort, but the fact that Aston Martin sports cars always suffered a power deficiency compared with their rivals, ensured that the prospects of the new single-seater being powerful enough to match the opposition were minimal. The final blow to the new car's chances was the decision to defer racing it until 1959. With

A cockpit view of the DBR4 on its début in the International Trophy at Silverstone in May 1959. *(T. C. March)*

In the International Trophy the cars flattered only to deceive and Salvadori took an excellent second place with DBR4/1 behind Brabham's Cooper. *(T. C. March)*

very few exceptions it took two to three seasons of racing experience and development before any newcomer to Grand Prix racing could expect substantial success. The Vanwall Special, for example, was first raced in 1954, but it was not until mid-1957 that Vanwall won a major race – and Tony Vandervell had a great deal of experience racing developed and modified Ferraris before embarking on his own Formula 1 programme.

The chassis of the Formula 1 car, typed the DBR4/250, was a very similar multi-tubular structure to that of the DBR1, but of course much narrower with a central seating position. At the front there was originally double wishbone and torsion bar front suspension as used on the DBR3, but this was changed to a layout of double wishbones, coil springs and Armstrong telescopic

dampers in 1958. A de Dion layout was selected at the back, with the de Dion tube located by a Watts linkage, longitudinal torsion bars and Armstrong dampers. Transmission was by the David Brown CG537 5-speed gearbox in unit with the final drive and incorporating a ZF limited slip differential. There was a right-hand gear change.

As fitted to the DBR4/250, the 6-cylinder engine had a capacity of 2493cc (83 x 76.8mm) and with three Weber 50 DCO carburettors and a compression ratio of 10.4:1 power output was 250 bhp at 7800 rpm. The engine was slightly offset in the frame (front to the right, back to the left) to permit an offset prop-shaft, but the driver still sat rather high, straddling the prop-shaft. The intakes for the carburettors, which protruded from the left of the bonnet, were housed in a large, prominent air-collector box and the twin exhausts ran high on the right side of the car. Rack-and-pinion steering from the DB4 was fitted (originally there had been a steering system incorporating Morris Minor parts). There were Girling disc brakes outboard front and rear and Borrani wire wheels with Rudge Whitworth-type knock-on hubs. Styling is a matter of taste, but in the writer's view the lines were clumsy and ungainly, with an excessively long nose, they appeared to lack good aerodynamics (no lessons had been learned from Frank Costin's work for Vanwall) with the air-box projecting into the airstream, a high, near vertical wrap-round screen added as an afterthought and a gap in the cockpit between the front of the fuel tank and the bodywork of the tail.

The DBR4s were eventually raced, in the form described, in 1959, by when only two years of the existing Formula remained, but the first car had been tested with Roy Parnell and Roy Salvadori at the wheel at the Motor Industry Research Association Establishment in December 1957. David Brown decided to concentrate on the sports car programme in 1958. John Wyer has written, 'The car would have been highly competitive in 1958 and we had no trouble in going faster than the Vanwall and 250F Maserati, but by the time the car did appear the rear-engine revolution was well under way and everything front-engined was out of date.' In fact, Maserati as a works team withdrew at the end of 1957 and Vanwall's main opposition in 1958 had come from the Ferrari Dino 246 with which Hawthorn won the Driver's Championship. Apart from the fact that Brooks with the front-engined Ferrari came close to winning the 1959 Driver's Championship, BRM raced front-engined cars in 1958 and 1959 (and won the Dutch Grand Prix in the latter year), Wyer's contention is partially supported by best comparative practice lap times, as shown in the accompanying table.

Silverstone (British Grand Prix, 1958)

Moss (Vanwall)	1 min 39.4 sec
Schell (BRM)	1 min 39.8 sec
Hawthorn (Ferrari)	1 min 40.4 sec

Silverstone (International Trophy, 1959)

Moss (BRM)	1 min 39.2 sec
Brooks (Ferrari)	1 min 40.1 sec
Salvadori (Aston Martin)	1 min 40.4 sec

Aintree (British Grand Prix, 1957 – cars running on alcohol-based fuels)

Moss (Vanwall)	2 min 0.2 sec
Behra (Maserati)	2 min 0.4 sec
Brooks (Vanwall)	2 min 0.4 sec

Aintree (British Grand Prix, 1959)

Salvadori (Aston Martin)	1 min 58.0 sec
Schell (BRM)	1 min 59.2 sec
Shelby (Aston Martin)	1 min 59.6 sec
Moss (BRM)	1 min 59.6 sec

Silverstone and Aintree showed the Astons at their best, for they flattered only to deceive at Silverstone in 1959, and at Aintree both Salvadori and Shelby made a supreme effort. A really fast circuit like Monza showed a very different picture:

Monza (Italian Grand Prix, 1958)

Moss (Vanwall)	1 min 40.5 sec
Hawthorn (Ferrari)	1 min 41.8 sec
Behra (BRM)	1 min 43.2 sec
Gregory (Maserati)	1 min 44.9 sec

Monza (Italian Grand Prix, 1959)

Brooks (Ferrari)	1 min 39.8 sec
Schell (BRM)	1 min 41.6 sec
G. Hill (Lotus)	1 min 42.9 sec
Salvadori (Aston Martin)	1 min 44.7 sec
Shelby (Aston Martin)	1 min 46.4 sec

Originally both Roy Salvadori and Jack Brabham had agreed to drive for Aston Martin, but once Brabham learned that Coventry Climax had produced a full 2495cc version of their twin-cam 4-cylinder engine and that Esso had agreed to provide enough money for Cooper to retain both Brabham and Salvadori, the Australian changed his mind, decided to stay with the Cooper team and tried to persuade Salvadori to do the same. Salvadori's allegiance was to John Wyer and there was no going back and he was joined in the Feltham team by Carroll Shelby, who had been driving obsolescent Maserati 250Fs with considerable verve.

The new cars made their début in the International Trophy race at Silverstone in May 1959 and Salvadori's fastest practice lap of 1 min 40.4 sec with DBR4/1 was joint third fastest with Brabham (Cooper). Moss (BRM) led briefly in the opening laps, but spun off at Copse because of brake problems. For the reminder of the race Brabham led, with Salvadori, second, and these were the finishing positions, with Salvadori setting fastest lap in 1 min 40.0 sec (which equalled the lap record). Shelby with DBR4/2 held fourth place until lap 49, when he retired at Stowe in a cloud of blue smoke. Shelby's car had run its bearings and it was clear from the team's inspection of the engine afterwards that Salvadori's car would not have lasted much longer. This was in a 146-mile race, far shorter than a full-length Grand Prix. To discover this major and fundamental problem in the team's first race smacks of inadequate testing.

Aston Martin missed the Monaco Grand Prix (and somehow evaded adverse press comment) and the DBR4s next appeared at Zandvoort, where they were fitted with new and stiffer con-rods on the advice of the Glacier bearing company. Joakim Bonnier (*front*-engined BRM) was fastest in practice in 1 min 36.0 sec, while Shelby was on the fourth row of the grid with a time of 1 min 38.5 sec and Salvadori was back on the fifth row with a time of 1 min 39.7 sec. After only four laps Salvadori was out of the race because of a broken con-rod. Shelby's car survived another 22 laps until con-rod failure caused the engine to seize at Hondenvlak and the Aston Martin spun viciously out of the race. Bonnier won the race after an exciting dice with Brabham.

Once again Aston Martin missed the next race, the French Grand Prix, and reappeared at the British race at Aintree. Although Team Manager Reg Parnell was cheerfully telling the drivers that the bearing problem had been solved, the cars were still restricted to 7250 rpm (instead of the 7800 rpm for which they were designed). Salvadori, encouraged by Parnell and using full revs, achieved a place on the front row of the grid, joint fastest with Brabham in 1 min 58.0 sec, but this necessitated a change of engine before the race. Despite a pit stop because fuel was sloshing

everywhere and a spin later in the race, Salvadori struggled on to finish sixth, a lap in arrears. Shelby was in ninth place when he retired after 68 laps of this 75-lap race because of valve trouble. In 1959 the German Grand Prix was held on the banked Avus circuit and so, not surprisingly, Aston Martin gave the race a miss. Even the Coopers failed and the works Ferraris took the first three places. The Feltham team next appeared at the Portuguese Grand Prix held on the Monsanto circuit at Lisbon. It was a winding, twisting circuit of great difficulty and the starting grid was dominated by the Coopers, which took the first four places. Salvadori (2 min 13.38 sec) and Shelby (2 min 13.58 sec) were back on the fifth row – Moss took pole position with Rob Walker's Cooper-Climax in 2 min 2.89 sec. There was an immense time difference between the competitive runners and the rest, and the Astons were hopelessly in the latter category. The race was won by Moss (Cooper-Climax) with Salvadori sixth, three laps in arrears, and Shelby eighth, four laps in arrears.

The team appeared at the next race, the Italian Grand Prix at Monza, with Salvadori with an arm in bandages and a burnt face after the Tourist Trophy disaster and at the wheel of DBR4/3, a new car with the centre-section of the body integral with the chassis and with a new one-piece de Dion tube. Inevitably the cars were well back on the grid and Salvadori, faster of the two entries, was only 17th fastest in 1 min 44.7 sec, with Shelby on the next row back in 1 min 46.4 sec. Salvadori worked his way up to seventh place in the race, only to retire when the engine broke a valve. Shelby finished tenth. As Aston Martin did not enter the United States Grand Prix, this marked the end of the team's season. Jack Brabham (Cooper) won the World Championship from Tony Brooks (Ferrari) and Stirling Moss (Cooper and BRM).

At this point both Aston Martin and Lotus were in complete disarray. Whilst Colin Chapman, working with much more limited finances than Aston Martin, designed and built the Lotus 18 rear-engined Grand Prix contender that won two World Championship races in 1960, Aston neither withdrew nor took serious steps to improve the situation. It *seems* that DBR4/1 was sold to Australian Lex Davison with a 3-litre engine before the start of the 1960 season and that DBR4/2 was scrapped, for certainly these cars were not available to the works drivers in

Carroll Shelby with DBR4/2 in the 1959 Portuguese Grand Prix on the Monsanto circuit near Lisbon. He finished eighth. *(Geoffrey Goddard)*

Maurice Trintignant with the lighter, more compact, but even more less competitive DBR5/1 in the 1960 International Trophy at Silverstone. He finished tenth. *(T. C. March)*

Shelby's DBR4/2 in front of the pits during practice for the 1959 Italian Grand Prix at Monza. *(Geoffrey Goddard)*

1960. DBR4/3 was retained and DBR4/4 was apparently only completed in 1960.

Aston Martin toyed with the possibility of building a rear-engined car and during early 1960 a chassis was assembled. The team's main efforts, however, were devoted to the DBR5, a lighter, shorter version of the 1959 design with substantially modified engine and in its final form independent rear suspension. This attempted refinement of an existing design – and lack of radical thinking – was part of the malaise that hampered all Aston Martin racing efforts.

The wheelbase of the DBR5 (typed the DP201) was reduced to 7ft 3in (from the 7ft 6in of the DBR4). At the front there was now torsion bar independent suspension, a two-piece prop-shaft

was used to lower the driving position and the rear suspension was modified so as to incorporate a one-piece de Dion tube running in front of the gearbox, which was the lighter, more positive Maserati 5M-60.

Wyer, however, made the biggest changes to the RB6 engine. A new 80-degree cylinder head had been designed with the assistance of Associated Motor Cycles and was based on the technology used in the AJS 7R racing motorcycle engine. This resulted in a reversal of the induction and exhaust sides of the engine so that the inlet ports were on the right and the exhaust on the left. New magnesium blocks were cast to be used with the new heads. Experiments were made running the new engines on Amal

Another view of Trintignant with DBR5/1 hounded by Ireland's Lotus in the 1960 British Grand Prix. This time the Frenchman finished 11th. *(T. C. March)*

At Silverstone Salvadori drove DBR5/2, but retired because of an engine misfire and handling problems.
(Geoffrey Goddard)

carburettors (as used on the 7R) without success and with Weber 50 DCO instruments it was soon discovered that the angle of the inlet ports was such that the carburettor float levels were affected and the engines were misfiring badly. At a late stage the decision was made to use Lucas fuel injection and this resulted in a reduction in power output to 245 bhp at 7500 rpm.

Originally Jim Clark negotiated to drive for the team, but he in fact drove for Lotus, and veteran driver Maurice Trintignant joined Salvadori in the Aston Martin team. Once against the team's first race was the International Trophy at Silverstone. At the start of practice Moss lost control of his Walker-entered Cooper and spun into Salvadori's DBR5/2, tearing off the front suspension. The engine (which was running on Webers) and gearbox were transferred back to DBR4/3 back at Feltham and Salvadori started from the third row of the grid with a time of 1 min

57.6 sec. Moss (Cooper) took pole in 1 min 50.4 sec. Salvadori retired after four laps with the inevitable engine misfire and Trintignant finished tenth, four laps in arrears. Innes Ireland won with the new Lotus 18-Climax.

Aston Martin again missed the Monaco race and entered only DBR5/1 for Salvadori in the Dutch Grand Prix. Moss tried the car during practice, was very unimpressed and could not lap below 1 min 40 sec, while Salvadori by a supreme effort achieved 1 min 37.8 sec. The team also tried DBR4/3 in practice. Moss's pole time with his Lotus was 1 min 33.2 sec. At Zandvoort, the fastest 15 were paid starting money, but the next five were also allowed to start. After 30 years there is an element of confusion as to what exactly happened. Only *Autosport* published a full list of practice times and their list of the fastest 15 in fact listed '14' cars and drivers with Salvadori 13th fastest. They have clearly omitted

Daigh (Scarab), who, unlike team-boss Reventlow, qualified. In any event David Brown withdrew the Aston Martin and Reventlow pulled out both Scarabs. Brabham (Cooper) won the race from Innes Ireland (Lotus).

Feltham made only one other outing in 1960, at the British Grand Prix at Silverstone, where both cars were back on Weber carburettors and Salvadori's DBR5/2 was fitted with independent torsion bar rear suspension. Brabham took pole position in 1 min 34.6 sec, while Salvadori, whose car was handling even worse than ever, was on the fourth row with a time of 1 min 39.4 sec and Trintignant recorded 1 min 43.8 sec. Early in the race Salvadori stopped to complain about the steering and he retired after 45 miserable laps, weary of battling with the ill-handling DBR5. Trintignant finished 11th, five laps in arrears.

In 1959 the Aston Martins had handled well and braked superbly, lacking acceleration. By 1960 the team had progressed backwards and not only were the cars pathetically slow, but the handling had deteriorated. The team did not race again, but it was not until late August that David Brown announced that the team would not be competing in the remaining Formula 1 events. He added that the change in Formula for 1961 allowed insufficient time for the development of new designs.

12 Grand Touring Cars: 1959–62

In 1955 Tadek Marek had started work on a new 6-cylinder 3670cc (92 x 92mm) engine. Featuring twin overhead camshafts and all-alloy construction, the engine, typed the DP186, was bench-tested in 1956 and from 1957 was used to power the DBR2 sports-racing car. At the London Motor Show in 1958 Aston Martin unveiled the DB4 powered by this engine in 240 bhp form, with a strong platform chassis and a body designed by Touring. This body featured Touring's 'Superleggera' system of construction of light alloy panels fixed to a tubular frame, transmission was by a Borg & Beck 10in single-plate clutch, David Brown 4-speed gearbox and a Salisbury hypoid bevel rear axle. At the front suspension was by unequal-length wishbones, coil springs and Armstrong telescopic dampers. The rear suspension incorporated a rigid axle with coil springs, Armstrong dampers, parallel trailing links and a Watts linkage. There was rack and pinion steering and Dunlop disc brakes front and rear.

A year later Aston Martin revealed the DB4GT at the London Motor Show. The wheelbase had been reduced from 8ft 2in to 7ft 9in, there was a twin-plate clutch, a close-ratio David Brown 4-speed gearbox with synchromesh on all ratios and a Powr-lok limited slip differential. Girling disc brakes were fitted. With three twin-choke Weber carburettors (in place of the SUs of the DB4), twin-plug head and twin distributors Aston Martin claimed a power output of 302 bhp at 6000 rpm. The body was a much shorter, two-seater coupé constructed in 18-gauge magnesium aluminium alloy, with sloping cowled headlamps and a 30-gallon fuel tank with twin chromium-plated filters.

The works-entered Aston Martin DB4GT prototype DP199/1, driven by Stirling Moss, won the race for Closed Cars at the International Trophy meeting at Silverstone in 1959. *(T. C. March)*

1959

The works prototype, DP199/1, was raced in the Grand Touring event at the International Trophy meeting at Silverstone on 2 May, when the model was neither in production nor homologated. Reg Parnell was more than a little anxious that the DB4GT would be disqualified. Stirling Moss, who also drove a DBR1 at this meeting, won the event from a rather motley field that included Jaguar saloons and Colin Chapman at the wheel of a Lotus Elite. As raced at Silverstone the DB4GT had a power output of 267 bhp at 5700 rpm.

This same car was entered at Le Mans, with the 3-litre engine from DBR3/1 detuned for endurance racing with a compression ratio of 8.9:1 (compared with 9.25:1 at Silverstone) and a power output of 238 bhp at what has been said to be 6500 rpm (but this engine speed seems dubious and probably peak power was developed at 6000 rpm). Among other modifications was the installation of an oil tank for the dry sump engine in the boot. It was a works entry for privateers

Patthey and Calderari. The DB4GT survived for only 21 laps before succumbing to bearing failure.

At the end of the year another DB4GT, 0103/L, the third production car, was prepared for Frank de Arellano of San Juan, Puerto Rico, by the Works Experimental Department, and Moss drove it on 29 November in the GT race at Nassau in the Bahamas. He won a 5-lap heat, but retired whilst leading the final.

1960

Five lightweight cars were built for 1960, one of which (0124/R) was acquired by Tommy Sopwith's Équipe Endeavour and two (0125/R and 0151/R) were bought by John Ogier to race under the banner of his Essex Racing Stable. Both teams enjoyed a substantial measure of works support, but there is little evidence available as to the precise nature of the modifications to the cars.

At Goodwood on Easter Monday, 18 April, the Équipe Endeavour car was driven by Stirling

In 1960 John Ogier's Essex Racing stable competed with two Lightweight DB4GTs, 0125/R and 0151/R. The former was registered 18 TVX, but when Salvadori drove it into second place in the 1960 Tourist Trophy at Goodwood it bore the registration 440 PPB. *(Geoffrey Goddard)*

In the same race Innes Ireland drove 0151/R, registered 17 TVX, and finished third. *(Geoffrey Goddard)*

At Montlhéry in the Paris 1000 Kms race in October 1960, Roy Salvadori and Innes Ireland shared 0125/R, now wearing its correct registration, and finished sixth, trounced by the Ferrari 250GTs. Here Ireland is coming off the banking. *(Geoffrey Goddard)*

Moss in the race for Closed Cars and he won from the Jaguar 3.8 saloons of Roy Salvadori and Jack Sears. Jack Sears drove the DB4GT at Aintree on 30 April, and in the absence of strong opposition won another race for Closed Cars. As *Autosport* commented, 'It was easy for Jack Sears, who soon established a clear lead, lapping around 2 min 15 sec, to the horror of Tommy Sopwith, who almost "did his nut" in the pits, giving his various slow-down signals.' Another easy victory for Sears followed in a GT race at Oulton Park on 7 May, although the bonnet was not properly closed and was lifting under braking so that it obscured his vision. A third victory followed at Snetterton. It seems that the first of the Essex cars, 0125/R, made its début in the hands of Jonathan Sieff in the Rouen Grand Prix for sports cars on 12 June. Sieff finished sixth overall. On August Bank Holiday Monday Sears was again at the wheel of the Sopwith car and won the 10-lap Wrotham Cup for GT cars from Sir Gawaine Baillie with a Lotus Élite entered by the same team.

In 1960 there was a distinct absence of events for GT cars, for the class was only just receiving international recognition. A major exception, however, was the three-hour Tourist Trophy at Goodwood on 20 August. Here the two Ogier

DB4GTs of Roy Salvadori (0125/R) and Innes Ireland (0151/R) faced six Ferrari 250GTs, including a car entered by Rob Walker for Stirling Moss. Although Salvadori took the lead briefly, it proved very much Moss's race. Salvadori finished second, two laps in arrears, after a tyre burst at Lavant, because the Borrani wheel was slightly off-centre and the tyre had been rubbing on the bodywork, while Ireland finished third, also two laps in arrears, after an unscheduled pit stop to repair a trailing exhaust system. A week later at Brands Hatch Moss won again with the Ferrari, for 'The strangely quiet and superbly prepared 250GT Ferrari simply glided round, gaining all the time from Jack Sears in the very noisy Aston Martin DB4.' Sears with the Équipe Endeavour DB4GT was 18 sec behind the Ferrari at the end of this 10-lap race.

The Essex cars were then entered in the Paris 1000 Km race at Monthléry driven by Ireland/ Salvadori (0125/R) and Jim Clark/Tony Maggs (0151/R). The Clark/Maggs car was conspicuously quicker, but was delayed at the start and later retired because of valve failure. Ireland/Salvadori were completely outpaced by the Ferrari opposition and gassed by a leaking exhaust manifold eventually took sixth place.

1961

At the 1960 Earls Court Show the company introduced a version of the DB4GT with lighter Zagato bodywork of superb lines and proportions. Only 19 of these cars were completed, in the main finished at Newport Pagnell, although all bodies were made in Italy. These superbly curving bodies, hand-made with the result that no two were exactly the same, exuded a sense of power and muscle. Power in this form was said to be 314 bhp, but the real figure would be about 285 bhp. The real figure was also the same as that claimed for the rival Ferrari 250GT, but the Aston Martin was a good 25 per cent heavier. In addition the Ferrari had better roadholding and better steering. But the DB4GTs were almost theatrically noisy, could be chucked about with abandon by skilled drivers, hold dramatic opposite-lock drifts and had an immense appeal to British drivers and entrants, as well as spectators. The Zagato-bodied cars were seriously raced in 1961 GT events and the most successful team was John Ogier's Essex Racing Stable, which acquired two

Zagatos, but also retained a 1960 car.

Early in the year, on 25 March, Salvadori drove 0151/R for Ogier in a 12-lap race at Snetterton, but the DB4GT seemed down on power and he trailed across the line behind the Ferraris of Mike Parkes (Équipe Endeavour) and Graham Whitehead. Next came the Easter Goodwood meeting and in the Fordwater Trophy for GT cars two DB4GTs were entered. Mike Parkes won the race with the Équipe Endeavour Ferrari, Innes Ireland finished second with Ogier's 0151/R and Stirling Moss was third with a Zagato. This was the 1960 Earls Court car, 0200/R, entered in Rob Walker's name and running far from well in the race, although Moss had taken pole position in practice.

Two DB4GTs appeared at the Le Mans Practice Days, 8 and 9 April. French Moroccan driver Kerguen was at the wheel of Charles Pozzoli's new Zagato, 0180/L, which was almost certainly being run in close liaison with the Aston Martin distributor for France, Marcel Blondeau. Kerguen lapped in 4 min 30.8 sec (111.29 mph). The second car was a normal DB4GT driven by Claude Le Guizec, and although its chassis number is unknown it appears to have been owned by the French Aston Martin distributor.

When the new Jaguar E-types made their début at Oulton Park on 15 April, they finished first and third (Graham Hill and Salvadori), but were split by 0151/R, driven by Innes Ireland. Ogier's DB4GT, 0151/R, was in action again on 28 May, when it was driven by Jim Clark and Bruce McLaren in the Nürburgring 1000 Km race. It was plagued by gearbox problems in practice, and although Clark led the field away, settling into eighth place (despite an unscheduled pit stop because a stone had jammed under the clutch pedal), he retired at the Flugplatz on lap 25 because of a broken oil pipe.

For Le Mans, on 10–11 June, the Essex Racing Stable took delivery of its two new light green Zagatos, both much lightened cars with modifications that included a magnesium gearbox casing. 0182/R (registered 1 VEV) was driven by Jack Fairman/Bernard Consten and 0183/R (registered 2 VEV) was driven by Australian drivers Lex Davison/Bib Stilwell. Essex had a team of ex-works mechanics, Eric Hind, Alan Woods and Ian Moss, and, because David Brown was planning to re-enter racing, a strong measure of works support. Pozzoli's white Zagato, 0180/L, was driven by Kerguen/'Franc' (Claude Dewez). Early in the race both Essex Zagatos retired

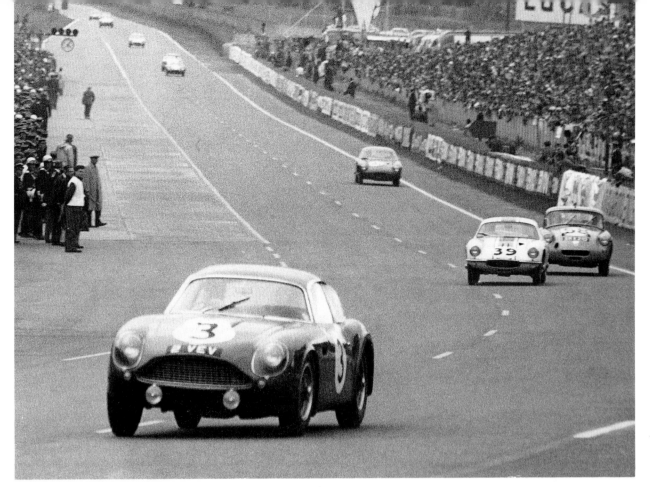

At Le Mans in 1961 the Essex Racing Stable entered DB4GT Zagato 0183/R at Le Mans for Davison/Stilwell, but it retired after 2½ hours with gasket failure. This car had a much modified engine and gearbox. *(Geoffrey Goddard)*

In the same race DB4GT 0180/L Zagato was entered for Kerguen/'Franc'. It was holding ninth place in the 23rd hour of the race when it too retired. *(Geoffrey Goddard)*

because of blown cylinder head gaskets, the result of the failure to tighten the head studs when the engines were cold after practice. It was not necessary on the ordinary DB4GTs, so the team's failure to do it on this occasion was not surprising. The Kerguen/'Franc' car ran with train-like reliability (its head studs had been tightened) until the 24th hour, when, in ninth place (but well behind the GT Ferraris) it failed to start after a pit stop. Incidentally, at 1166kg, the Kerguen/'Franc' Zagato was the heaviest car in the race. Subsequently this car was driven by Kerguen in the 3 Hours race at Clermont-Ferrand (it retired for reasons unknown), in the Inter-Europa Cup at Monza (fourth) and the Paris 1000 Km race at Montlhéry (14th with 'Franc').

The Ogier team next appeared at the British Grand Prix meeting at Aintree and Lex Davison with 0183/R scored an easy win in the 51-mile GT race from Jack Sears (Coombs's E-type) and Sir John Whitmore (0151/R). Once again in August the Tourist Trophy was held as a three hour-race for GT cars at Goodwood. Essex entered a trio of cars, Salvadori (0182/R), Clark (0183/R) and Ireland (0151/R). The race was, however, dominated by the Ferrari 250GTs of Moss (who

The Essex Racing Stable entered three DB4GTs, all driven to the circuit on the road, in the 1961 Tourist Trophy. The Ferrari 250GTs of Moss and Parkes took the first two places, but Salvadori finished third with Zagato 0182/R, seen here during a pit stop. *(Geoffrey Goddard)*

With Zagato-bodied 0183/R Jim Clark finished fifth in the 1961 Tourist Trophy. *(Geoffrey Goddard)*

In the Tourist Trophy Innes Ireland drove 0151/R into fourth place. *(Geoffrey Goddard)*

won with a Dick Wilkins/Rob Walker entry) and Parkes (second with the Équipe Endeavour/Maranello Concessionaires car). Parkes was much harder on tyres than Moss and also lost 90 seconds in a pit stop to have part of the undertray removed. The Aston Martins lacked the pace of the Ferraris and their efforts were crippled by phenomenal tyre wear. Salvadori, who finished third, made four pit stops and had 13 tyres changed, while fourth-place man Clark was lighter on tyres, but his car seemed slower. Ireland finished fifth after three stops to change tyres. In practice and the race the Astons consumed a total of 80 tyres. The Essex Stable won the Team prize, and after the race Ogier drove off in 0182/R to spectate at the following day's Snetterton race meeting.

On the day of the Italian Grand Prix Tony Maggs drove 0182/R in the larger-capacity of two Coppa Inter-Europa GT races at Monza. Normally the cars were driven to the race, but on this rare occasion the team used a transporter.

The race was won by Pierre Noblet (Ferrari 250GT), but Maggs drove non-stop to finish second and Kerguen finished fourth with 0180/L. The Essex team ran in comparatively few races and their last outing of the year was the Paris 1000 Km event at Montlhéry on 22 October. Here 0182/R was driven by Clark/Ireland and 0183/R by Maggs/Whitmore. Both cars were reluctant starters (the Essex Zagatos were always plagued by fuel vaporisation problems), they were no real match for the Ferraris and after delays Clark/Ireland finished fifth and Maggs/Whitmore ninth.

1962

In 1962 Ferrari introduced the 250GT0 and this rendered the Zagatos almost completely obsolete. Essex and Kerguen continued to race their cars and in a monumental error of judgement Coombs acquired a Zagato (0190/L) to race alongside his 250GT0. Salvadori, to his dismay, was expected to drive the Zagato, while Graham Hill drove the GTO. The Coombs team made only the one entry with the Zagato, at Brands Hatch on 27 May, and Salvadori finished second to Innes Ireland (UDT-Laystall 250GTO). After this John Coombs rapidly disposed of the car.

David Brown was planning to return to racing at Le Mans, and while continuing to support Essex, now expected something in return. While Tony Maggs drove 0182/R to third place in a GT race at Oulton Park on 7 April behind Parkes (250GTO) and Hill (E-type), 0183/R had been lent to the works for the Le Mans Practice Weekend. Aston Martin fitted the still far from fully developed 3995cc engine to be used in Project 212. After a change during practice to megaphone exhausts and fitting larger carburettor chokes, 'Franc' lapped second fastest on the Saturday in 4 min 12.9 sec, but the best that Kerguen could manage was 4 min 28.2 sec. The car was much slower on the Sunday.

On Easter Monday Graham Warner (of The Chequered Flag sports car dealers) drove 0182/R in the 15-lap Sussex Trophy race at Goodwood, where he finished seventh overall, trounced by Ferrari and Jaguar opposition, while at the International Trophy meeting at Silverstone the following month Jim Clark finished fourth with 0182/R, and Mike Salmon was sixth with 0200/R, the original 1960 Earls Court Show car.

Aston Martin persuaded Ogier to lend to the works 0183/R for them to run in the name of Équipe Nationale Belge in the Spa Grand Prix meeting on 20 May. Ogier was far from keen, but reluctantly agreed. The works team entered Lucien Bianchi in the 15-lap GT race for large-capacity cars and 0193/R was fitted with a magnesium-block 3750cc engine of the type to be used in 1963 in the works 214 cars. On a wet but drying track, well covered with oil after a day's racing, Bianchi went into the lead on lap 2, but on the following lap went off the road at Burnenville, completely wrecking the Zagato. Mike Salmon finished fifth with his Zagato. There were red faces at Feltham, and after an interval 'returned' to Ogier what proved to be a completely new car, the 1962 DP209 Lightweight version, but retaining the original chassis number, registration and log book. The engine was now believed to develop a genuine 300 bhp plus, the body was restyled with lower, flatter roofline, broader rear wings, a deeper, longer tail with more vertical rear window, greater bodywork

There were two DB4GT Zagatos entered at Le Mans in 1962. No 12 lightweight 0193/R, was entered by Jean Kerguen for himself and 'Franc', but retired with a blown gasket. No 14, 0200/R, the car driven by Peter Salmon and Ian Baillie, was the 1960 Earls Court Show car, had been driven by Moss at Goodwood on Easter Monday 1961 and was fitted with a special engine. It retired because of a seized piston. *(Geoffrey Goddard)*

overhang front and rear, a very large racing fuel filler and with the front sidelights mounted within the grille opening. The new car was also much lighter. It was some while before the Essex Stable raced again.

Accordingly there were no Essex Stable entries at Le Mans, but two Zagatos did run, both of which retired in the early hours of the Sunday morning. Kerguen/'Franc' had a new 1962 Lightweight Zagato, 0193/R, which retired because of either transmission trouble or burnt exhaust valves (it depends which account you believe). Already Mike Salmon's DB4GT, in which he was partnered by Ian Baillie, had retired, eliminated by piston trouble after a spell of misfiring.

Essex returned to the fray on 15 July in the GT race held on the Circuit d'Auvergne at Clermont-Ferrand. The team entered only the 'new' 0183/R for young South African driver Tony Maggs, who finished seventh in a race won by Abate (Ferrari 250GTO), followed across the line by Alan Rees with the Essex Stable's Lotus 23 and four more Ferraris. On the way back from this race the engine block (which was still the 3.7-litre magnesium as fitted to the 'original' car earlier in the year) cracked. On a wet track at Brands Hatch on August Bank Holiday Monday Salmon finished sixth with his Zagato in the 25-lap Peco Trophy race.

At the Tourist Trophy at Goodwood, the two Essex cars were entered for Jim Clark and Graham Warner, while Mike Salmon drove his own Zagato. Clark made a superb start, holding fourth place with 0183/R, but Warner had a miserable race with the original car. It was misfiring and smoking badly, made an early pit stop and despite the mechanics changing a couple of plugs it still ran on only four cylinders and was retired. John Surtees with his red Bowmaker Racing Ferrari 250GTO was dominating the race, but the situation changed dramatically, as described by Gregory Grant in *Autosport*: '[Surtees] was coming up fast to double Jim Clark for the second time at Madgwick, the Scotsman

unaccountably spun the Aston Martin, whilst moving for Surtees to go through. Surtees swung the wheel round viciously to try to miss the gyrating Zagato, but hit it fair and square, both cars landing in the ditch. The drivers scrambled out unhurt, but both machines were badly damaged. John was bitterly disappointed, but said laconically: "Well that's motor racing for you!" He was also upset that the lovely Berlinetta was more than somewhat bent. Jim just could not understand how he had suddenly lost it, but thought that it might have been due to brand-new tyres on the rear wheels. The car swerved so quickly that Jim thought he had a soft tyre.' Later in the race Robin Benson with another Ferrari crashed at Madgwick into the two stricken cars, causing even more damage. Salmon retired his Zagato because of a jammed gear-lever. Ferraris took the first three places.

0193/R was repaired for Clark/Whitmore to drive in the Paris 1000 Kms race; initially Clark held sixth place, spun, fell back to 11th and climbed up to second place when the leaders made their pit stops. Unfortunately the car retired shortly after Sir John Whitmore had taken over because of a holed piston. This race marked the end of John Ogier's relationship with the DB4GT.

The serious racing days of the model were now over, although Kerguen continued to race 0193/R in international events. In the Dakar 6 Hours race in April 1963, Kerguen, partnered by Duffour, finished second, albeit nine laps behind the winning Ferrari 250GTO of Noblet/Guichet. Kerguen, partnered by Dewez, ran the car at Le Mans, but retired because of rear axle failure after an off-course excursion on oil dropped by McLaren's works Aston Martin, and Kerguen finished a rather hopeless 18th at Clermont-Ferrand. DB4GTs continued to be raced in minor events; indeed their racing career never really ended, but have been seen less and less as values have escalated.

13 Project Cars: 1962–3

1962

Although Aston Martin had given a great deal of support to the Essex Racing Stable, dealers, especially the French distributor Marcel Blondeau, urged the company to run a works team again, even on a limited scale, as this would help boost sales. So the decision was made to construct a car complying with the current Prototype rules, with a capacity limit of 4000cc for 'Experimental' cars, and enter it at Le Mans in 1962.

The new car, designated Project 212, was very much a development of the DB4GT. The chassis was broadly similar, but much lighter, built up from rectangular box-section members with integral riveted light alloy floor panels. At the front the suspension was similar to that of the DB4GT, with unequal-length wishbones, coil springs and Armstrong telescopic dampers. A de Dion layout, adopted from a prototype Lagonda saloon, was used at the rear with torsion bars,

trailing links and a Watts linkage.

To power the 212, Aston Martin used what was basically the all-alloy DP186 6-cylinder engine, as fitted to the DB4GT, linered out to 96mm; the existing stroke was retained and this gave a capacity of 3996cc. With three Weber 50 DCO carburettors and a compression ratio of 9.5:1, a power output of 345 bhp at 6000 rpm was claimed. This was, however, a test-bed figure and as installed in the car the power developed was 327 bhp. Transmission was by a Borg & Beck 7½in triple-plate clutch, the David Brown S532 gearbox (with magnesium casing) – a 4-speed all-synchromesh gearbox – as used on the DB4GT and a spiral bevel final drive.

DP212/1 was the only car of its type built and it was probably the best-looking Aston Martin ever. Constructed in magnesium-aluminium alloy, the body featured sweeping graceful lines, with simple oval air intake, faired headlamps and foglamps and a long, graceful tail. As originally

At Le Mans in 1962, DP212/1 was driven by Graham Hill and Richie Ginther (seen here). The car retired with piston failure after 79 laps. *(Geoffrey Goddard)*

built, the rear wings partially enveloped the wheels, but the openings in the wings were enlarged before the car was raced. The only problem was that this body had not been fully aerodynamically tested and this was to lead to problems at Le Mans. There were Girling disc brakes (12in. at the front, 11.7in. at the rear) and Borrani wire wheels with Rudge-type knock-off hubs featuring triple-eared hub caps.

The new car was driven at Le Mans by BRM works drivers Graham Hill and Richie Ginther. In practice Hill lapped in 4 min 16 sec. He made a brilliant start in the race, led on the first lap and early on was timed on the Mulsanne straight at 167.8 mph. The Aston Martin led again before stopping to refuel, but lost a lot of time in the pits because of a faulty dynamo, and it was in ninth place when it retired after 79 laps because of piston failure caused by a fractured oil pipe. John Wyer had regarded Le Mans as a reconnaissance rather than a serious attempt to win and was well satisfied. The only problem had been the handling at high speed, for the 212 suffered from aerodynamic lift, and this shortcoming exposed the team's lack of adequate pre-race testing.

1963

Encouraged by the performance in 1962, David Brown sanctioned the construction of a team of three cars for the following season, two cars for the GT category and a Prototype.

The prototype, DP215/1, was in many ways a development of DP212/1. There was a new light, heavily drilled and substantially cross-braced chassis with alloy floor panels. At the front suspension was by upper wishbones, reversed lower wishbones and coil spring/damper units, while at the rear the DP215 featured a fully independent layout with wide-based double wishbones and coil spring/damper units. The engine was very similar to that of the 1962 car apart from dry sump lubrication with a 5½-gallon tank that actually contained 4 gallons of oil. Aston Martin decided to fit the SG537 combined 5-speed gearbox and final drive, as had been fitted to the DBR1 and had given so much trouble, so it was inevitable that this would lead to problems. All three cars built in 1963 featured lower, longer 20-gauge magnesium-alloy bodywork, but, after extensive testing, chopped tails with spoilers were

Aston Martin returned to Le Mans in 1963 with a team of three cars. This is the Prototype, DP215/1, driven by Phil Hill/Lucien Bianchi, lights blazing and leading the Rover-BRM. *(Geoffrey Goddard)*

DP215 retired at Le Mans because of transmission failure. Here the car is seen just before it was withdrawn. Lucien Bianchi and Phill Hill discuss the situation and to their left is John Wyer. *(Nigel Snowdon)*

DB4GT/0195/R driven by Bruce McLaren/Innes Ireland blew its engine on the Mulsanne straight, depositing oil all over the road and causing a multi-car accident. *(David Phipps)*

adopted and, because of the dry sump lubrication, DP215/1 had a lower bonnet line. The air intakes were smaller and there were NACA ducts in the nose. The wheelbase (7ft 10in.), overall length (14ft 6in.) and width (5ft 6in.) was common to all four but the 1963 cars were two inches lower at 4ft 0in and had wider front track (4ft 7in.) and narrower rear track (4ft 5in.) than the 1962 car, which had a track of 4ft 6in. front and rear.

The two GT cars, the DP214, were allocated DB4GT chassis numbers (0194/R and 0195/R), but both used chassis the same as that of the DP215. This was contrary to the regulations, but Wyer rightly assumed that the team would get away with it. The non-standard bodywork was permitted under the regulations, as was an increase in bore by 1mm. As fitted to the DP214s, engine capacity was 3749cc (93 x 92mm) and on a 9.1:1 compression ratio and with three Weber twin-choke 50 DCO carburettors 317 bhp was developed at 6000 rpm. The engine was 8½in further back in the chassis than on the production car. The transmission incorporated the standard 4-speed gearbox of the DB4GT, but there was a special Salisbury back axle incorporating a limited slip differential and shorter than the production axle to provide space for the wider rear wheels and DBR1 brake calipers. Supposedly the suspension was the same as for the production cars, but the DP214s incorporated at the front lightened, standard, lower wishbones with much shorter upper wishbones and the roll centre height and camber angle could be adjusted to suit different circuits. It was compulsory to use the same wheel size as the production cars, 16in., but throughout the year, with one notable exception, 5½in. rims at the front and 6½in. at the rear were used.

DP215 was not ready for the Le Mans Test Days in April, so the team took along DP212/1 (now with chopped tail) and the two DP214s. The drivers were Lucien Bianchi, Jim Kimberly, Bruce McLaren and Jo Schlesser, but so far as Wyer was concerned it was purely a testing exercise and no dramatic lap times were set, compared to the Ferraris, which dominated both the Prototype and GT classes at the time. And Ferrari dominated the race in June, taking the first six places. The P215 driven by Phil Hill/Bianchi survived for just over two hours until 6.01 pm. Hill had been in third place at the end of the first lap, but he was forced to make a pit stop at the end of lap 5 for the car to be checked after running over debris from Masson's crashed René Bonnet, and after 29 laps Hill abandoned the P215 because of gearbox trouble. It has been suggested that the gearbox was damaged by the earlier incident, but that is unlikely. During practice Hill with DP215/1 was timed on the Mulsanne straight at 319.6 km/h (198.6 mph). Steady driving brought the McLaren/Kimberly car through to seventh place, but at 8.20pm with McLaren at the wheel, 0195/R blew its engine at Les Hunaudières, covering the track with oil and setting off a multi-car accident that eliminated Dewez's Aston Martin, Salvadori's E-type Jaguar, Jean-Pierre Manzon's René Bonnet and Bindo Heinz's Alpine (the driver of which was trapped in the burning wreckage of his car and died).

Autosport commented, 'Bruce McLaren was terribly upset when he returned to the pits after

Aston Martin No. 8 blew up, and oil vapour possibly precipitated the multi-car pile-up on the Hunaudières section. No one could possibly put any blame on McLaren for this; few drivers save their engines like the New Zealander does, and it was just another of those unfortunate incidents which are amongst the hazards of motor racing.' In fact the problem was piston failure – the team was using a faulty batch – and the Aston Martin had dropped a very real sea of oil. The same problem eliminated 0194/R driven by Kimberly/Schlesser at 2.10 am on the Sunday morning, when it had risen to third place, but fortunately without any tragic outcome.

On 30 June Aston Martin entered the DP215 for Jo Schlesser in the 25-lap Sports and Prototype race at the French Grand Prix meeting at Reims. Schlesser made a superb start, powering into the lead, but because of gearbox problems he missed a couple of gear changes and retired because of bent valves. By the Guards Trophy at Brands Hatch on August Bank Holiday Monday, DP215/1 had been rebuilt with the gearbox from DP212/1 in unit with the engine. In the event, the car, to be driven by McLaren, was withdrawn after the New Zealander had crashed in the German Grand Prix the previous day, but interestingly Roy Salvadori drove all three works Astons during practice so that he could report his findings to John Wyer. Ireland finished a poor sixth (second in his class) with 0195/R, while Kimberly spun and hit the bank at Dingle Dell with 0194/R.

Next came the Tourist Trophy at Goodwood on 24 August, a race restricted to GT cars and run over 130 laps of the 2.4-mile Sussex circuit. 0194/R was entered for Innes Ireland and 0195/R for Bruce McLaren, but the team ran into problems during scrutineering and the RAC Chief Scrutineer insisted that the cars run on 5½in. rear rims, because the usual wider rims had not, through an oversight, been homologated. Even so Ireland and McLaren were third and fourth fastest in practice behind the Ferrari 250GTOs of Graham Hill and Mike Parkes. McLaren drove a steady race, rising to third place, dropping back to ninth after a long pit stop and retiring because of valve problems. Ireland drove the race in a fiery rage and this emphasized the handling problems on the narrow rims; when he tried to take the lead from Graham Hill he spun three times at Woodcote, taking Hill with him, and he eventually finished seventh, two laps

In the Tourist Trophy at Goodwood the RAC scrutineers insisted on the DP214s running with 5.5.in. rims, with which they were homologated. This is Bruce McLaren, who drove a steady race with 0195/R, but retired with valve problems. *(Nigel Snowdon)*

Innes Ireland, however, with 0194/R went flat out and after a succession of spins finished seventh. *(Geoffrey Goddard)*

At Monza in September 1963 Salvadori scored one of the greatest success of his career by winning the Coppa Inter-Europa with 0194/R by the narrowest of margins from Mike Parkes (Ferrari 250GT0). *(Geoffrey Goddard)*

in arrears.

The last ever works Aston Martin entry was in the three-hour Coppa Inter-Europa at Monza on 8 September, and there the team entered 0194/R for Roy Salvadori and 0195/R for Lucien Bianchi. There was a strong entry of Ferrari 250GT0s and as the Astons were only fourth and sixth fastest in practice, their prospects seemed poor. Roy Salvadori, however, drove one of the finest races in his career and the following account is from his biography, published by Patrick Stephens Limited in 1985:

'Mike Parkes with a 250GT0 was fastest in practice on a damp track in 1 min 49.4 sec and although I did very little practice, so as to conserve my car, I was fourth fastest in 1 min 54.6 sec. The Aston was handling superbly, it was very fast and the gear ratios, thanks to inspired guesswork by the team manager, John Horsman, were just right.

'In the race Parkes led, but I kept him firmly glued in my sights. Driving really hard, I closed up on him and I knew that I was putting him under pressure. At half-distance Parkes made his routine refuelling stop; he was stationary long enough for me to pull out a lead of about 1 min 12 sec, and then I made my stop. The Aston Martin pit work was very slick, partly because the team was using pressurized refuelling system, and I rejoined the race just behind the Ferrari.

'The remainder of the race turned into the closest possible duel. I was leaving my braking to the last possible moment, far later than I would have thought conceivable with a heavy GT car, and both Parkes and I were right on the limit. I found that I had the edge on the straight and could just nose past the Ferrari. But the 250GT0, thanks to its 5-speed gearbox . . . was quicker out of the corners and the vital corner was the corner before the pits, the last before the finishing line . . .

At Le Mans in 1964 0194/R driven by Mike Salmon/Peter Sutcliffe ran strongly, at one stage holding ninth place, until it was disqualified six hours before the finish for taking on oil sooner than the regulations permitted. *(Nigel Snowdon)*

'I knew if I was to win the race I had to break the tow and pull out a couple of seconds over the Ferrari so that Mike could not re-pass me before the finishing line. The chance did not come until a couple of laps from the end, when we caught two slower cars on the approach to Lesmo. They obviously had not seen us and I thought if I could scramble past them just before the apex of the corner, then Mike would be forced to hold back and take them on the exit. It was a very risky manoeuvre, I eased off a fraction giving Mike the impression that I was going to follow the two cars through the corner, got my timing to absolute perfection and dived through on the inside. This caught Mike off-balance and he was forced to follow the two cars through the corner. On the exit to the corner he got on to the grass and this gave me the chance to pull out several cars' lengths. Mike chased me hard to the finish, but I still led by a second or two as we crossed the line. For me it had been a fantastic race, not least because Mike was great to race against and completely trustworthy!'

Salvadori's average speed of 120.23 mph was

faster than the previous GT lap record, he set a new class lap record of 124.27 mph and Bianchi finished third. Wyer's long career with Aston Martin had ended on a fine note, for he left the company at the end of September to join the Ford GT40 project.

Later in September the two DP214s were entered at Montlhéry in the name of the French distributor Marcel Blondeau and it was another successful outing. Le Guezec (0194/R) won the Coupe de Paris with Dewez (0195/R) second and Schlesser (0195/R) won the Coupe du Salon with Le Guezec (0194/R) fifth.

Once David Brown had decided to withdraw from racing once more, there was no future for John Wyer at Aston Martin Lagonda Limited and without John Wyer the team never again entered racing.

Postscript

In 1964 the two DP214s were sold to a private owner, Dawnay Racing (run by the Hon John Dawnay, now Viscount Downe). After both cars retired in the Daytona Continental 2000 Kms race, Mike Salmon finished second with 0194/R in the GT race at the May Silverstone meeting. Brian Hetread crashed 0195/R during practice for the Nürburgring 1000 Kms race, the driver suffered fatal injuries and the car was subsequently scrapped. Mike Salmon/Peter Sutcliffe shared 0194/R at Le Mans, holding eighth place on the Sunday morning, when they were disqualified for taking on extra oil before the permitted number of laps had been completed. Subsequently at the Martini-sponsored Aston Martin Owners' Club meeting at Silverstone Salmon won a 10-lap scratch race for Aston Martins and won the GT division of the Martini Trophy race.

14 Lola-Aston Martin: 1967

In 1963 Eric Broadley had entered the Lola coupé at Le Mans, a promising mid-engine coupé powered by a Ford V8 4.2-litre engine. Undoubtedly the Lola needed a great deal of development work, but its immense promise was evident. Ford were planning their entry into motor racing and entered into an arrangement with Broadley whereby he would work for Ford, and the Lola ultimately formed the basis of the Ford GT40. Broadley's stay with Ford was short-lived and he was soon back in business on his own. For 1965 Lola produced the T70 Group 7 sports car, with monocoque sheet steel and alloy chassis based on an aluminium centre-structure with box-like side-members and three main structural bulkheads. Front suspension was by double wishbones (upper top links and wide-based lower wishbones) and rear suspension by inverted lower wishbones, top links and twin radius rods. A glass-fibre body was fitted (unstressed and acting purely as an aerodynamic covering). There were rack-and-pinion steering, cast magnesium wheels and outboard Girling disc brakes front and rear. The power unit was either a Chevrolet or Ford V8 used with a Borg & Beck twin-plate clutch and ZF 5-speed or Hewland LG500 4-speed gearbox. The cars proved immensely successful and one of the most enthusiastic supporters of the T70 was John Surtees, whose red Chevrolet-powered car entered by Team Surtees was a consistent contender. Surtees had raced Lola Formula 1 cars for the Bowmaker Yeoman team and had great confidence in Broadley.

Surtees, who was determined to set up his own team, crashed a T70 very badly during the Can-Am series, but made an almost miraculous recovery and was racing again in 1966. He had been driving for Ferrari since 1963, but left Ferrari in mid-1966 after a disagreement with team manager Dragoni and for the remainder of the year drove for Cooper in Formula 1. Team Surtees continued to enter a T70, usually driven by David Hobbs in British events, and Surtees won the Can-Am series with a T70. At the 1967 Racing Car Show, Lola announced the Group 6 Sports Prototype Mark III coupé. Team Surtees confirmed that they would be racing these cars with new Aston Martin V8 engines supplied by

the works and one of these engines was exhibited. The main difference between the Mark III and its predecessors was the gull-wing coupé body (with the doors opened by a central T-bar) and quickly detachable front and rear body sections.

The Aston Martin engine was the new DP218 designed by Tadek Marek and which powered the production DBSV8 announced in September 1969. As raced by Surtees, the 90-degree V8 all-alloy four overhead camshaft engine had a capacity of 5064cc (98 x 83mm) and with four Weber 48 IDA carburettors was claimed to develop 450 bhp at 6000 rpm. Dry sump lubrication was featured, the crankshaft ran in five main bearings and there was a Lucas magneto driven from the exhaust camshaft on the right-hand bank of cylinders.

Testing with the Aston Martin engine in an open T70 in the autumn of 1966 revealed many engine problems and it was not until March 1967 that the now much developed V8 engine was installed in the Mk III coupé, typed in this form T73 and with the first car having chassis number SL73/101. When the car was tested at Snetterton, Surtees discovered that there were vibration problems and that the engine could not be persuaded to rev above 6100 rpm. Frantic work was carried out on the engine and further testing at the Motor Industry Research Association resulted in bodywork modifications that included lowering the rear engine decking and fitting a spoiler at the rear. At the Le Mans Test Days in April the Lola-Aston Martin appeared in immaculate dark green, with the arrowhead in white on the nose and the shaft running to the tail that was to characterize Surtees' entries.

Surtees achieved third fastest lap at the Test Days in 3 min 31.9 sec, compared with Bandini (Ferrari P4) in 3 min 25.5 sec and Parkes (Ferrari P4) in 3 min 27.6 sec, and was faster than the 7-litre Fords. On the Mulsanne straight the Fords were timed at around 205 mph, compared with 186 mph for the Lola (which it had been hoped would achieve 200 mph at Le Mans). During the second day's testing the Lola ran into engine problems, a portent for the future.

Team Surtees missed the Spa 1000 Kms race intended as the first event and the Lola-Aston Martin made its début at the Nürburgring driven

Two views of the original Lola-Aston Martin SL73/101 on the Saturday of the Le Mans Test Days in 1967.

In the 24 Hours race SL73/101 was driven by Irwin/de Klerk and retired early in the race after a series of problems. *(Nigel Snowdon).*

by Surtees and Hobbs, and running on fuel injection. During the first day's practice the Lola with Hobbs at the wheel shed a front wheel because of a loose retaining nut, but despite this and other problems Surtees was second fastest in 8 min 39.6 sec. At the start the engine fired, then cut out and was very reluctant to start again, and at the end of the first lap Surtees was back in 12th place. Surtees moved up to seventh, but on lap 8 a rear wishbone broke at the Fuchsröhre, the rear wheels locked up, he narrowly missed Steinemann's abandoned Porsche and was lucky to bring the car safely to a halt.

By Le Mans a second Lola-Aston Martin had been completed, SL73/121, with a long alloy tail (to improve air flow to the engine and hopefully also improve straight-line speed). Both cars were fitted with fuel injection. The newer car was driven by Surtees/Hobbs and the older car by Chris Irwin/de Klerk. Surtees was 13th fastest in

practice in 3 min 33.7 sec. After only three laps Surtees was out of the race because of a holed piston, the result of overheating caused by the new tail, which had not been adequately tested. The second car of Irwin/de Klerk was plagued by mechanical problems: a broken camshaft driveshaft (that was replaced), loss of oil pressure, overheating and a broken crankshaft damper and it retired after 2½ hours' racing.

Aston Martin had put a great deal of effort and money into the racing V8, but it had been expecting too much for the car to be competitive in such a short space of time. The resources that were available now had to be applied to developing the V8 for production and the project was abandoned. A fortnight later Surtees ran the newer car with a Chevrolet engine at Reims. Both Lola-Aston Martins have survived, but both are now fitted with 5.3-litre production Aston Martin engines.

15 Aston Martin- Nimrod and Others: 1982-85

Following the failure of the Lolas at Le Mans in 1967, many observers formed the view that the Aston Martin V8 engine was not suitable for use in a serious competition car, not simply because of the engine's failure on that occasion, but because of its weight, bulk and power limitations. A limited number of enthusiasts believed otherwise and a number of V8 cars were modified and developed for competition work. In 1977 and 1979 Robin Hamilton, an Aston Martin enthusiast, a Service Agent and later dealer, had fielded much-developed production cars at Le Mans and elsewhere and he was soon planning an Aston Martin-powered car built from scratch for long-distance sports car racing. The original scheme was that the car should race as early as 1980, but it did not in fact appear until the start of the new Group C Category in 1982.

Hamilton discussed the project at length with Eric Broadley of Lola. Broadley, assisted by Andrew Thornby and with aerodynamic studies carried out by the French consultant Max Sardou, was planning the T600 GTP car for American IMSA sports car racing (and this was eventually announced in March 1981) and from this was developed the T610 for European Group C. With vivid memories of the 1967 Aston Martin fiasco, Broadley was initially sceptical of Hamilton's project, but soon became convinced that Hamilton was serious and had the funds to meet the cost of the project.

For the new car, much later to be named the Nimrod, Broadley adapted the T600 chassis, which in this form became known as the T385. The design incorporated a full-length monocoque constructed in bonded and riveted honeycomb and sheet aluminium, with tubular members running from the rear bulkhead to carry the engine, transmission and rear suspension. A feature of the design was the wide, flat floor in the cockpit area, as Hamilton was projecting a limited production road-going version, and there was coupé bodywork with gull-wing doors. The Nimrod had a wheelbase of 9ft 0in. (but this was adjustable), front track of 5ft 2.5in. and rear track of 4ft 10in.

Apart from the monocoque itself, most of the car was built up by Hamilton's team, although Lola magnesium suspension uprights were used

front and rear. At the front, the suspension, mounted inboard, was by upper rocking arms and lower wishbones, at the rear there were trailing arms, transverse upper links and inverted wishbones, and there were adjustable roll-bars front and rear. Rack-and-pinion steering was fitted and the radiator was mounted almost horizontally in the nose. Lockheed ventilated disc brakes were used front and rear and there were alloy wheels, 16in. diameter and 11in. wide at the front, 16/19in. diameter and 15in. wide at the rear. The V8 engine was developed by Aston Martin subsidiary Tickford, mounted largely unstressed, and was used with the Hewland VG 5-speed trans-axle and roller spline drive-shafts. With its curved roofline, otherwise rather angular lines and large tail-fins, the Nimrod looked superb.

Following the acquisition of a 50 per cent shareholding in Aston Martin Lagonda Limited by Victor Gauntlett's Pace Petroleum in 1981, Gauntlett, who had become Chairman of Aston Martin Lagonda, made a thorough investigation of the project and decided that Pace Petroleum would support it (but not Aston Martin Lagonda, because of its financial difficulties). Peter Livanos, the Aston Martin Lagonda distributor in the United States, also joined the consortium. The name Nimrod was chosen and in September 1981 Nimrod Racing Automobiles Limited was incorporated, with Hamilton, Gauntlett and Livanos as shareholders and contribution from each of £250,000. When the differences between Group C in Europe and IMSA in the United States became known and it was clear that Livanos would not be able, as he wished, to race a Nimrod in most events in the United States, he withdrew from the company and the financial gap was filled by Gauntlett and Hamilton. Viscount Downe, President of the Aston Martin Owners' Club, also decided to buy and race a car with sponsorship from Pace Petroleum and this car was managed by Richard Williams.

After testing at Silverstone by Derek Bell, the first car, NRAC1/001, built to IMSA specification and fitted with Hamilton's 1977 engine, was shown to the press at Goodwood, where it was driven by James Hunt and Stirling Moss. In this form it appeared at the Dubai Grand Prix meeting

The works Nimrod, NRAC2/003 driven by Tiff Needell/Geoff Lees/Bob Evans in the 1982 Silverstone 6 Hours race. It retired because of a broken rotor arm. *(Nigel Snowdon)*

in October 1981, for a 'shakedown' with Bell at the wheel again. While Tickford struggled to produce reliable and sufficiently powered engines, many observors had, and as it was to prove rightly, concluded that the Nimrods were condemned to mediocrity by an excess of weight (1050kg) and a paucity of power. By mid-1982 power output was hopefully reliable 570bhp with maximum rpm of 7200 rpm using Lucas mechanical fuel injection, but in the interests of reliability the Downe car was usually restricted to 6250 rpm (and 6500 rpm on the Mulsanne Straight at Le Mans). The development of these Aston Martin engines has been riddled, however, by claims and counter-claims in relation to power outputs and the accuracy of the figures above may be doubtful. The

engines remained unreliable all year.

Two new cars were built by the Silverstone 6 Hours race, NRAC2/003 painted green and silver for the works team and NRAC2/004 painted white and blue for Lord Downe. At Silverstone the works car was driven by Needell/Lees/Evans, whilst Salmon/Mallock drove the Downe car. During the four weeks since delivery of the Nimrod to the Downe team, the car had been completely rebuilt and changes included major modifications to the suspension geometry, together with resiting of the engine cooling and plumbing arrangements. The works team also had present the prototype Nimrod, now rebuilt to Group C specification. There was a minor problem in scrutineering because the cars just fell

The Downe Nimrod at Silverstone in 1982. Driven by Mallock/Salmon, it finished sixth. *(Nigel Snowdon)*

At Le Mans in 1982 the white and blue Nimrod, NRAC2/004, driven by Mallock/Salmon/Phillips and entered by Viscount Downe finished fifth, crossing the line on five cylinders. *(Nigel Snowdon)*

short of the minimum height requirement of 100cm, but this was easily overcome. Silverstone was dominated by Lancia and Porsche, but in the absence of other serious opposition the Nimrods ran reasonably well. Despite a very excessive oil consumption Mallock/Salmon finished sixth overall, while the works car, after 148 laps, retired because of a broken rotor arm.

As expected the two Nimrods ran into problems with the scrutineer at Le Mans over the minimum height rule. On the works car, again driven by Needell/Lees/Evans, the problem was circumvented by raising the ride height by 0.5cm and mounting a small 'spacer' above the windscreen. On the Downe car a much larger 'spacer' was fitted, as the team was not prepared to risk upsetting the handling with suspension modifications. Again Mallock/Salmon were the drivers, but they were joined by Simon Phillips, who was contributing to the costs of running in the event. Both cars ran steadily, if unspectacularly, with the works car rising to seventh place and the Downe car ninth after 3½ hours' racing. Within minutes the works car was out of the race. Just before the kink on the Mulsanne straight a rear tyre failed, the back end broke away and Needell spun viciously along the straight and into the Armco. Although the car was badly damaged, Needell was unhurt. Despite burnt-out exhaust valves caused by falling fuel pressure and a succession of pit stops the Mallock/Salmon/Phillips car eventually crossed the line on five cylinders to take seventh place at 111.80 mph. Porsche 956 cars took the first three places.

The problems with the Aston Martin engines continued and the only solution seemed to be to run them at lower revs than prescribed by Tickford. Both cars next appeared at the Spa 1000 Kms race, although both teams were facing financial problems. In practice Downe's car appeared with a modified nose featuring slim fins angled slightly forwards. The works car driven by Needell/Lees retired with less than an hour to go to the finish because of a broken valve head. It was the 16th Tickford engine that had broken on the works car during the year and Tickford had the temerity to charge £22,000 for each. The Downe car was delayed by two long pit stops, because of an oil leak cause by a leaking cooler (after some hesitation the works team loaned their only spare) and subsequently when it was discovered that the right rear air jack had fallen off (and it was this that probably caused the

damage to the oil cooler). Mallock/Salmon managed, however, to make up enough ground to be classified 11th (seventh Group C car).

The Nimrod's final race in 1982 was the Brands Hatch 1000 Kms, and as the works team had run out of money, only the Downe car driven by Mallock/Salmon appeared. At this race the Downe car, running with sponsorship from Bovis, was fitted with a full-width front wing to improve downforce. The race was run in torrential rain, stopped because of the crash of the two Ford C100s, restarted after an interval and then cut short because of poor light. The Nimrod finished ninth (seventh in the Group C class). On the strength of the Downe car's performance at Spa, Nimrod took third place overall in the Maker's championship, but that in reality was nothing more than a reflection of the weakness, Porsche apart, of the opposition. What was remarkable was that the Downe team had through restricting revs survived the season on one engine, although it had been rebuilt by the team several times during the year. In November there was a run-off over a standing kilometre over parallel runaways for publicity purposes at St Mawgan airfield in Cornwall between the works Nimrod driven by Needell and Evans and a No 42 Squadron Nimrod reconnaissance aircraft. In wet conditions the car won with times of 21.8 and 22.6 sec (attaining about 160 mph), compared with 25.6 and 23 sec recorded by the aircraft.

Whether the Tickford engines were as bad as Hamilton claimed or whether they had been badly treated by the Nimrod team, the constant engine failures had brought Nimrod to its knees. Gauntlett could no longer afford support and, after trying without success to raise sponsorship, Hamilton abandoned racing in Europe and planned a full season of IMSA racing in the United States. Although the Porsche 962 did not appear until 1984, the opposition in IMSA was strong and included the obsolescent but still very competitive 935 from Stuttgart, so Nimrod's prospects of success were slim. At the Daytona 24 Hours race in February, two cars were entered, one, NRAC1/002 to IMSA specification, running as the Pepsi Challenger and driven by Waltrip/ A. J. Foyt/Maldanado/Needell, and the other, NRAC2/003 to Group C specification, by Olsen/ Graham/Lyn St James. Both cars were eliminated by sump baffle problems. In the Miami Grand Prix, cut short to 1 hr 45 min by heavy rain, Gonzales finished 14th (with 002) and

The red-painted EMKA at Le Mans in 1983. Driven by Tiff Needell/Steven O'Rourke/Nick Faure, it had a far from trouble-free race and finished 17th. *(Nigel Snowdon)*

Bundy 20th (with 003). Because of the reduced distance of the race there were no driver changes.

Again the two cars were entered at Sebring. The IMSA car, 002, driven by Olsen/Gonzales, retired early when Gonzales missed a gear and bent a valve. Olsen was switched to join Lyn St James/Smith in 003, intended to qualify and not expected to last the distance. This car rumbled round to finish fifth and first Group C finisher and it was the team's best result of the year. Just 003 ran at Road Atlanta, but Lyn St James crashed. Because of the team's financial situation, 002 was sold to Jack Miller and at Riverside Raceway in the 6 Hours race Olsen/St James retired after running over débris from the crashed Jaguar XJR-5. Nimrod missed the Lime Rock 3 Hours race for financial reasons, but Miller ran his newly acquired car for Olsen and himself; they retired because of transmission

problems. The team's final outing was in the Mid-Ohio 6 Hours race in which 003 was entered for Olsen/Overby and crashed by Overby. Nimrod was forced to pull out of racing, the team was sold up and the planned NRAC3/006 car with carbon-fibre and Kevlar honeycomb monocoque was never completed.

In the meantime Aston Martin-powered cars continued to race in Europe. Over the winter Lord Downe's 004 had been rebuilt by Ray Mallock and Richard Williams with a completely new and much sleeker body with much improved downforce, lightened chassis and revised suspension geometry. The Downe team continued to race with sponsorship from Bovis Construction and Pace Petroleum.

A completely new contender in 1983 was the EMKA, financed by Steve O'Rourke, former manager of the Pink Floyd rock group (the car was named for his daughters Emma and Katherine), in partnership with Michael Cane. The new car, designated C83/1 was designed by Len Bailey (whose previous designs included Gulf-Mirages and the Ford C100). Bailey produced a very neat aluminium monocoque incorporating the compulsory flat bottom and air tunnels into which the air was forced by a 'lip' on the nose, just about as far as any designer could go to exploit ground effect within the very restrictive rules of Group C. Developed with modifications proposed by Bailey, the Tickford Aston Martin V8 engine was 4.5in. shorter than that used in the Nimrods, was of slightly lower weight (by about 50 lb), was still rated at 570 bhp (at slightly lower revs) and was attached directly to the rear bulkhead so as to form a stressed member with the bulkhead. The EMKA featured a very forward driving position, together with side-mounted water and oil radiators. At the front there were magnesium suspension uprights, unequal-length double wishbones and inboard-mounted coil spring/damper units. The rear suspension consisted of lower wishbones, upper A-brackets (the latter mounted on the casing of the Hewland VG5 combined gearbox/final drive unit) and coil spring/damper units mounted on the bell housing. The bell housing also mounted the rear bodywork and wing. AP ventilated disc brakes were fitted front and rear and the 16in. alloy wheels had a width of 11in. at the front and 15in. at the rear.

The dark red EMKA made its début at the 1983 Silverstone 1000 Kms race, in which it was driven by Needell/O'Rourke/Allan, and the rebuilt Downe Nimrod was driven by Mallock/Salmon. After delays caused by a broken distributor cap and a loose plug lead the EMKA was in 13th place when

The Downe team made a late entry at Spa in 1983, but the Nimrod driven by Mallock/Salmon was eliminated by failure of a con-rod-bolt.

At Le Mans in 1984 both Nimrods crashed and brought about the end of the Downe entries. Here the Mallock/ Olsen car leads the Group 44 Racing-entered Jaguar XJR-5 of Watson/Ballot-Lena/Adamowicz. *(Nigel Snowdon)*

it retired because of rear wheel bearing failure on the last lap. The Nimrod lost time in the pits for bodywork repairs after a collision with a hare, but eventually finished seventh.

Next for both cars was Le Mans, but it has to be said there were no prospects of either achieving any worthwhile success. Porsche domination of Group C was overwhelming. In practice the Nimrod was 16th fastest and the EMKA 27th. Both cars were plagued by problems in the race. The EMKA was delayed by stops to replace a holed radiator, a door, the oil tank, a rear wishbone and the rear hub bearings, and stops were made later in the race to repair a door and sort out a loose rear wing. Needell/O'Rourke/Faure eventually finished 17th. The Nimrod driven by Mallock/Salmon/Earle was delayed by alternator and battery problems, gear selector trouble (the team stripped the gearbox and replaced a selector fork), burnt-through lines to the oil and fuel gauges (which resulted in oil loss

that under the regulations could not be topped up), and as a result of the oil loss the Nimrod's engine broke a con-rod. It was a miserable saga of problems and unreliability.

The EMKA was not raced again in 1983, but the Downe Nimrod made two further Championship appearances. At Spa the car was powered by the 1982 engine and was running well in seventh place when it was eliminated by failure of a con-rod bolt. In the very wet Brands Hatch race the Nimrod retired because of crown wheel and pinion failure. In late September Mallock/Salmon finished fourth in a Thundersports race at Brands Hatch.

Early in 1984 Downe entered 004 in the Daytona 24 Hours race for Mallock/Sheldon. John Cooper, who had bought 005 from Hamilton, entered it for himself/Bob Evans/Paul Smith and Jack Miller ran 002 for himself/Ramirez/Vicki Smith. It was at this race that the Porsche 962 made its début. Fastest of the Nimrods in qualifying was Mallock, seventh quickest in 1 min 56.82 sec compared with the pole position 1 min 50.99 sec of Mario/Mike Andretti with the 962. Two of the Nimrods finished the race. Cooper/Evans/Smith took seventh place, whilst the Downe entry, once again plagued by problems, including the change of three suspension uprights and a wheel bearing and cylinder head gasket failure, crawled across the line into 16th place. The Miller/Ramirez/Smith car was eliminated by final drive failure.

After Daytona John Cooper abandoned plans to race 005 and the car, bought by Peter Livanos, was brought into the Downe team. It was immediately rebodied on similar lines to 004, but the latest body was lighter and used clip-on panels and titanium springs were fitted. The EMKA team withdrew, partly because of lack of sponsorship and partly because a proposed new rule in Group C, reducing fuel allowance by 15 per cent that favoured the normally aspirated cars, but was later abandoned. Even so Livanos decided to go ahead with turbocharging on 005. Tickford produced an engine with twin Garrett T04B turbochargers, twin intercoolers, a wastegate control and lower compression pistons. It could best be described as 'lightly turbocharged' and was said to develop 710 bhp, but the actual figure under race conditions was 650 bhp. It proved a complete disaster.

In the Silverstone 1000 Kms race the turbocharged 005 was driven by Mallock/Olsen and 004 by Salmon/Sheldon/Attwood. 005 displayed a voracious appetite for oil and retired because of damaged pistons. Although some development continued, the Nimrod was not again raced in turbocharged form. The normally aspirated entry was pathetically slow and retired because of a dropped valve.

The same two cars ran at Le Mans, 004 driven

The Cheetah-Aston Martin driven on its début at Spa in 1984 by Mallock/de Dryver/Hytten. It was eliminated by crankshaft damper failure. *(Nigel Snowdon)*

The EMKA returned to racing in 1985 and despite problems it finished 11th at Le Mans driven by Needell/O'Rourke/ Evans. The car was now sponsored by Dow Corning and ran in white, blue and black livery. *(Nigel Snowdon)*

by Salmon/Sheldon/Attwood and 005 by Mallock/ Olsen. It was to prove a disastrous race for the Nimrods and brought Viscount Downe's racing activities to an end. At 9.21 pm, after a little over six hours' racing (Le Mans started at 3 pm, because of European elections in 1984, instead of the usual 4 pm), 004 with Sheldon at the wheel suffered a burst left rear tyre on the approach to the kink on the Mulsanne Straight whilst travelling at over 200 mph. The Nimrod thudded into the Armco, the almost full fuel tank burst and caught fire and the disintegrating car cartwheeled over the barriers. Although Sheldon was badly burnt and had suffered broken wrists, he was able to free himself from the wreckage and he made a full recovery. Sadly a marshal was killed. Close behind the Aston was Jonathan Palmer (Porsche), who breaked heavily,

desperately trying to avoid debris from the Nimrod. Behind Palmer came Olsen with 005, who tried to swerve round the Porsche, but lost adhesion on the loose surface at the edge of the track and spun into the Armco. Both cars were eventually rebuilt, but neither was raced again.

Another new Aston Martin-powered contender appeared at Spa in 1984, the Cheetah G604, designed and built by Chuck Graemiger, a Swiss engineer with extensive experience in the single-seater field. In 1983 Graemiger had raced the Cosworth-powered G603 Cheetah without success, but this led to litigation brought by Louis Kessel, who had provided finance, had been responsible for the building of the carbon-fibre body and who had driven the car that year. These proceedings, which related to Kessel's claim for the design rights to the Cheetah, delayed

At Spa in 1985 the usually unreliable Cheetah finished tenth with de Dryver/Dieudonné at the wheel. *(Nigel Snowdon)*

progress on the G604, financed by Gatoil, a Swiss oil refining company, and to be powered by the Tickford Aston Martin engine.

The G604 eventually appeared at Spa in 1984 (it had been entered at Le Mans, but missed the race because of the legal wrangles). Graemiger's advanced design was based on a full-length carbon-fibre composite monocoque, the first use of the construction in sports car racing. The Aston Martin V8 engine acted as a fully stressed member and was used with a Hewland VG 5-speed gearbox/final drive unit. At the front there were double wishbones and outboard coil spring/damper units and at the rear rocking arms, lower wishbones and coil spring/damper units. Side-mounted radiators were fitted. The

car was much lighter than the Nimrod and the EMKA at 870 kg, so it seemed to have reasonable prospects of success. The car was driven by de Dryver/Hytten/Mallock and after overheating problems in both qualifying and the race, it retired because of the failure of an engine crankshaft damper. Subsequently the Cheetah was entered at Imola, but was plagued by engine trouble during the qualifying and non-started.

Gatoil planned a full season for the car in 1985 and extensive modifications were made, including revision of the suspension, modification of the underbody ground-effect tunnels, widening the body and replacing the side radiators with a single radiator in the nose.

The EMKA also returned to racing in 1985 and

it too was substantially modified, with revised rear suspension, larger hubs, removal of most of the underbody ground effects and new bodywork. Sponsorship came from the Dow Corning silicones group and there was new white, blue and black paintwork.

At the first Group C race of the year at Mugello, a very poorly supported 1000 Kms event, the Cheetah was plagued in qualifying by throttle and handling problems. The throttle problems persisted in the race and the car was retired when it lost its rear wing. The drivers were de Dryver/Brancatelli, and the same drivers were at the wheel at Monza. It survived only until the third lap, when Brancatelli abandoned it out on the circuit with what was believed to be ignition failure – in fact the master switch had accidentally been turned off and the car was perfectly healthy. At Silverstone, Cooper/ Brindley drove the Cheetah. The car lost its rear bodywork on the warming-up lap, joined the race late, was further delayed by starter motor trouble and retired because of rear suspension failure. Sadly this promising project rapidly became regarded as a joke. The EMKA was driven by Needell/O'Rourke/Evans and ran much better, but it retired because of rear suspension failure.

Both cars next appeared at Le Mans. Once again the Cheetah's race was soon over. Entered for de Dryver/Cooper/Bourgoignie, it was again plagued by problems during qualifying, it was delayed by suspension problems in the race and after just under five hours' racing it crashed after losing a wheel, the result of drive-shaft failure. In contrast, the EMKA driven by Needell/O'Rourke/ Faure ran well. During qualifying it was timed on the Mulsanne Straight at a surprisingly quick

216 mph (compared with 183 mph for the Cheetah) and it led the race briefly (thanks to a very early refuelling stop) when the fastest cars began their first round of refuelling. After problems during the night hours the EMKA finished 11th overall – although the throttle return spring failed on the finishing straight on the last lap.

Needell/Cooper drove the Cheetah at Hockenheim and were eliminated by piston failure. The EMKA reappeared at Spa in the hands of Needell/O'Rourke/Weaver, but retired early in the race because of loss of fuel pressure, whilst the Cheetah driven by de Dryver/ Dieudonné ran reasonably well to its only finish of the season in tenth place. At Brands Hatch in September the EMKA was driven by Needell/ O'Rourke/Galvin and although at one stage it held fourth place, it retired because of a broken suspension top link. The Cheetah (Brindley/ Regout) joined the race very late because of a leaking fuel metering unit and retired because of a broken stub axle. The Cheetah was also entered in the last race of the year at Fuji, and on a flooded track, which caused most of the European entries to withdraw, completed 12 or so laps before pulling out. By the end of the year Gatoil were weary of the Cheetah's constant failures and the car was withdrawn.

After 1985 no Aston Martin-powered car competed in Group C. None had been successful and the lion's share of the failure of the Aston Martin-powered contenders could be laid at the door of engine builders Tickford. It was only when the Aston Martin works team raced the AMR1 in 1989 that the true potential of the V8 engine was seen.

Group C Cars: 1989

The decision that Aston Martin would build a Group C contender was made in mid-1986. It was a joint decision made between Victor Gauntlett, Chairman of Aston Martin, Peter Livanos, Aston Martin distributor in the United States and Hugh McCaig, who headed the Ecurie Ecosse team that had previously raced C2 cars. Following the announcement that Aston Martin and Ecurie Ecosse had joined forces in its development and construction, a development contract was granted to Ecurie Ecosse and Ray Mallock, whilst Richard Williams, who had managed Lord Downe's Nimrods, was taken on as team manager in charge of development. Engine development was entrusted to the Reeves Callaway company in Connecticut. The designer of the car was Max Boxstrom, formerly with Brabham, and the founder of the Dymag Wheels Company based in Chippenham. Not long after the plans had been formulated, in September, 1987, Ford acquired a 75 per cent shareholding in Aston Martin Lagonda Limited, and despite initial fears at that stage that they would try to axe the project, no objection was raised and development went ahead.

The prototype AMR1 (AMR1/01) was first revealed to Aston Martin and Ford personnel at Newport Pagnell in October 1988 and did not in fact run until late November 1988. The car was based on a monocoque formed by only three mouldings, was constructed in carbon-composite with Kevlar skins and honeycomb floors. The three principal components forming the monocoque consisted of the outer shell, the floor and the seat-back panel. The bodywork was

Le Mans 1989 and preparation work on the Redman/Los/Roe car, AMR1/02 *(Roger Stowers)*

A superb shot of the highly developed Aston Martin V8 twin overhead camshaft engine used in the AMR1. Again this photograph was taken at Le Mans. *(Roger Stowers)*

manufactured using carbon-fibre moulds. The AMR1 closely followed Formula 1 practice by featuring a 'coke-bottle'-shape monocoque, with a wide wing under the nose, and air expelled through large front ducts forward of the doors, a full-length rear tunnel and angled engine and trans-axle. The radiator was mounted below the rear wing.

At the front, suspension was by double wishbones and coil spring/dampers, with the rear suspension by double wishbones and inboard-mounted coil spring/dampers suspended from the semi-stressed engine and trans-axle units. Callaway Engineering had already produced the 4-valve production Aston Martin engine and so were well equipped to undertake development of the racing unit. As early as April 1988 5.3-litre V8s in racing specification were being tested and by August Callaway had completed two 6.0-litre

units. Originally the 5.3-litre racing engine, which was intended only for testing purposes, developed 570 bhp at 7500 rpm, but the 6-litre version had an output of 680 bhp and as raced power topped 700 bhp. Callaway had also been working on a 6.4-litre version of the V8 engine, but that was abandoned because of a change in the racing regulations. Transmission was by a trans-axle built by the team itself, but incorporating Hewland gears. A British Zytec engine management system was used. Later, after development work, the engine could run safely and consistently at 8500 rpm. The AMR1 was fitted with 17in. Dymag wheels, 14in. wide at the front and 15in. at the rear, with 14in. AP discs and three-pot calipers. Overall length was 15ft 8in., width 6ft 6in. and height 3ft 4in. The cars were painted white, blue and red and the only sponsors to be shown on the car were Mobil and Goodyear.

It was not until early 1989 that the final decision to go ahead with the project on a budget of £26 million was announced. At the same time it became known that there were two subsidiary companies, Aston Martin Racing Developments Limited and Proteus Technology Limited (Protech). The company had taken spacious premises at Milton Keynes and Richard Williams closed down his own company, R. S. Williams Limited in Brixton, to concentrate on managing the team.

In the early part of the year the team was plagued by minor problems, not unexpected with a totally new design, and during testing at Donington Park in January, David Leslie crashed, the result of the failure of a rear hub, badly damaging AMR1/01. At the Le Mans test days the team suffered two engine failures, totally unexpected because the Callaway-developed engines were very reliable, contrasting strongly with their Tickford predecessors.

Because of these problems Protech missed the first round in the World Sports Prototype Championship at Suzuka on 9 April and as a result incurred a fine of £250,000. This fine was based on the rules that state that all cars registered to compete in the Prototype Championship had to attend all rounds, with the exception of one European race. By the race at Dijon-Prenois in France on 21 May, the second chassis AMR1/02 was ready and this was driven in the French race by David Leslie and veteran Brian Redman. Much of qualifying was spent sorting out suspension problems of a minor nature and coping with excess downforce. As raced at Dijon the power output of the V8 unit was 670/680 bhp. In this 480-kilometre race Leslie/Redman ran steadily, but unspectacularly, to finish 17th.

For the Le Mans 24 Hours race Protech had two cars ready, AMR1/02, driven by Michael Roe/Costas Los, and AMR1/03, driven by David

At Le Mans AMR1/03 was shared by David Leslie, Ray Mallock and David Sears. It retired because of inexplicable engine failure during the night hours. Note the black band on the left wing, a mark of respect to John Wyer who had died in April. *(Nigel Snowdon)*

At around noon on the Sunday Redman takes over from David Sears. Although Sears drove in the final hours, Brian Redman brought the car across the line to finish 11th, the first time ever at Le Mans for this veteran driver. *(Roger Stowers)*

Only the one AMR1, chassis 04, was entered in the Championship round at Brands Hatch. Development work was continuing steadily, weight had been reduced, there was improved suspension and aerodynamics and the car was now much more competitive. David Leslie and Brian Redman drove into a more than satisfactory fourth place. *(Nigel Snowdon)*

Two cars were entered in the Wheatcroft Gold Cup at Donington Park and the ever-improving AMR1s finished sixth (Leslie/Roe with 05) and seventh (Redman/Sears with 07). This superb close-up shot is of the sixth place car. Note the Ecurie Ecosse badge on the wing. *(Nigel Snowdon)*

Aston Martins were still far from competitive, and at a little after 2.30 am on the Sunday morning Sears abandoned 03 at Mulsanne Corner because of engine failure; an electrical problem had meant that the car had been running without a tachometer for some while and it was initially believed that it had been over-revved, but this was not in fact the reason for the failure and the cause was never clearly established. AMR1/02 driven by Roe/Los/Redman ran steadily through the race to finish 11th overall.

The performance at Le Mans was more than acceptable to the team, which was well on course with its development programme. The biggest problem revealed had been aerodynamic failings, which limited the speed down the Mulsanne Straight to 217 mph compared with the 245 mph of the fastest cars. Protech now exercised their right to miss a round in the European series, did not enter the Spanish race at Jarama, and next

appeared at Brands Hatch on 23 July. Here only one car, the new AMR1/04, was entered for David Leslie/Brian Redman. A host of minor changes, including aerodynamic improvements, had been made. In the early laps of the race Leslie battled with Neilsen's Jaguar XJR-9 and Belm's Spice, but fell back as the race progressed; Leslie/Redman finished fourth after a spate of retirements in the closing laps of the race.

Next came the race at the Nürburgring on 22 August. Here only 04 was entered for Leslie/Redman. The most significant change since Brands Hatch was the adoption of carbon-fibre brakes, but development was continuing and the weight of the car had been considerably reduced. Although the Aston Martin ran steadily, it spent most of the race in mid-field, mainly because of its lack of high-speed handling, and it eventually finished eighth. For the Donington Park race on 3 September Protech prepared two cars, AMR1/05

Leslie/Ray Mallock/David Sears. At this stage the for Leslie/Roe and AMR1/04 for Redman/Sears. Weight reduction continued apace, and the 962kg. of the car at the Nürburgring had now been reduced to 912kg. (the newer car weighed 906kg.). Redman/Sears fought their way through to fourth place, with Leslie/Roe fifth. Sears was slowed by clutch slip and a broken anti-roll bar at the front, but crossed the line in seventh place, with Leslie/Roe sixth.

Two cars were again entered at Spa-Francorchamps. Leslie/Roe drove 05, whilst Brian Redman/Stanley Dickens were at the wheel of 04. When Roe was holding eighth place with 05, a con-rod failed and the Aston Martin was out of the race. Dickens/Redman rose to ninth place and finished seventh, thanks to two late retirements. There remained only the race in Mexico on 29 October and here Aston Martin fielded only a single car, 05 for Leslie/Redman. More progress had been made in the reduction of weight and a lighter gearbox was now fitted. As a result of testing of the Version II engine at Donington Park in October, one of these units

that revved to 7750 rpm was fitted. Early in the race the Aston Martin held tenth place and it eventually finished eighth.

Throughout the year the AMR1 had shown considerable promise and as a result the team was well advanced for 1990 on the improved AMR2, but Aston Martin racing plans ended in disarray. It had always been something of a mystery that Ford had been prepared to allow two of their companies to run cars in Group C, and sadly for all those involved in the AMR project Ford decided to axe it. Two reasons were given, firstly that there was some doubt as to whether the Le Mans 24 Hours race would be held – to win this was Aston Martin's prime goal – and also because of Protech's failure to acquire a suitable 3.5-litre engine for the new era of normally aspirated power units that was coming into force. Although never spelled out in as many words, this meant that Fords were not prepared to make available the Cosworth Formula 1 engine that was used to power the Benetton and (now) Jordan Grand Prix cars.

Appendix 1

Specification of David Aston Martin Competition Cars

DB2 (1950–53)

Specification (1950)
Note: As this was also a production car, many of the details given also relate to the production model.

Engine:	6-cylinder twin overhead camshaft 2580cc (78 x 90mm) with twin SU H4 carburettors, a compression ratio of 6.5:1 and a power output of 105 bhp at 5000 rpm.
Clutch:	9in dry single-plate.
Gearbox:	David Brown 4-speed and reverse in unit with the engine and with the standard 3.7:1 final drive ratio, overall ratios of top, 3.77:1; third, 5.02:1; second, 7.48:1; first, 11.03:1 and reverse, 11.03:1. With the close-ratio gearbox, the overall ratios were top, 3.77:1; third, 4.75:1; second, 7.05:1; first, 11.03:1 and reverse, 11.03:1.
Final drive:	Salisbury hypoid bevel with standard ratio of 3.77:1 and optional alternative ratios of 3.5, 3.67 and 4.1:1.
Chassis:	Rectangular tube main members.
Front suspension:	Independent by trailing links, torsion bars and coil spring/damper units.
Rear suspension:	Live axle, parallel trailing links, Panhard rod and coil spring/damper units.
Steering:	Worm and roller, 2⅔ turns lock to lock.
Brakes:	Girling hydraulic two-leading shoe at the front, leading and trailing shoe at the rear, 12in. drums.
Wheels:	16in. centre-lock wire-type, knock-off hubs.
Fuel capacity:	19 gallons.
Oil capacity:	15 pints.
Wheelbase:	8ft 3in.
Track:	4ft 6in front and rear.
Overall length:	13ft 6.5in.
Overall width:	5ft 5in.
Overall height:	4ft 5.5in.
Ground clearance:	6.5in.
Turning circle:	35ft.
Weight:	21.87 cwt (dry).

Development

June 1949:	Prototype cars, two with 2-litre 4-cylinder push-rod engines and one with 6-cylinder engine ran at Le Mans.
April 1950:	Production coupé first exhibited at the New York Motor Show.
June 1950:	Works cars ran at Le Mans with engines developing 125 bhp at 5000 rpm.
September 1950:	Production drophead coupé announced.
January 1951:	Production cars became available with 'Vantage' engine, SU HV6 carburettors, 8.16:1 compression ratio and a power output of 125 bhp at 5000 rpm.
May 1951:	Appearance at Silverstone of two 'lightweight' works cars with lightened chassis and body panels. Al-fin brake drums and Borrani wheels. Power output of 128 bhp at 5000 rpm. One car fitted with aluminium cylinder head.
June 1951:	All three works cars at Le Mans fitted with aluminium cylinder heads, three Weber 35 DCO carburettors and with a power output of 138 bhp at 5500 rpm.

DB3

Specification (1952)

Engine:	6-cylinder twin overhead camshaft 2580cc (78 x 90mm), with three Weber twin-choke 36 DCF5 carburettors, compression ratio of 8.16:1 and a power output of 140 bhp at 5200 rpm.
Clutch:	9in. dry single-plate with carbon thrust withdrawal mechanism.
Gearbox:	David Brown 5-speed and reverse with overall ratios of top, 3.415:1; fourth, 4.11:1, third, 5.24:1; second, 7.768:1; first, 11.919:1 and reverse, 8.63:1.
Final drive:	David Brown hypoid bevel with ratio of 4.11:1.
Chassis:	Twin-tubular constructed from 4in. 16-gauge chrome molybdenum longitudinal members with three 5in. 14-gauge cross-members and rear frame extension fabricated from 2in. tubes.

Front suspension:	Independent by trailing links and transverse torsion bars.
Rear suspension:	De Dion axle, trailing links and torsion bars.
Steering:	Rack-and-pinion, two turns lock to lock.
Brakes:	Front: two-leading shoe drum with Al-fin drums of 13in. diameter and 2.5in. width. Rear: leading and trailing shoe drum mounted inboard with Al-fin drums of 11in. diameter and 2.25in. width.
Wheels:	16in. centre-lock wire-type, knock-off hubs and steel rims to take 6.00 x 16in. tyres.
Fuel capacity:	32 gallons.
Oil capacity:	24 pints.
Wheelbase:	7ft 9in.
Track:	4ft 3in front and rear.
Overall length:	13ft 2.5in.
Overall width:	5ft 1.5in.
Overall height:	3ft 4in (to top of aero screen).
Ground clearance:	5in.
Frontal area:	13.27 sq. ft.
Turning circle:	32ft.
Weight:	19.31 cwt (with 9 gallons fuel).

Development

September 1951:	Prototype appeared in the Tourist Trophy.
May 1952:	Cars ran in the Monaco Grand Prix with 2922cc engines.
June 1952:	DB3/1 ran at Le Mans with hard-top body.
July 1952:	All cars henceforth fitted with the S430/63R 4-speed gearbox.

DB3S

Specification (1953)

Engine:	6-cylinder twin overhead camshaft 2922cc (83 x 90mm) with three Weber twin-choke 35 DCO carburettors, compression rate of 8.5:1, maximum torque of 182 lb.ft. at 3800 rpm and power output of 182 bhp at 5500 rpm.
Clutch:	9in. dry single-plate with hydraulically operated carbon ring withdrawal mechanism.
Gearbox:	David Brown 4-speed and reverse with overall ratios of top, 3.727:1 (1:1); third, 4.69:1 (1.26:1); second, 6.97:1 (1.87:1); first, 10.88:1 (2.29:1) and reverse, 10.88:1 (2.29:1)
Final drive:	David Brown spiral drive with ratio of 3.727:1 and light alloy casing.

Chassis:	Twin-tubular constructed from 4in. 16-gauge chrome molybdenum steel longitudinal members with three 14-gauge 4in. and 5in. cross-members.
Front suspension:	Independent by trailing links and torsion bars.
Rear suspension:	De Dion axle, trailing links and transverse torsion bars.
Steering:	Rack-and-pinion, two turns lock to lock.
Brakes:	Front: two-leading shoe drum with Al-fin drums of 13in. diameter and 2.5in. width. Rear: leading and trailing shoe drum mounted inboard with Al-fin drums of 12in. diameter and 2.5in. width.
Wheels:	16in. centre-lock wire-type, knock-off hubs and steel rims to take 6.00 x 16in. tyres.
Fuel capacity:	35 gallons.
Oil capacity:	24 pints.
Wheelbase:	7ft 3in.
Track:	4ft 1in. front and rear.
Overall length:	12 ft 9.75in.
Overall width:	4ft 10.75in.
Overall height:	3ft 5.5in. (to scuttle).
Ground clearance:	5.5in.
Frontal area:	11.1 sq. ft.
Turning circle:	30ft.
Weight:	19.25 cwt (with 35 gallons fuel).

Development

May 1953:	Prototype appeared at Charterhall.
September 1953:	Outboard rear brakes fitted to DB3S/2 in Tourist Trophy.
January 1954:	Outboard rear brakes and Girling automatic adjusters on all cars. Cars ran at Buenos Aires with raised 9.4:1 compression ratio (to suit the 100/130 octane Avgas used in this race) and developed 194 bhp at 5500 rpm.
May 1954:	All three cars at the International Trophy meeting at Silverstone were fitted with new twin-plug cylinder heads and Weber 45 DCO carburettors which boosted power output to 225 bhp at 6000 rpm.

The new coupés appeared with bodywork developed with the aid of the Vickers wind tunnel facilities.

DB3S/1 fitted with Lockheed disc brakes on the front wheels.

June 1954:	At Le Mans DB3S/1 ran with Wade supercharger, single Weber 52 DCO carburettor, 7:1 compression ratio and a power output of 240 bhp at 6000 rpm.
October 1954:	Production DB3S announced at the Earls Court Show with single-plug coil ignition, triple Solex carburettors, 180 bhp and drum brakes. Bodywork reprofiled.
April 1955:	Works cars rebodied. Girling disc brakes and wheels with offset Borrani rims fitted. Car with 2493cc (83 x 76.8mm) engine entered in the British Empire Trophy.
September 1955:	Car with 2992cc (84 x 90mm) engine ran in the Tourist Trophy.
May 1956:	Triple Weber carburettors and claimed 210 bhp engine adopted on production cars. Appearance of fixed head coupé to production specification at the May Silverstone meeting (not raced).
July 1956:	New cars DB3S/9 and DB3S/10 with reprofiled nose, headlamps under perspex covers and streamlined headrest at Rouen.
April 1957:	DB3S/10 with CAV fuel injection and wishbone and coil spring front suspension raced in the British Empire Trophy.

DBR1

Specification (1957)

Engine:	6-cylinder twin overhead camshaft 2922cc (83 x 90mm) with three Weber twin-choke 45 DCO carburettors, two plugs per cylinder, compression ratio of 9:1 and power output of 240 bhp at 6250 rpm.
Clutch:	7½in. triple-plate.
Gearbox:	David Brown CG537 non-synchromesh 5-speed and reverse in unit with the final drive and with ratios of top, 0735:1, fourth, 0.8184:1, third, 1.035:1, second, 1.458:1, and first, 2.11:1.
Final drive:	ZF, limited slip differential.
Chassis:	Multi-tubular space-frame constructed from chrome molybdenum tubing.
Front suspension:	Independent by trailing links and torsion bars.
Rear suspension:	De Dion axle, trailing links and transverse torsion bars.
Steering:	Rack-and-pinion, two turns lock to lock.
Brakes:	Girling single-caliper, non-servo disc, 12.5in. at front, 11.5in. at rear.
Wheels:	Borrani 16in. centre-lock wire-type with triple-eared knock-off hubs and 6.00 x 16 and 6.50 x 16in. tyres front and rear.
Fuel capacity:	40 gallons.
Oil capacity:	36 pints (dry sump).
Wheelbase:	7ft 6in.
Track:	4ft 3.5in. front and rear.
Overall length:	13ft 2.5in.
Overall width:	5ft 4in.
Overall height:	3ft 2.5in. (to scuttle).
Ground clearance:	5in.
Turning circle:	39ft.
Weight:	15.75 cwt (dry).

Development

August 1956:	Raced at Le Mans with 2493cc engine.
April 1957:	Raced in the British Empire Trophy with less rounded nose, smaller headrest and dished Borrani wheels in place of the original offset wheels.
August 1957:	Raced at Spa with 2922cc engine, 95-degree cylinder head, 9.25:1 compression ratio and a power output of 252 bhp at 6000 rpm.
March 1958:	Raced at Sebring with the new seven-bearing crankshaft.
May 1958:	Appearance of experimental DBR3/1 with wishbone and longitudinal torsion bar front suspension and 2992cc (92 x 75mm) engine at Silverstone.
September 1958:	Two cars ran in the Tourist Trophy with 2992cc (84 x 90mm) engines and these engines were used throughout 1959.
March 1959:	At Sebring the DBR1 ran with seven-bearing crankshaft and Weber 50 DCO carburettors.
June 1959:	Cars raced at Le Mans with shorter, more rounded tails, partly valanced front wheels, valanced rear wheels and re-routed exhaust system emerging under the tail.
September 1959:	DBR1/1 appeared in practice for the Tourist Trophy with Maserati gearbox; race cars fitted with built-in pneumatic jacks.

DBR2

Specification (1957)

Engine:	6-cylinder twin overhead camshaft 3670cc (92 x 92mm), with six Weber single-choke 48 DOE carburettors (three twin-choke 50 DCO substituted after first race), single plug per cylinder, compression ratio of 9.25:1 and a claimed power output of 287 bhp at 5750 rpm.
Clutch:	7½in. triple-plate.
Gearbox:	David Brown SC532 all-syncromesh 5-speed and reverse in unit with the engine and with ratios of top, 0.89:1; fourth, 1:1; third, 1.28:1; second, 1.73:1 and first, 2.5:1.
Final drive:	ZF, limited slip differential.
Chassis:	Multi-tubular backbone.
Front suspension:	Independent by trailing links and torsion bars.
Rear suspension:	De Dion axle, trailing links and transverse torsion bars.
Steering:	Rack-and-pinion, two turns lock-to-lock.
Brakes:	Girling single-caliper, non-servo disc, 12.5in. at front, 11.5in. at rear.
Wheels:	Borrani 16in. centre-lock wire-type with triple-eared knock-off hubs.
Wheelbase:	7ft 9in.
Track:	4ft 5in. front and rear.

Development

June 1957:	DBR2/1 ran at Le Mans with six Weber single-choke carburettors.
September 1957:	DBR2/1 and DBR2/2 ran at Silverstone with three Weber twin-choke carburettors.
April 1958:	DBR2/1 and DBR2/2 ran at Oulton Park with 3910cc (95 x 92mm) engines developing 284/298 bhp at 5500/5700 rpm.
June 1958:	DBR2/1 and DBR2/2 exported to the United States 'on loan' with 4164cc (98 x 92mm) engines.
December 1959:	DBR2/2 driven by Moss in the Bahamas with twin-plug cylinder head and power output of 315 bhp at 6000 rpm.

DBR4 and DBR5 (1959–60)

Specification (1959)

Engine:	6-cylinder twin overhead camshaft 2493cc (83 x 76.8mm) with three Weber 50 DCO carburettors, twin plugs per cylinder, a compression ratio varying between 10.4:1 and 9.57:1 and a power output of 250 bhp at 7800 rpm.
Clutch:	7½in. triple-plate.
Gearbox:	David Brown CG537 5-speed and reverse in unit with the final drive.
Final drive:	ZF, limited slip differential.
Chassis:	Multi-tubular space-frame constructed from chrome molybdenum tubing.
Front suspension:	Independent, by double wishbones and coil spring/damper units.
Rear suspension:	De Dion axle, trailing links and transverse torsion bars.
Steering:	Rack-and-pinion, two turns lock-to-lock.
Brakes:	Girling single-caliper, non-servo disc, 12.5in. at front, 11.5in. at rear
Wheels:	Borrani 16in. centre-lock wire-type with twin-eared knock-off hubs to take 5.50 x 16 and 7.00 x 16in. tyres front and rear.
Wheelbase:	7ft 6in.
Track:	4ft 3.5in. front and rear.

Development

December 1957:	Prototype, MP192, with wishbone and torsion bar front suspension and Morris Minor rack-and-pinion steering tested by Roy Salvadori and Roy Parnell at the Motor Industry Research Association establishment and in January and February 1958 tested at Goodwood.
April 1959:	DBR4 announced (now with DB4 steering box and wishbone and coil spring front suspension) and raced in the International Trophy at Silverstone the following month.
September 1959:	DBR4/3 appeared at Monza with centre-section of the body integral with the chassis and with one-piece de Dion tube.
May 1960:	Appearance at Silverstone of the much modified and rather lighter DBR5 with 7ft 3in. wheelbase, 80-degree cylinder head with reversed porting, torsion bar front suspension, one-piece de Dion tube and Maserati 5M-60 gearbox.
July 1960:	DBR5/2 appeared at the British Grand Prix with independent rear suspension.

DB4GT and DB4GT Zagato (1960–61)

Specification (1960)
Note:
1. As these were production cars, many of the details given also relate to production models.

2. Variations relating to the DB4GT Zagato are given in parenthesis.

Engine:	6-cylinder twin overhead camshaft 3670cc (92 x 92mm) with three Weber twin-choke Weber 45 DCOE4 or DCOE9 carburettors, twin plugs per cylinder, a compression ratio of 9:1 (Zagato 9.7:1) and a claimed power output of 302 bhp (Zagato 314 bhp) at 6000 rpm.
Clutch:	9in. dry twin-plate.
Gearbox:	David Brown 4-speed and reverse all-syncromesh with overall ratios of top, 3.54:1 (1:1); third, 4.42:1 (1.25:1); second, 6.6:1 (1.74:1); first, 8.82:1 (2.49:1) and reverse, 8.58:1 (2.43:1).
Final drive:	Salisbury hypoid bevel with ratio of 3.54:1 and Powr-lok limited slip differential.
Chassis:	Steel platform and tubular steel framework.
Front suspension:	Unequal-length double wishbones, coil spring/damper units and anti-roll bar.
Rear suspension:	Live axle, coil spring/damper units, parallel trailing links and transverse Watts linkage.
Steering:	Rack-and-pinion, 2½ turns lock to lock.
Brakes:	Girling disc, no servo, front 12in., rear 11in.
Wheels:	Borrani 16in. centre-lock wire-type, knock-off hubs with triple eared hubcaps, to take 6.00 x 16 tyres.
Fuel capacity:	30 gallons (certain cars had additional two 6-gallon tanks in the wings).
Oil capacity:	23 pints.
Wheelbase:	7ft 9in.
Track:	4ft 6in. front, 4ft 5.5in. rear.
Overall length:	14ft 3⅜in. (Zagato 14ft 0in.).
Overall width:	5ft 6in. (Zagato 5ft 5.25in.).
Overall height:	4ft 2in.
Ground clearance:	6.25in.
Turning circle:	35ft.
Weight:	24.98 cwt (kerb weight) (Zagato 24.6 cwt).

Development
May 1959:	Prototype car, DP199/1, entered in the Grand Touring race at the BRDC Silverstone meeting.
June 1959:	DP199/1 entered at Le Mans with 3-litre engine from DBR3/1.
October 1959:	Production DB4GT announced at London Motor Show.
April 1960:	Appearance of the 'lightweight' DB4GT at Goodwood.
October 1960:	DB4GT Zagato announced at London Motor Show.
June 1962:	DP209 lightweight version delivered to Essex Racing Stable.

DP212

Specification (1962)
Engine:	6-cylinder twin overhead camshaft 3996cc (96 x 92mm), with three Weber twin-choke 50 DCO carburettors, compression ratio of 9.5:1 and a power output of 327 bhp at 6000 rpm.
Clutch:	7½in. three-plate.
Gearbox:	David Brown 5-speed and reverse with ratios of top, 0.89:1; fourth, 1.00:1; third, 1.28:1; second, 1.73:1; first, 2.51:1; and reverse, 2.14:1
Final drive:	David Brown spiral bevel with alloy casing.
Chassis:	Rectangular box-section members with light alloy floor panels.
Front suspension:	Independent by unequal-length double wishbone and coil/spring damper units
Rear suspension:	De Dion axle, torsion bars and telescope dampers.
Steering:	Rack-and-pinion, two turns lock-to-lock.
Brakes:	Girling single-caliper non-servo disc, 12in. at front, 11⁷⁄₁₆in. at rear.
Wheels:	Borrani 16in. centre-lock wire-type with triple-eared knock-off hubs and 6.00 x 16 and 6.50 x 16in. tyres front and rear respectively.
Fuel capacity:	40 gallons.
Oil capacity:	21 pints.
Wheelbase:	7ft 10in.
Track:	4ft 6in front and rear.
Overall length:	14ft 6in.
Overall width:	5ft 6in.
Overall height:	4ft 2in.
Ground clearance:	5in.
Turning circle:	36ft.
Weight:	19.25 cwt (dry).

Development
June 1962:	Raced at Le Mans.
April 1963:	Appeared at Le Mans Practice days with chopped tail.

Appendix 2:
Race Performances of Aston Martin Competition Cars

Note:

1. The results relate mainly to works cars, but exclude works entries competing in very minor events such as Aston Martin Owners' Club meetings

2. The results for private entrants are included where they achieved a significant success and are marked thus*

3. All entries are sports cars, unless indicated

1948

Spa 24 Hours, Spa Francorchamps, 10–11 July	St J. Horsfall/L. Johnson (DB1, LMA/48/1)	1st, 72.07 mph

1949

Le Mans 24 Hours, 25–26 June	A. Jones/N. Haines (DB2, LMA/49/2)	7th (and 3rd in 3000cc class)
	T. A. S. O. Mathieson/P. Maréchal (DB2, LMA/49/1)	Crashed
	L. Johnson/C. Brackenbury (DB2, LMA/49/3)	Retired, water pump
Spa 24 Hours, Spa Francorchamps, 9–10 July	L. Johnson/C. Brackenbury (DB2, LMA/49/3)	3rd (and 2nd in 4000cc class)
	St J. Horsfall (Speed Model, J6/707/U)*	4th (and 2nd in 2000cc class)
	L. Macklin/N. Haines (DB2, LMA/49/1)	5th (and 3rd in in 4000cc class)

1950

Inter-Europa Cup, Monza, Sports Class, 26 March, 2 hours	N. Macklin (DB2 LML/49/4)*	2nd
Le Mans 24 Hours, 24–25 June	N. Macklin/G. Abecassis (DB2, LML/50/8)	5th (and 1st in 3000cc class)
	C. Brackenbury/R. Parnell (DB2, LML/50/7)	6th (and 2nd in 3000cc class)
	E. Thompson/J. Gordon (DB2, LML/49/3)	Retired, broken crankshaft
Production Car race, Silverstone, 20 August, 1 hour	R. Sommer (DB2, LML/50/8)	10th (and 2nd in 3000cc class)
	R. Parnell (DB2, LML/50/7)	12th (and 3rd in 3000cc class)
	E. Thompson (DB2, LML/50/9)	15th (and 4th in 3000cc class)
Tourist Trophy, Dundrod, 16 September, 3 Hours	R. Parnell (DB2, LML/50/7)	4th (and 1st in the 3000cc class)
	G. Abecassis (DB2, LML/50/9)	5th (and 2nd in the 3000cc class)
	L. Macklin (DB2, LML/50/8	8th (and 3rd in the 3000cc class)

1951

Mille Miglia, 28–29 April, 972 miles	T. H. Wisdom/A. Hume (DB2, LML/50/8)*	11th (and 1st in over 2000cc Closed Car class)

Production Car race, Silverstone, 5th May, 1 hour	R. Parnell (DB2, LML/50/50) G. Abecassis (DB2, LML/50/55)	6th (and 1st in the 3000cc class) Retired, gearbox
Le Mans 24 Hours	L. Macklin/E. Thompson (DB2, LML/50/8) G. Abecassis/B. Shawe-Taylor (DB2, LML/50/55) R. Parnell/D. Hampshire (DB2, LML/50/50)	3rd (and 1st in the 3000cc class) 5th (and 2nd in the 3000cc class) 7th (and 3rd in the 3000cc class)
Tourist Trophy, Dundrod, 15 September, 319 miles	B. Shawe-Taylor (DB2, LML/50/50) G. Abecassis (DB2, LML/50/55) L. Macklin (DB3/1)	7th (and 2nd in the 3000cc class) Retired, clutch Retired, engine bearings

1952

Mille Miglia, 3–4 May, 992 miles	T. H. Wisdom/A. Hume (DB2, LML/50/8) R. Parnell/Gerboli (DBR2, LML/50/50) G. Abecassis (DB2, LML/50/55)	12th (and 1st in over 2000cc Touring class) 13th (and 2nd in over 2000cc Touring class) Retired, clutch
Production sports car race, Silverstone, 10 May, 50 miles	R. Parnell (DB3/3) G. Abecassis (DB3/5) L. Macklin (DB3/5) G. E. Duke (DB3/1)	2nd (and 1st in 3000cc class) 3rd (and 2nd in 3000cc class) 4th (and 3rd in 3000cc class) Retired, damaged steering
Prix de Berne, Bremgarten, 18th May, 81 miles	G. E. Duke (DB2, LML/50/55) R. Parnell (DB2, LML/50/50)	4th 5th
British Empire Trophy, Douglas, Isle of Man, 29 May, 202 miles	G. E. Duke (DB3/1)	Retired, broken crankshaft
Monaco Grand Prix, 2 June, 195 miles	P. J. Collins (DB3/4) R. Parnell (DB3/3) L. Macklin (DB3/5)	7th Retired, broken connecting rod Retired, broken connecting rod
Le Mans 24 Hours, 14–15 June	R. Parnell/E. Thompson (DB3/1) R. D. Poore/P. D. C. Griffith (DB3/3) L. Macklin/P. J. Collins (DB3/5)	Retired, final drive Retired, water pump Retired, final drive
Jersey Road Race, 10 July, Two 32-mile qualifying heats and 64-mile final	G. Abecassis (DB3/4) R. Parnell (DB3/5)	3rd 4th
International sports car race, Boreham, 2 August, 102 miles	R. Parnell (DB3/5) G. Abecassis (DB3/4)	3rd (and 1st in 3000cc class) Retired, fuel filter
Goodwood 9 Hours race, 16 August	P. J. Collins/P. D. C. Griffith (DB3/5) G. Abecassis/P. D. Poore (DB3/4) R. Parnell/E. Thompson (DB3/3)	1st, 75.42 mph Retired, clutch Retired, fire in pits

1953

Sebring 12 Hours race, 8 March	R. Parnell/G. Abecassis (DB3/5) P. J. Collins/G. E. Duke (DB3/4)	2nd (and 1st in 3000cc class) Retired, accident
Mille Miglia, 25–26th April, 992 miles	R. Parnell/L. Klementaski (DB3/3) P. J. Collins/M. Keen (DB3/4) G. Abecassis/P. D. C. Griffith (DB3/5) T. H. Wisdom/P. Bolton (DB2, LML/50/55)	5th 16th Retired, steering Retired, rear axle
Production Sports race, Silverstone, 9 May, 50 miles	R. Parnell (DB3/3) P. J. Collins (DB3/4) G. E. Duke (DB3/2)	3rd (and 1st in 3000cc class) 4th (and 2nd in 3000cc class) Retired, clutch
Charterhall, 23 May, Unlimited sports cars, 30 miles	R. Parnell (DB3S/1)	1st, 78.40 mph
Le Mans 24 Hours, 13–14 June	R. Parnell/P. J. Collins (DB3S/2) G. E. Abecassis/R. F. Salvadori (DB3S/3) R. D. Poore/E. Thompson (DB3S/4)	Crashed Retired, clutch Retired, valve failure
British Empire Trophy, Douglas, Isle of Man, 18 June, three 31-mile heats and 62-mile final	R. Parnell (DB3S/1)	1st, 73.96 mph
Silverstone, 18 July, Sports car race, 102 miles	R. Parnell (DB3S/4) R. F. Salvadori (DB3S/3) P. J. Collins (DB3S/2)	1st, 89.41 mph 2nd 3rd
Charterhall, 15 August, Unlimited sports cars, 40 miles	R. Parnell (DB3S/1)	1st, 72.07 mph
Goodwood 9 Hours race, 22 August	R. Parnell/E. Thompson (DB3S/2) P. J. Collins/P. D. C. Griffith (DB3S/4) R. F. Salvadori/R. D. Poore (DB3S/3)	1st, 78.94 mph 2nd Retired, broken con-rod
Tourist Trophy, Dundrod, 5 September, 823 miles	P. J. Collins/P. D. C. Griffith (DB3S/4) R. Parnell/E. Thompson (DB3S/2) R. F. Salvadori/R. D. Poore (DB3S/3)	1st, 81.71 mph 2nd Crashed
Snetterton, 12 September, Unlimited sports cars, 13.5 miles	R. Flockhart (DB3S/1)	2nd (1st in 3000cc class)
Sports car handicap, 27 miles	R. Flockhart (DB3S/1)	Unplaced

Castle Combe, 3 October, Sports cars over 1500cc, 18 miles	R. Parnell (DB3S/1)	1st, 81.43 mph
Casablanca 12 Hours race, 20 December	R. F. Salvadori/M. Sparken (DB3/3)*	4th

1954

Buenos Aires 1000 Kms race, 24 January	P. J. Collins/D. P. C. Griffith (DB3S/4) R. Parnell/R. F. Salvadori (DB3S/2) R. Mieres/Tomasi (DB3S/3)	3rd Retired, distributor shaft Retired, final drive failure
Sebring 12 Hours race, 7 March	R. Parnell/R. F. Salvadoi (DB3S/2) C. Shelby/C. Wallace (DB3S/3) P. J. Collins/P. D. C. Griffith (DB3S/4)	Retired, broken con-rod Retired, brakes Retired, brakes
Mille Miglia, 1–2 May, 992 miles	R. Parnell/L. Klementaski (DB3S/2) P. J. Collins/P. D. C. Griffith (DB3S/4)	Crashed Crashed
Silverstone, 15 May, Sports car race, 73 miles	R. F. Salvadori (DB3S/6) P. J. Collins (DB3S/1) A. G. Whitehead (DB3S/7)	7th (and 1st in 3000cc class) 8th 12th
Aintree, 29 May, Sports car race, 30 miles	C. Shelby (DB3S/3)	2nd
Le Mans 24 Hours, 12–13 June	R. Parnell/R. F. Salvadori (DB3S/1) C. Shelby/P. Frère (DB3S/3) P. J. Collins/'B. Bira' (DB3S/6) A. G. Whitehead/J. Stewart (DB3S/7)	Retired, gasket failure Retired, stub axle Crashed Crashed
Supercortemaggiore Grand Prix, Monza, 27 June, 1000 kilometres	C. Shelby/A. G. Whitehead (DB3S/3)*	5th
Silverstone, 18 July, Sports cars over 1500 cc, 73 miles	P. J. Collins (DB3S/1) R. F. Salvadori (DB3S/5) C. Shelby (DB3S/3)	1st, 86.34 mph 2nd 3rd
Tourist Trophy, Dundrod, 11 September, 69 miles	R. D. Poore/A. G. Whitehead (DB3S/3) P. J. Collins/P. D. C. Griffith (DB3S/2) R. Parnell/R. F. Salvadori (DB3S/1)	13th Retired, final drive Retired, accident damage
Aintree, 2 Ocober, Sports cars over 2500cc, 51 miles	P. J. Collins (DB3S/2) R. Parnell (DB3S/1) R. F. Salvadori (DB3S/5)	2nd 3rd 5th

1955

British Empire Trophy, Oulton Park, 2 April, Three qualifying heats and 69-mile final	R. Parnell (DB3S/5, 2.5-litre)	3rd
Goodwood, 11 April, Sports cars over 2000cc, 12 miles	R. F. Salvadori (DB3S/1)*	1st, 83.40 mph
Mille Miglia, 30 April–1 May, 992 miles	P. J. Collins/L. Klementaski (DB3S/5)	Retired, con-rod bolt
Ibsley, 30 April, Sports cars over 2750cc, 31 miles	R. F. Salvadori (DB3S/1)*	1st, 80.95 mph
Silverstone, 7 May, Sports car race, 117 miles	R. Parnell (DB3S/6) R. F. Salvadori (DB3S/7) P. J. Collins (DB3S/2) P. D. C. Walker (DB3S/1)	1st, 93.58 mph 2nd 6th 7th
Spa Grand Prix, Spa-Francorchamps, 8 May, 175 miles	P. Frère (DB3S/8)	1st, 107.80 mph
Hyères 12 Hours race, Île d'Or, 29 May	A. Gaze/D. McKay (DB3S/102)* L. Cosh/R. Cobden (DB3S/104)* T. Sulman/J. Brabham (DB3S/103)*	2nd 3rd 4th
Snetterton, 28 May, Sports cars over 2000cc, 14 miles	P. J. Collins (DB3S/2)*	2nd
Crystal Palace, 30 May, Norbury Trophy, Sports cars over 2000cc, 14 miles	R. F. Salvadori (DB3S/1)*	2nd
Le Mans 24 Hours, 11–12 June	P. J. Collins/P. Frère (DB3S/6) R. F. Salvadori/P. D. C. Walker (DB3S/7) C. A. S. Brooks/J. Riseley-Prichard (DB3S/8)	2nd Retired, broken crankshaft Retired, dynamo

Snetterton, 25 June, Eastern Counties '100', 100 miles	R. F. Salvadori (DB3S/1)*	1st, 86.30 mph
Aintree, 16 July, Sports car race, 51 miles	R. F. Salvadori (DB3S/7) P. J. Collins (DB3S/6) R. Parnell (DB3S/5) P. D. C. Walker (DB3S/8)	1st, 81.32 mph 2nd 3rd 4th
Crystal Palace, 30 July, Unlimited sports cars, 14 miles	R. F. Salvadori (DB3S/5)	1st, 73.16 mph
Charterhall, 6 August, *Newcastle Journal* Trophy, 40 miles	R. Parnell (DB3S/5)	6th
Goodwood 9 Hours race, 20 August	P. D. C. Walker/R. D. Poore (DB3S/7) P. J. Collins/C. A. S. Brooks (DB3S/6) R. Parnell/R. F. Salvadori (DB3S/8)	1st, 82.24 mph 3rd Retired, hub failure
Oulton Park, *Daily Herald* Trophy, 27 August, 221 miles	R. Parnell (DB3S/8) P. J. Collins (DB3S/2)*	1st, 81.16 mph 3rd
Aintree, 3 September, Unlimited sports cars, 51 miles	R. F. Salvadori (DB3S/1)*	3rd
Tourist Trophy, Dundrod, 17 September, 623 miles	P. D. C. Walker/R. D. Poore (DB3S/7) R. Parnell/R. F. Salvadori (DB3S/8) P. J. Collins/C. A. S. Brooks (DB3S/6)	4th 7th Retired, con-rod bolt

1956

Sebring 12 Hours race, 25 March	R. F. Salvadori/C. Shelby (DB3S/7) S. Moss/P. J. Collins (DB3S/6) R. Parnell/C. A. S. Brooks (DB3S/8)	4th Retired, oil pump drive Retired, oil pump drive
Goodwood, 2 April, Sports cars over 1500cc, 36 miles	S. Moss (DB3S/5)*	1st, 89.18 mph

British Empire Trophy, Oulton Park, 14 April, Three qualifying heats and 44-mile final	R. Parnell (DB3S/5, 2.5-litre)	11th (1st in heat)
Aintree, 21 April, Unlmited Sports cars, 30 miles	R. F. Salvadori (DB3S/5)*	1st 83.20 mph
Silverstone, 5 May, Sports cars over 1500cc, 73 miles	R. F. Salvadori (DB3S/5) S. Moss (DB3S/8) P. J. Collins (DB3S/7) R. Parnell (DB3S/6)	1st, 94.79 mph 2nd Crashed Crashed
Spa Grand Prix, 13 May, Spa-Francorchamps, 105 miles	R. Parnell (DB3S/5) H. David (DB3S/118)*	2nd 3rd
Grand Prix des Frontières, Chimay, 20 May, 149 miles	A. G. Whitehead (DB3S/1)*	3rd
Nürburgring 1000 Kms race, 27 May	P. J. Collins/C. A. S. Brooks (DB3S/5) R. F. Salvadori/P. D. C. Walker (DB3S/8)	5th Retired, broken de Dion tube
Aintree, 23 June, Unlimited sports cars, 30 miles	R. F. Salvadori (DB3S/5)*	1st, 81.33 mph
Rouen Grand Prix, 8 July, 3000cc sports cars, 203 miles	S. Moss (DB3S/6) C. A. S. Brooks (DB3S/7) R. F. Salvadori (DB3/10) P. J. Collins (DB3S/9)	2nd 4th 5th Retired, engine
Le Mans 24 Hours, 28–29 July	S. Moss/P. J. Collins (DB3S/9) P. D. Walker/R. F. Salvadori (DB3S/10) C. A. S. Brooks/R. Parnell (DBR1/1)	2nd Crashed Retired, engine
Brands Hatch, 6 August, Sports car over 1900cc, 19 miles	A. G. Whitehead (DB3S/1)*	2nd
Oulton Park, *Daily Herald* Trophy, 18 August, 110 miles	S. Moss (DB3S/9) C. A. S. Brooks (DB3S/8) R. Parnell (DB3S/7) R. F. Salvadori (DB3S/6)	1st, 76.99 mph 2nd 3rd 4th

Goodwood, 8 September, Goodwood Trophy, 50 miles	C. A. S. Brooks (DBS/7) R. F. Salvadori (DB3S/9)	1st, 88.19 mph 2nd

1957

British Empire Trophy, Oulton Park 6 April, Sports Cars over 2000cc, 69 miles	R. F. Salvadori (DBR1/1) N. Cunningham-Reid (DB3S/10)	2nd 3rd
Goodwood, 22 April, Sussex Trophy, 50 miles	R. F. Salvadori (DBR/1) C. A. S. Brooks (DB3S/9)	2nd 3rd
Spa Grand Prix, 12 May, Spa-Francorchamps, 132 miles	C. A. S. Brooks (DBR1/2) R. F. Salvadori (DBR1/1)	1st, 103.97 mph 2nd
Brands Hatch, 19 May, Unlimited sports cars, 12 miles	G. Hill (DB3S/5)*	3rd
Snetterton, 19 May, Unlimited sports cars, 27 miles	P. N. Whitehead (DB3S/7)*	3rd
Formule Libre, 27 miles	P. N. Whitehead (DB3S/7)*	3rd
Nürburgring 1000 Kms race, 26 May	C. A. S. Brooks/N. Cunningham-Reid (DBR1/2) R. F. Salvadori/L. Leston (DBR1/1) P. N. Whitehead/A. G. Whitehead (DB3S/10)	1st, 82.39 mph 6th 9th
St. Étienne, 31 May, 2 hours	A. G. Whitehead (DB3S/6)*	4th
Le Mans 24 Hours, 22–23 June	R. Salvadori/L. Leston (DBR1/1) C. A. S. Brooks/N. Cunningham-Reid (DBR1/2) P. N. Whitehead/A. G. Whitehead (DBR2/1)	Retired, oil pipe Crashed Retired, gearbox
Aintree, 20 July, Sports car race, 51 miles	R. F. Salvadori (DBR1/2)	2nd
Brands Hatch, 5 August, Kingsdown Trophy, 15 miles	A. G. Whitehead (DB3S/6)*	3rd

RACB Grand Prix, Spa-Francorchamps, 25 August, 3 hours	C. A. S. Brooks (DBR1/2) R. F. Salvadori (DBR1/1) A. G. Whitehead (DB3S/6)*	1st, 118.56 mph 4th 6th
Snetterton, 1 September, Sports cars over 2700cc, 27 miles	P. N. Whitehead (DB3S/7)*	2nd
Silverstone, 14 September, Sports cars over 1500cc, 44 miles	R. F. Salvadori (DBR2/2) N. Cunningham-Reid (DBR2/1) C. A. S. Brooks (DBR2/1) S. Lewis-Evans (DBR1/1)	1st, 96.08 mph 3rd 4th 6th

1958

Sebring 12 Hours race, 22 March	S. Moss/C. A. S. Brooks (DBR1/2) R. F. Salvadori/C. Shelby (DBR1/1)	Retired, gearbox Retired, broken chassis
Goodwood, 7 April, Sussex Trophy, 50 miles	S. Moss (DBR2/1)	1st, 89.74 mph
British Empire Trophy, Oulton Park, 12 April, Three 55-mile qualifying heats and 69-mile final	S. Moss (DBR2/1) C. A. S. Brooks (DBR2/2)	1st, 87.45 mph (1st in heat) 2nd (2nd in heat)
Aintree, 19 April, Unlimited sports cars, 45 miles	R. F. Salvadori (DBR2/2) C. A. S. Brooks (DBR1/1)	2nd Retired, final drive
Silverstone 3 May, Sports cars over 1500cc, 73 miles	R. F. Salvadori (DBR2/2) C. A. S. Brooks (DBR2/1) S. Moss (DBR3/1)	4th 5th Retired, bearings
Targa Florio, 11 May, 626 miles	S. Moss/C. A. S. Brooks (DBR1/3)	Retired, gearbox
Belgian Sports Car Grand Prix, Spa-Francorchamps, 25 May, 132 miles	P. Frère (DBR2/2) C. Shelby (DBR2/1)	2nd 3rd
Nürburgring 1000 Kms race, 1 June	S. Moss/J. Brabham (DBR1/3) R. F. Salvadori/C. Shelby (DBR1/1) R. F. Salvadori/S. Lewis-Evans (DBR1/1) P. N. Whitehead/A. G. Whitehead (DB3S/6)*	1st, 84.07 mph Retired, gearbox Crashed 6th

Le Mans 24 Hours, 21–22 June	P. N. Whitehead/A. G. Whitehead (DB3S/6)*	2nd
	S. Moss/J. Braham (DBR1/3)	Retired, con-rod
	C. A. S. Brooks/M. Trintignant (DBR1/2)	Retired, gearbox
	R. F. Salvadori/S. Lewis-Evans (DBR1/1)	Crashed
Tourist Trophy, Goodwood, 13 September, Four hours	S. Moss/C. A. S. Brooks (DBR1/2)	1st, 88.33 mph
	R. Salvadori/J. Brabham (DBR1/1)	2nd
	C. Shelby/S. Lewis-Evans (DBR1/3)	3rd
Riverside Grand Prix, 11 October, 203 miles	R. F. Salvadori (DBR1/1)	6th

1959

Sebring 12 Hours, 21 March	R. F. Salvadori/C. Shelby (DBR1/1)	Retired, broken gearbox
Goodwood, 30 March, Sussex Trophy, 50 miles	A. G. Whitehead (DBR1/5)*	3rd
Silverstone 2 May:		
International Trophy FORMULA 1, 146 miles	R. F. Salvadori (DBR4/1)	2nd
	C. Shelby (DBR4/2)	Retired, broken con-rod
Sports cars to 3000cc, 73 miles	S. Moss (DBR1/2)	2nd
	A. G. Whitehead (DBR1/5)*	5th
GRAND TOURING CARS, 35 miles	S. Moss (DP199/1)	1st, 86.94 mph
Dutch Grand Prix, Zandvoort, FORMULA 1, 31 May, 195 miles	R. F. Salvadori (DBR4/1)	Retired, broken con-rod
	C. Shelby (DBR4/2)	Retired, broken con-rod
Nürburgring 1000 Kms race, 7 June	S. Moss/J. Fairman (DBR1/1)	1st, 82.50 mph
Le Mans 24 Hours, 20–21 June	R. F. Salvadori/C. Shelby (DBR1/2)	1st, 112.57 mph
	M. Trintignant/P. Frère (DBR1/4)	2nd
	S. Moss/J. Fairman (DBR1/3)	Retired, engine
	H. Patthey/J. Calderari (DP199/1)	Retired, bearings
British Grand Prix, Aintree, FORMULA 1, 18 July 225 miles	R. F. Salvadori (DBR4/1)	6th
	C. Shelby (DBR4/2)	Retired, valve failure

Portuguese Grand Prix, Monsanto, FORMULA 1, 23 August, 209 miles	R. F. Salvadori (DBR4/1) C. Shelby (DBR4/2)	6th 8th
Tourist Trophy, Goodwood, 5 September, 6 Hours	C. Shelby/J. Fairman/S. Moss (DBR1/2) M. Trintignant/P. Frère (DBR1/4) S. Moss/R. F. Salvadori (DBR1/4)	1st, 89.41 mph 4th Retired, fire damage
Governor's Trophy, Bahamas, 4 December, Qualifying heat and final	S. Moss (DBR2/2)	1st, 90.95 mph

1960

Oulton Park, 2 April, Sports cars over 1500cc, 28 miles	J. Clark (DBR1/3)*	3rd
Goodwood, 18 April, GRAND TOURING CARS, Fordwater Trophy, 24 miles	S. Moss (DB4GT, 0124/R)*	1st, 83.03 mph
Aintree, 30 April, CLOSED CARS, 30 miles	J. Sears (DB4GT, 0124/R)*	1st, 78.08 mph
Oulton Park, 7 May, GRAND TOURING CARS, 28 miles	J. Sears (DB4GT, 0124/R)*	1st, 79.43 mph
International Trophy, Silverstone, FORMULA 1, 14 May, 146 miles	M. Trintignant (DBR5/1) R. F. Salvadori (DBR4/3)	10th Retired, engine misfire
Le Mans 24 Hours, 24–25 June	J. Clark/R. F. Salvadori (DBR1/3)*	3rd
British Grand Prix, FORMULA 1, Silverstone, 16 July, 225 miles	M. Trintignant (DBR5/1) R. F. Salvadori (DBR5/2)	11th Retired, handling
Brands Hatch, 1 August, Wrotham Cup, GRAND TOURING CARS, 27 miles	J. Sears (DB4GT, 0124/R)*	1st, 77.56 mph

Tourist Trophy Goodwood, GRAND TOURING CARS, 20 August, 3 hours	R. F. Salvadori (DB4GT, 0125/R)* I. Ireland (DB4GT, 0151/R)*	2nd 3rd
Brands Hatch, 27 August, RedEx Trophy, GRAND TOURING CARS, 27 miles	J. Sears (DB4GT, 0124/R)*	2nd
Paris 1000 Kms Race, Montlhéry, 23 October, GRAND TOURING CARS	I. Ireland/R. F. Salvadori (DB4GT, 0125/R)*	6th

1961

Snetterton, 25 March, GRAND TOURING CARS, 27 miles	R. F. Salvadori (DB4GT, 0125/R)*	3rd
Goodwood, 3 April, Fordwater Trophy, GRAND TOURING CARS, 24 miles	I. Ireland (DB4GT, 0151/R)* S. Moss (Zagato, 0200/R)*	2nd 3rd
Oulton Park, 15 April, Oulton Park Trophy, GRAND TOURING CARS, 69 miles	I. Ireland (DB4GT, 0151/R)*	2nd
Aintree, 15 July, GRAND TOURING CARS, 51 miles	L. Davison (Zagato, 0183/R)* Sir J. Whitmore (DB4GT, 0151/R)*	1st, 81.86 mph 3rd
Tourist Trophy, Goodwood, 19 August, GRAND TOURING CARS, 3 hours	R. F. Salvadori (Zagato, 0182/R)* J. Clark (Zagato, 0183/R)* I. Ireland (DB4GT, 0151/R)*	3rd 4th 5th
Coppe Inter-Europa, Monza, 10 September, GRAND TOURING CARS, 3 hours	A. Maggs (Zagato, 0182/R)* F. Kerguen (Zagato, 0180/L)*	2nd 4th
Paris 1000 Kms race, 22 October, GRAND TOURING CARS	J. Clark/I. Ireland (Zagato, 0182/R)*	5th

1962

Oulton Park, GRAND TOURING CARS over 2000cc, 7 April, 69 miles	A. Maggs (Zagato, 0182/R)*	3rd
Spa Grand Prix, Spa-Francorchamps, GRAND TOURING CARS, 20 May, 132 miles	M. Salmon (Zagato, 0200/R)*	5th
Nürburgring 1000 Kms race, 27 May	B. McLaren/A. Maggs (DBR1/1)*	5th
Le Mans 24 Hours, 23–24 June	G. Hill/R. Ginther (DP212/1)	Retired, piston

1963

Le Mans 24 Hours, 15–16 June	J. Kimberly/J. Schlesser (DB4GT, 0194/R) B. McLaren/I. Ireland (DB4GT, 0195/R) P. Hill/L. Bianchi (DP215/1)	Retired, piston Retired, piston Retired, transmission
Reims, Sports cars and Prototypes, 30 June, 129 miles	J. Schlesser (DP215/1)	Retired, bent valves
Guards International Trophy, Brands Hatch, Sports cars over 2000cc, 5 August, 133 miles	I. Ireland (DB4GT, 0195/R) J. Kimberly (DB4GT, 0195/R)	6th Retired, accident
Tourist Trophy, Goodwood, GRAND TOURING CARS, 24 August, 312 miles	I. Ireland (DB4GT, 0194/R) B. McLaren (DB4GT, 0195/R)	7th Retired, Valve trouble
Coppa Inter-Europa, Monza, GRAND TOURING CARS, 8 September, Three hours	R. F. Salvadori (DB4GT, 0194/R) L. Bianchi (DB4GT, 0195/R)	1st, 120.23 mph 3rd
Coupe du Salon, Montlhéry, GRAND TOURING CARS, 22 September, 37 miles	J. Schlesser (DB4GT, 0195/R)* C. Le Guezec (DB4GT, 0194/R)*	1st, 73.21 mph 5th
Coupe de Paris, Montlhéry, GRAND TOURING CARS, 22 September, 50 miles	C. Le Guezec (DB4GT, 0194/R)* C. Dewez (DB4GT, 0195/R)*	1st 2nd

1964

Silverstone, GRAND TOURING CARS, 2 May, 73 miles	M. Salmon (DB4GT, 0194/R)*	2nd
Martini Trophy, GT and sports cars, 4 July, 152 miles	M. Salmon (DB4GT, 0194/R)*	1st (over 2000cc), 97.62 mph

1989

Dijon-Prenois, 21 May, 300 miles	D. Leslie/B. Redman (AMR1/02)	17th
Le Mans 24 Hours, 10–11 June	B. Redman/C. Los/M. Roe (AMR1/02) D. Leslie/R. Mallock/D. Sears (AMR1/03)	11th Retired, engine
Brands Hatch Trophy, Brands Hatch, 23 July, 299 miles	D. Leslie/B. Redman (AMR1/04)	4th
ADAC Trophy, Nürburgring, 20 August, 299 miles	D. Leslie/B. Redman (AMR1/04)	8th
Wheatcroft Gold Cup, Donington Park, 3 September, 300 miles	D. Leslie/M. Roe (AMR1/05) B. Redman/D. Sears (AMR1/04)	6th 7th
Spa-Francorchamps, 17 September, 302 miles	B. Redman/S. Dickens (AMR1/04) D. Leslie/M. Roe (AMR1/05)	7th Retired, con-rod
Trofeo Hermanos Rodriguez, Mexico City, 29 October, 199 miles	B. Redman/D. Leslie (AMR1/05)	8th

Appendix 3

Individual Histories of Aston Martin Competition Cars

Note:
It is not intended that this Appendix should in any way usurp the *Aston Martin Register*, the 'bible' of Aston Martin enthusiasts. The aim is to give a more detailed history of the cars, the changes made to them, the changes of ownership in the cars' early days and the prices that were being asked for them in the market place.

DB3

DB3/1

The first car that ran in the 1951 Tourist Trophy. Driven by Geoff Duke at the 1952 Easter Goodwood meeting, the International Trophy meeting at Silverstone and in the British Empire Trophy in the Isle of Man. It became in effect the team's spare car and, as such, with hard top, was brought into the team for Le Mans in 1952. Powered by a supercharged engine (as far as can be ascertained a Wade supercharger was fitted as on DB3S/1 at Le Mans in 1954) and used in practice for the 1953 Mille Miglia. It was subsequently driven by Dennis Poore at Thruxton. Aston Martin sold the car to Buenos Aires resident Eric Forrest Greene and took it with them for him to drive in the 1954 Buenos Aires 1000 Kms race. Forrest Greene crashed, the car caught fire and the driver died of his burns the following day. The car was stored for many years and rebuilt by his son, J. Forrest Greene.

DB3/2

Registered XMY 80, this car was built with touring equipment and full-width screen for the personal use of David Brown. In 1953 it was raced as a works car by Geoff Duke at Silverstone in May and it was driven by Eric Thompson at a couple of minor events at Thruxton and Snetterton. Barthel bought it for 1955 and ran it in minor events. It was maintained at Rob Walker's Pipbrook Garage at Dorking and advertised for sale in September 1955. It was bought by David Howard and raced by him in 1956. Offered by Mayford Motors of Woking in August 1957 at £1475.

DB3/3

Team car built for the 1952 season, initially with 2580cc engine and raced in this form at the International Trophy at Silverstone. Ran with 2922cc engine at Monaco (Parnell), retired because of con-rod failure, damaged in multi-car accident. Hastily repaired by Henri Chapron in Paris with shortened tail, ran and retired at Le Mans, badly damaged in pits

fire at the Goodwood 9 Hours race. Achieved distinction by being driven to fifth place in the 1953 Mille Miglia by Parnell (highest placed finish by British car in the history of the race). Subsequently driven by Parnell at Silverstone and Poore in minor races at Thruxton and Snetterton. Sold to French driver Mike Sparken, who had fitted a Vignale coupé body of classic lines. With Salvadori as co-driver and with works support Sparken finished fourth in the Casablanca 12 Hours race in December 1953. This resulted in a drive for Sparken with the Gilby Engineering Maserati A6GCS in the sports car race at the British Grand Prix meeting in July 1954 (the car was usually driven by Salvadori, but he was at the wheel of a works Aston Martin). Early in 1954 Sparken finished fifth in the Circuit d'Agadir and fourth in the Criterium du Sénégal. Sparken acquired a Ferrari *Monza* for 1955 and it is believed that DB3/3 was written off in a road accident.

DB3/4

Team car built for the 1952 season, initially with 2580cc engine. Driven by Abecassis at Silverstone (3rd), Collins at Monaco with 2922cc engine (7th), and was crashed heavily in practice at Le Mans by Griffith (non-started). It was subsequently driven by Abecassis at Boreham (retired), Abecassis/Poore in the Goodwood 9 Hours race (retired) and Abecassis at Shelsley Walsh Hill climb (2nd in class). Remained with the team for 1953 and entered at Sebring (Collins/Duke – crashed), Mille Miglia (Collins/Kean – 16th) and Silverstone (Collins – 4th). It was sold by the works in 1954 and thereafter no racing history as it was rebuilt with a DB3S body with road equipment.

DB3/5

Team car built for the 1952 season initially with 2580cc engine. Driven by Macklin at Silverstone (4th), with 2922cc engine at Monaco (retired), and by Macklin/Collins at Le Mans (retired). Parnell drove into 4th place in the Jersey Road race, 3rd place at Boreham and, driven by Collins/Griffith, it won the Goodwood 9 Hours race. In 1953 Parnell/Abecassis drove it into 2nd place at Sebring and Abecassis/Griffith retired it in the Mille Miglia because of steering problems. For 1954 this car was sold to Nigel Mann and fitted with a fixed head coupé body which aped the DB3S, especially its wire-mesh grille. Mann partnered by Charles Brackenbury finished 6th in the 1954 Hyères 12 Hours race despite a fire, and later finished 14th in La Baule Grand Prix. Entered at Le Mans in 1954, it did not run. At some stage in 1955 the car was rebuilt in open form,

DB3/2: Built as a demonstrator and DB's personal transport, this car was acquired by D. R. Barthel and raced by him as shown here with full-width windscreen and number plate. It was offered for sale by R. R. C. Walker's Pippbrook Garage, which prepared the car, as shown in this advertisement in *Autosport* in September 1955.

but it is not certain when. Mann, partnered by Mortimer Morris Goodall, again finished 6th at Hyères (the fixed head bodywork may still have been on the car) and it appears that it was a reserve at Le Mans in 1955, but did not start. The car subsequently went to Hong Kong and then the United States.

DB3/6

Supplied to Robert 'Bob' Dickson in 1953 as FHH 534 and raced in a number of hill climbs and races, including the British Empire Trophy (12th), the sports car race at the British Grand Prix meeting (retired) and the Tourist Trophy (6th, co-driver Desmond Titterington). In 1954 it was fitted with a remarkable gull-wing body and a Jaguar C-type engine. Although it is known that it was raced by R. H. Dennis at Goodwood in 1955, its racing days were to all intents and purposes over. In 1989 it was sold at auction by Christie's, less engine and body, for £180,000.

DB3/7

Like a number of other DB3s, this car was fitted with fixed head coupé bodywork, but with the difference that it was fitted from new. The first private owner was Tom Meyer, who entered the car in a number of endurance events. With Philip Fotheringham-Parker as co-driver he retired in the 1953 Spa 12 Hours race, he and Tony Gaze finished 6th in the Pescara 12 Hours and with Fotheringham-Parker again he was 12th in the Goodwood 9 Hours race. Meyer crashed in the 1954 Mille Miglia and took a couple of places in minor Scandanavian events that year. In October 1954 DB3/7 was advertised by HW Motors at £2250 and it was bought by Angela Brown, David Brown's daughter, who was later to marry George Abecassis of HWM. When Meyer had the car it was distinguished by a very ugly rectangular air intake with vertical and horizontal cross-bars, but Angela Brown had a new bonnet made with a simple oval air intake without a grille. She ran the car in a number of minor events in 1955 and offered it for sale in December 1955:

'Unique opportunity to acquire the only Aston Martin DB3 competition chassis fitted with aerodynamic saloon body, which was specially constructed for use on road or track. The workmanship and finish are of the highest order, and the special instruments are fitted into a beautifully made walnut facia.

'The car has been maintained by the factory and fitted with a special high-output cylinder head. Brakes and suspension have had the latest modifications.

'Finished in deep carriage green with beige leather upholstery, this Aston Martin is one of the best-looking cars on the road today. It contains a truly aerodynamic form with reasonable luggage accommodation and the generous use of moulded perspex and alloy panel work on steel has resulted in the combination of great

DB3/5: It is remarkable just how many DB3s were at one time or another fitted with fixed-head bodywork. This is DB3/5 as rebodied for Nigel Mann in 1954 and looking like an ineptly styled DB3S. Later the fixed head was removed.

DB3/7: In 1953 this car fitted with fixed-head coupé bodywork was bought by Tom Meyer and driven by him and Fotheringham-Parker into 12th place in the Goodwood 9 Hours race. It was offered for sale by HW Motors in October 1954 and bought by Angela Brown.

strength and light weight, so that the car is always entirely free from rattles.

'With a maximum in excess of 140 mph and a choice of axle ratio, this car is offered in perfect condition throughout at £1995.'

It was acquired by Charles Sgonina, who owned, at different times, many competition Aston Martins.

DB3/8

Supplied new in 1953 to Ken Downing (former Connaught driver) as NUV 925, and driven by him in minor events without success. Parnell drove it to win a race at the AMOC meeting at Snetterton in 1953. For 1954 it was acquired by Sir Jeremy Boles, who entered both it and a Connaught A-series for Don Beauman (a close friend of Mike Hawthorn). Boles drove the car himself in minor events and Beauman won his class of the Dutch Sports Car Grand Prix, but was well down the field on general classification. The car was not raced after the end of 1954 and Beauman, who had driven a works Jaguar at Le Mans in 1955, was killed at the wheel of the Connaught in the Leinster Trophy that year.

DB3/9

Supplied to New Zealand driver Tony Gaze as TPB 639, this car had a career that was short and not so sweet. After driving the car at the International Trophy meeting at Silverstone (14th) and Charterhall (15th), Gaze entered it in the Oporto Grand Prix. He crashed, the car caught fire and was completely burnt out.

DB3/8: Don Beauman with Sir Jeremy Boles's DB3/8 on his way to a class win at Zandvoort in August 1954

DB3/10

This DB3, registered TPB 641, was the first of many competition Aston Martins supplied to Graham Whitehead. It was the most successful of the private DB3s and at certain races received a degree of works support. Whitehead finished 7th in the sports car race at the International Trophy meeting at Silverstone, 5th in the Caen Grand Prix, 5th in a handicap race at Roubaix, 5th (with Tony Gaze) in the Tourist Trophy at Dundrod, 5th in the sports car race at the Autumn Goodwood meeting and 5th (with half-brother Peter) in the Casablanca 12 Hours race. In October 1953 Whitehead had offered the car for sale and in 1954 it was run as part of 'The Vermin Stable' by P. A. Everard. The name was derived from the reference by Aneurin Bevan to Conservatives as being vermin. The car was maintained by Rob Walker's Pipbrook Garage at

DB3/9: Before and after: Tony Gaze with DB3/9 before the start of the 1953 Portuguese Grand Prix and the remains of his car after the crash.

Dorking, scored many minor success and was advertised in March 1955 at £1950. It was acquired by Cuff-Miller, who with Hinde as co-driver finished 15th in the 1955 Goodwood 9 Hours race. Everard moved on in 1956 to the ex-Bob Chase/Alan Brown sports Cooper-Bristol, fitted with a 2.6-litre Aston Martin engine.

DB3S

DB3S/1

The works prototype, registered YMY 307, extensively raced by the works in 1953–4. For full details of its successes see Appendix 2. It was regarded by the works as the team spare. Ran at Le Mans in 1954 with Wade-supercharged single-plug engine, fitted with twin-plug 225 bhp engine for other races in 1954 and rebodied for 1955 with bodywork incorporating small tail fins in the rear wings. Loaned to Graham Whitehead to drive in Penya Rhin Grand Prix at Barcelona, 1954 (6th). Sold to Roy Salvadori for 1955, but borrowed back by the works for the International Trophy meeting and the Swedish Grand Prix. Salvadori scored many successes,

including wins at Goodwood and Snetterton. Bought for 1956 by Graham Whitehead, who drove it at Agadir (10th), Grand Prix des Frontières (3rd), Oporto (7th), Oulton Park (7th) and also took 1st and 2nd places in races at Brands Hatch. Whitehead tried to improve the braking by fitting a servo unit operated from the back of the gearbox (this was also tried by the works), but this was not successful.

Graham Whitehead advertised the car in September 1956: 'Aston Martin DB3S fitted with twin-plug cylinder head. Servo brakes and latest modifications. Recent complete overhaul of engine and chassis, including fitting brand new gearbox. Always maintained by experienced mechanics – further details, A. G. Whitehead, Shinfield court, Three Mile Cross, Reading.' Whitehead was still advertising the car in February 1957 with a quoted price of £2400 ono. The car was eventually sold to N. C. F. Taylor through, it seems, Retfords of Nottingham, and his successes included joint BTD at the Cambridge University Automobile Club Sprint at Snetterton in March 1960. At one stage the car was fitted with a production body. Kenneth Yeates bought the car in 1960 through, it seems, Ashmores of West Bromwich. Yeates fitted Jaguar Mk X disc brakes at the front (stretching and reshaping the front wings to accommodate the wider wheels), and the car was used in and damaged during the filming of *The Green Helmet*.

In 1965 the author drove the car for *Sporting Motorist* magazine and commented:

'The appearance of the car is still magnificent, and it is in excellent condition both bodily and mechanically. The engine at present develops about 220 bhp and peaks at 6200 rpm, but nevertheless will potter along happily in top gear at 1500 rpm. Incidentally, with the 6.50 x 16 rear tyres fitted, the gearing gives 24 mph per 1000 rpm in top gear. When racing the car, Yeates will normally take off at the start at about 3500 rpm and tries to restrict himself to 5800 rpm.

'... There is no doubt that the DB3S still possesses, even by today's standards, exceptionally high cornering power and very easy handling. It is possible to bring in a great deal of power while the car is on lock in a corner and furthermore the handling is always predictable and consistent. On this car, the fitting of disc brakes has had only a slight effect on the handling, and the brakes themselves are exceptionally good.'

'... Kenneth Yeates finds that the car gives about 18 mpg on the road and 11 mpg under racing conditions. He has always regarded it as a working car. By this he does not mean using the car on the road, as he does this as little as possible out of consideration for other road users. He believes, however, that the car should pay its way in prize and starting money sufficiently to

DB3S/1: Photographed in 1966 when out on a driving session with the author for the long defunct magazine *Sporting Motorist*. It was perfectly tractable on the road and displayed superb handling. Note the offset front wheels to accommodate disc brakes (fitted at the front only). At this time Kenneth Yeates was trying to sell the car for £1250 or offers. *(The Author)*

cover racing expenses and a winter overhaul. This it is no longer able to do and so, unfortunately, YMY 307 is now seeking another owner.'

The car passed to Rupert Glydon and soon became a frequent competitor in the developing Historic Sports Car scene.

DB3S/2

Works car built for Le Mans 1953, where it crashed and subsequently finished 3rd in the sports car race at the Grand Prix meeting at Silverstone (Collins), won the Goodwood 9 Hours race (Parnell/Thompson) and finished 2nd in the Tourist Trophy (Parnell/Thompson). Driven by Parnell/Salvadori, it retired in both the 1954 Buenos Aires 1000 Kms and the Sebring 12 Hours races, and it was crashed heavily by Parnell in the Mille Miglia. It reappeared in the Tourist Trophy driven by Collins/Griffith, but retired. In September Collins took second place at Aintree. For 1955 the car was rebodied with rear wings incorporating small tail-fins and was sold to Peter Collins on the same basis as DB3S/1 had been sold to Salvadori, a low price, major maintenance by the works and the right for the works to call on the car when needed. It was registered UDV 609. In the sports car race at Silverstone in May, with DB3S/2 running as a works car, Collins finished a poor 7th and, again running as a works entry, Collins non-started in the Swedish Grand Prix after con-rod failure in practice. Running as a private entrant, Collins finished 5th in the sports car race at the Easter Goodwood meeting, 2nd at Snetterton and 3rd in the

Daily Herald Trophy at Oulton Park in August.

For 1956 the car was sold to Tom Kyffin, who ran the Torbay Speed Shop at Torquay and raced as Équipe Devone. Previous cars raced by Équipe Devone included the ex-Gould single-seater Cooper-Bristol and a Cooper-Bristol sports car built up by Alan Brown from the ex-Bob Chase Cooper-Alfa Romeo Formula 2 car. Kyffin raced the car, without much success, including an entry with Ken Wharton as co-driver in Paris 1000 Kms race at Montlhéry, in which the DB3S retired. As early as August 1956 Kyffin had advertised DB3S/2 from his Totnes home in the following terms: 'The ex-works Peter Collins ASTON MARTIN DB3S. Twin point head makes it the fastest private DB3S. Spares include extra gearbox, three axle ratios, Dunlop and Borrani wheels. £3300.' Kyffin was slow to find a buyer and in 1957 the car was sold to John Dalton (who had previously raced an Austin-Healey 100S). Dalton repainted the car dark blue, ran it in a few events with success, but sold it in 1958 to Barton Motors of Preston, acquiring DB3S/10 in part-exchange. DB3S/2 was eventually sold to Roy Bloxam, who part-exchanged his HWM-Jaguar, XPE 2. In October 1958 Bloxam's company, Gordon White & Co. Ltd., of Gerards Cross, offered it at £1495 ono and by July 1959 it was in the stock of the Chequered Flag at £1385, subsequently reduced to £1285.

DB3S/3

Works car for Le Mans 1953, but retired (Abecassis/Salvadori). Subsequently Salvadori drove it into 2nd place at Silverstone in July, Salvadori/Poore retired in the Goodwood 9 Hours race and Salvadori/Poore crashed in the Tourist Trophy. In 1954 it was driven by Mieres/Tomasi at Buenos Aires (retired) and Shelby/Wallace at Sebring (retired). When Shelby did a deal with John Wyer for the 1954 season, he was allocated DB3S/3 with single-plug engine and painted American white and blue colours. Shelby drove the car at Aintree in May (2nd), at Silverstone in May (3rd), in the Supercortemaggiore Grand Prix (fifth with Graham Whitehead) at Le Mans (retired with Frère) and the sports car race at the British Grand Prix meeting at Silverstone (3rd). Reg Parnell appeared with DB3S/3 at the AMOC St John Horsfall Trophy meeting at Silverstone and the writer remembers the excitement the car caused by its white and blue colours. The car was then repainted in Aston Martin's light green and it was driven in the Tourist Trophy by Poore/Graham Whitehead (13th) and at Aintree by Salvadori (2nd).

For 1955 DB3S/3 was sold to P. A. Everard to run with Jocelyn Stevens under the banner of 'The Vermin Stable' and registered HNR 1. Both drivers scored minor successes. For 1956 the car was sold to the Hon. S. Plunkett and driven by both him and Patsy Burt. Apparently the car was burnt out in a crash at Brands Hatch and the engine and the registration were transferred to DB3S/4.

DB3S/2: Eric Thompson at the wheel of DB3S/2, which he co-drove with Reg Parnell to a win in the 1953 Goodwood 9 Hours race. *(LAT)*

DB3S/4

Works car for Le Mans 1953, but retired (Poore/Thompson). Subsequently driven by Parnell at the July Silverstone meeting (1st), by Collins/Griffith in the Goodwood 9 Hours (2nd), and Collins/Griffith in the Tourist Trophy (1st). In 1954 Collins/Griffith drove it to 3rd place in the Buenos Aires 1000 Kms race, retired because of brake problems in the Sebring 12 Hours and crashed in the Mille Miglia. It was sold to Graham Whitehead, who raced it at Hyères, where it was crashed by co-driver Pat Griffith. Whitehead received the repaired car back from Feltham late in the year and raced it only briefly before taking delivery of a production DB3S. He advertised it in April 1955: 'DB3S, completely overhauled ready for 1955 season – offers to A. G. Whitehead, Shinfield Court, 3 Mile Cross, Reading.' It was eventually acquired by the Hon. S. Plunkett, who apparently transferred the engine and registration, HNR 1, from DB3S/3. It continued to be raced in a number of minor events without conspicuous success, and is shown on the jacket at the Clubmen's Championship at Silverstone in October 1965, where it was painted gaudy dark blue with red wheels and driven by J. Le Sage. It is now in New Zealand.

DB3S/5

Originally built as a road car for David Brown in late 1953 and registered 9046 H, but brought into the team following the disaster at Le Mans. Salvadori drove the car at the June 1954 Silverstone meeting into 2nd place (when the car had the 1953 air intake partially blocked), Dennis Poore set a class record with the car at Prescott and Salvadori drove the car to 5th place at Aintree in October (by when the nose had been reprofiled to incorporate the smaller 1954 air intake). Disc brakes, offset Borrani front wheels and new 'Gothic Arch' body fitted for 1955. For the British Empire Trophy race a 2493cc engine was fitted and in this form Parnell drove the car to a win in the 2700cc heat and 3rd place in the final. Collins drove the car in the Mille Miglia, but it retired. Parnell was third at the Grand Prix meeting at Aintree, Salvadori won at the Crystal Palace and Parnell finished a poor 6th at Charterhall.

For 1955 the car was sold to Roy Salvadori and entered in the name of Gilby Engineering, except when it was loaned back to the works. Moss won for Gilby at Goodwood on Easter Monday. The works borrowed the car for the British Empire Trophy and fitted a 2493cc engine. Parnell won his heat and was 11th in the handicap final. Salvadori won for Gilby at Aintree in April, he drove the car as a works entry to a win at Silverstone in May, Parnell drove the car to second

DB3S/3: Carroll Shelby at the wheel of DB3S/3 in the sports car race at the British Grand Prix meeting at Silverstone in July 1954. He finished third. *(T. C. March)*

place in the Production race at Spa (again as a works entry) and Collins/Brooks drove it as a works entry into fifth place at the Nürburgring. Back with Gilby, the car was driven by Salvadori at Aintree in June (1st).

C. T. Atkins bought the car for 1957 and it was driven with limited success by Graham Hill and Peter Blond. It was crashed with fatal results in the Gosport Speed Trials in 1958, was rebuilt, re-registered PAP 625 and used in the filming of *School for Scoundrels*. It was later raced extensively by Clive Aston. At one time also registered JAN 800 (see DB3S/108), it has now reverted to 9046 H.

DB3S/6

Built in 1954 with fixed head bodywork. Salvadori finished 7th at the May Silverstone meeting and it was driven by Collins/'B. Bira' at Le Mans (the Siamese driver crashed because of the car's aerodynamic instability). It was rebuilt for 1955 with 'Gothic Arch' open body, Girling disc brakes and Borrani offset wheels and registered 62 EMU. Parnell won at Silverstone in May, Collins/Frère finished 2nd at Le Mans, Collins finished 2nd at the Grand Prix meeting at Aintree, Collins/Brooks finished 3rd in the Goodwood 9 Hours race and Collins/Brooks retired in the Tourist Trophy. In 1956 the car was driven by Moss/Collins at Sebring (retired), Collins at the May Silverstone meeting (eliminated in the first-lap multi-car crash), Moss at Rouen (2nd with drum brakes) and Salvadori in the *Daily Herald* Trophy at Oulton Park (4th).

The body was converted to 1956 specification (as DB3S/9 and 10, but no headrest). For 1957 the DB3S/6 was sold to Graham Whitehead and over the next two seasons he achieved many success, mainly in minor events. In 1958 with half-brother Peter as co-driver he finished 6th in the Nürburgring 1000 Kms race and 2nd at Le Mans. The car was sold to Michael Bond for 1959 and he ran it through to 1961 with again, many successes in minor events. It does seem, however, that he tried to sell the car for it was advertised by The Chequered Flag Competition Cars Ltd. in January 1960:–

'DB3S the very famous 62 EMU. Discs, Webers, twin plug head. Recently completely works overhauled in superb condition ... £2185.'

Again the car was advertised in November 1960 at much reduced price:

'Here is a Clubman's "opportunity" to acquire a fabulous machine at a nebulous price ... £1495.'

The famous 62 EMU ex-works–Whitehead DB3S awaits a new owner. This Aston which has been maintained by Arthur Birks is in mint condition. Full specification including discs, twin-plug head, Appendix "C" modifications, etc. etc. Part exchanges are no problem. All details from

ROY BLOXAM
Austin House, Gerrards Cross, Bucks'

Arthur Birks was the Whiteheads' mechanic. The car continued to be raced in minor events and in 1965 was fitted with the single-plug engine from DB3S/4. It is one of the most famous of its type.

DB3S/6: Reg Parnell at the wheel on his way to a win in the sports car race at Silverstone in May 1955. *(T. C. March)*

DB3S/7

Built in 1954 with fixed head bodywork. Graham Whitehead finished 12th at the May Silverstone meeting and it was driven by Graham Whitehead/ Jimmy Stewart at Le Mans (Stewart crashed because of the car's aerodynamic stability). It was rebuilt for 1955 with 'Gothic Arch' open body, Girling disc brakes and Borrani offset wheels and registered 63 EMU. Salvadori finished 2nd at Silverstone in May, Salvadori/Walker retired at Le Mans, Salvadori won at the Grand Prix meeting at Aintree. Walker/Poore won the Goodwood 9 Hours race and Walker/Poore finished 4th in the Tourist Trophy. In 1956 Salvadori/Shelby finished 4th at Sebring, Parnell was eliminated in the multi-car crash at Silverstone in May, Brooks finished 4th at Rouen, Parnell finished 3rd in the *Daily Herald* Trophy at Oulton Park and Brooks won at the September Goodwood meeting. The body was converted to 1956 specification (as DB3S/9 and 10, but no head-rest).

For 1957 DB3S/7 was sold to Peter Whitehead, who raced the car very little. Whitehead finished 8th at Spa, took a couple of places at Snetterton and was the winner on scratch in the Leinster Trophy at Belfast (but this was primarily a handicap event). Jack Brabham drove DB3S/7 at the International Trophy at Silverstone, postponed to September following the Suez crisis, and finished 8th. The car was advertised in January 1958:–

DB3S/7: DB3S/7 in 1973 when the car was owned by Robert Cooper. *(The Author)*

'Peter Whitehead would dispose of his Aston Martin DB3S, twin plug head, disc brakes, raced by works in 1956 season. Whole car completely overhauled, new discs, etc., and brought up to full Appendix "C" specification. Eligible for World Championship events. Price including spares, £2750. Enquiries – Motorwork (Chalfont) Ltd.' The car was acquired by Jean Bloxam to replace DB3S/120 and temporarily bore her usual registration, JB 16. It was run in a number of minor events in 1959 without much success. Gordon White &

A view of the twin-plug engine of DB3S/7. *(The Author)*

Company (the Bloxams' Company) advertised the car in November 1959, by February 1960 it was in the stock of The Chequered Flag at £2185 and it was bought by solicitor and hotelier Brian Hetreed. After a number of minor successes in 1960 it was offered by The Chequered Flag (Competition Cars) Ltd at its recently opened premises at Edgware in March 1961. The price had dropped to £1365. Since then DB3S/7 has enjoyed an almost unbroken competition record and for many years has been owned by Richard Pilkington.

DB3S/8

New works car for 1955 with 'Gothic Arch' body. The car was fitted with single-plug engine and drum brakes for Paul Frère to drive in production form at Spa and Frère won. Converted back to full works specification. Brooks/Riseley-Prichard retired at Le Mans, Walker finished 4th at the Grand Prix meeting at Aintree, Parnell/Salvadori retired in the Goodwood 9 Hours race, Parnell won the *Daily Herald* Trophy at Aintree and Parnell/Salvadori finished 7th in the Tourist Trophy. In 1956 Parnell/Brooks retired at Sebring, Moss finished 2nd at the May Silverstone meeting, Salvadori/Walker retired at the Nürburgring, Salvadori finished 2nd at the Grand Prix meeting at Silverstone in July and Brooks finished 2nd in the *Daily Herald* Trophy at Oulton Park.

In late 1956 the body was updated to the same specification as DB3S/9 and 10 (but no head-rest), the car was sold in the United States to Joe Lubin and painted white and blue. Raced extensively, but details are vague. Subsequent owner had a major accident with the car and fitted the body from DB3S/118. Unused twin-plug engine fitted before the car was brought back to the UK. Completely restored to full works 'Gothic Arch' specification (other than head-rest to conceal roll-over bar). Registered 743 HYX (previous registration uncertain). In the Midlands Motor Museum 1978–85. See *Motor Sport*, November 1978.

DB3S/9

New team car for Rouen with new nose incorporating faired headlamps, reshaped air intake, no bonnet-top intakes and streamlined tail with head-rest. Collins retired DB3S/9 at Rouen, Moss/Collins finished second at Le Mans, Moss won the *Daily Herald* Trophy at Oulton Park and Salvadori finished second at the September Goodwood meeting. In 1957 Brooks finished 3rd at the Easter Goodwood meeting and DB3S/9 was the practice car at the British Empire Trophy and the Nürburgring.

In 1957 the car was painted red and sold to David McKay in Australia. It remains in Australia.

DB3S/10

New team car for Rouen 1956 with new nose incorporating faired headlamps, reshaped air intake, no bonnet-top intakes and streamlined tail with head-rest. Salvadori finished 5th at Rouen, and Walker (co-driving with Salvadori) crashed at Le Mans. For 1957 wishbone and coil spring front suspension was fitted. Cunningham-Reid finished 5th in the British Empire Trophy (CAV fuel injection fitted for this race only) and Graham and Peter Whitehead finished 10th at the Nürburgring.

For 1958 DB3S/10 was sold to John Dalton via Barton Motors (Preston) Ltd, registered JFD 40 and raced weekend after weekend in minor events with immense success during 1958/59. The car was advertised by Dalton through Alan Barton Ltd of Burton Road Garage, Derby, in October 1959. Alan Barton prepared the car, but any connection between Alan Barton and Barton Motors (Preston) Ltd is not known. DB3S/10 was bought by Charles Sgonina, raced extensively and after passing through a number of hands was acquired by Peter Livanos in the United States.

DB3S/11

Built by Aston Martin at Feltham in 1957 to full works specification from unsold production car DB3S/109. Raced extensively by Rod Carveth both in the United States and Australia. Crashed by subsequent owner in 1965 and eventually rebuilt.

DP155/1

Single-seater DB3S for Parnell to race in New Zealand in 1956. Subsequently sold to Geoff Richardson and built up by him as RRA Special with the body, much modified, from DB3S/105 and Jaguar 3.4-litre engine. Subsequently rebuilt with twin-plug DB3S engine and body restored to 'original' DB3S shape.

We offer the following high grade motor cars for cash, exchange or easy payment plan.

ASTON MARTIN DB3S.
One of the last Works cars to be completed. Twin plug head. Disc brakes. Whole car in absolutely superb condition.
£2,650.

New JAGUAR "D" Type.
One of the last made. British Racing Green.
£2,650.

ASTON MARTIN DB3S.
Ex-Works car. Twin plug head. Finished in blue. Really excellent condition. Ex-John Dalton. Registered March 1956.
£1,875.

H.W.M. ALTA-JAGUAR.
Ex-Scragg. Finished in green. This car has plated axle beam and suspension parts and is absolutely as new. A very fast motor car indeed. Suitable for either road work or track. Registered in 1952.
£975.

H.W.M.-JAGUAR
in reasonable condition. Very fast indeed.
£575.

BENTLEY Continental.
Latest model. Body work by H. J. Mulliner. Power steering. Finished in most attractive shade of light blue, with light blue upholstery. Genuine mileage 4,800. Present day list price £8,120.
Our price, £6,500.

BARTON MOTORS (PRESTON), LTD.,
Corporation Street,
· Preston.
Tel.: Preston 4664 (10 lines).

DB3S/10: Shown in an advertisement by Barton Motors (Preston) Ltd. in March 1958. John Dalton had made an offer for DB3S/10, offering DB3S/2 in part exchange, but it seems that Barton would not close the deal until they had a buyer for DB3S/2. Hence the fact that both cars were advertised. Roy Bloxam bought DB3S/2, part-exchanging HWM-Jaguar, XPE 2 (not the HWM advertised here).

DB3S/101

Production car registered 323 AHA (although it also appeared with the registration AHA 323) supplied to Ken Wharton for 1955. Wharton, a leading driver, had the car painted dark green with a yellow nose-band (as his 1953 Cooper-Bristol Formula 2 car). It was uncompetitive, and after two races, the British Empire Trophy and the sports car race at the May Silverstone meeting, he returned the car to Feltham in disgust. He was not convinced when Wyer asked Salvadori to try the car at Goodwood and Roy lapped with DB3S/101 almost as quickly as he had with DB3S/1 at the Easter Monday meeting. Later that year the car was acquired by Berwyn Baxter. Baxter had raced an ex-Ecurie

Ecosse C-type Jaguar and in 1955 had attempted to rejuvenate Kieft as the Kieft Sports Co. Ltd in Birmingham and entered works cars at Le Mans that year. Baxter drove DB3S/101 in minor events through to the end of 1957 and it was offered in the accompanying advertisement in April 1958. DB3S/101 was bought by W. F. 'Bill' Moss, previously the driver of ERA 'Remus' and later of Gemini Formula Junior cars. By October 1958 Moss was trying to sell DB3S/101 at £1600 and it passed through a number of owners, including Brian Joscelyne of the Aston Martin Owners Club and is now owned by Richard Forshaw. So far as the writer is aware, it has never had a major accident and it is still in magnificent condition.

DB3S/102

Delivered to A. F. G. 'Tony' Gaze, who had, albeit briefly, owned a DB3. It was registered OXE 472 and run as part of the Australian/New Zealand 'Kangaroo Stable' in 1955. In 1955 the car ran in a number of events, albeit without much success, apart from second place by Gaze/David McKay in the Hyères 12 Hours race, a poorly supported event. In 1956 McKay took the car back to Australia and its greatest claim to fame was an Australian Land Speed Record of 143.1 mph set by McKay at Carrathool in 1956 during a road test for *Modern Motor*. In the test McKay commented: 'Readers may remember the extensive engine "blow-up" in NZ early last year, and my subsequent wait for a new engine from the factory. The long delay was worth while, as the 1956 engine gives the full 210 bhp and has minor modifications and improvements over our 1955 units, which we suspected as giving a bare 180 bhp.' The new engine was of course, a twin-plug unit. McKay commented on changes made to the 'Kangaroo' cars, including moving the battery to under the passenger seat (on the scuttle on the production cars) and transferring the radiator header tank from its usual position near the exhaust manifolds to the scuttle. The car was raced in Australia for several years (McKay sold it after taking delivery of DB3S/9 in 1957) and it was crashed in 1970. It was subsequently rebuilt and is back in the UK with Richard Forshaw.

DB3S/103

'Kangaroo Stable' car delivered to Tom Sulman in 1955 and registered OXE 473. Raced in Europe in 1955 without much success except for a fourth place by Sulman/Brabham at Hyères. Raced by Sulman in Australia until 1971. Rebuilt and is now back in the UK with Frank Sytner.

DB3S/104

'Kangaroo Stable' car delivered to Lesh Cosh in 1955 and registered OXE 474. Raced in Europe in 1955 without much success except for a third place by Sulman/Dick Cobden at Hyères. Sold in the United

DB3S/101: Advertisement by the Kieft Sports Car Co Ltd in April 1958.

States in 1956, raced consistently and restored in the 1970s according to the AMOC with the body from DB3S/112.

DB3S/105

Supplied to Graham Whitehead in 1955. Whitehead was very unhappy with this production DB3S and has written (*Racing with the David Brown Aston Martins*, Volume 2 by Chris Nixon, Transport Bookman 1980): 'The cars were very good-looking, but I'm afraid that's as far as it went.' Co-driving with half-brother Peter, Graham Whitehead retired at Hyères in 1955, finished 8th at Lisbon and took a 5th at Brands Hatch. Whitehead advertised it in September 1955:

'1955 DB3S, low mileage, only raced four times. Maintained by first-class mechanics. Opportunity to acquire superb car for racing or road use.'

The DB3S passed to Lord O'Neil, who had new coupé body built for him by Panelcraft (see photograph) and the original body was fitted to the ex-single-seater rebuilt by Richardson as the RRA Special. After a chequered career overseas DB3S/105 has now been restored in the UK.

DB3S/101 Robert Cooper with *DB3S/101*: on his way to a class second at Prescott in 1970. *(The Author)*

DB3S/105: In 1956 this ex-Graham Whitehead car was rebuilt with a Panelcraft fixed-head coupé body for Lord O'Neill. It has now been restored to its original specification.

DB3S/106

Sold to Chan Lye-Choon and raced extensively in the Far East. Successes included 6th in the Macau Grand Prix in 1965 (after a lengthy pit stop to replace a blown gasket), 1st in the Macau Grand Prix in 1958 and 3rd in 1959. The car was subsequently sold and crashed in Malaya in 1963. Rebuilt by Clive Aston, who has retained the car.

DB3S/107

No known history. According to the AMOC, probably in Venezuela.

DB3S/106: Chan Lye-Choon with DB3S/106 on his way to a win in the 1958 Macau Grand Prix.

DB3S/108

Registered JAN 800, but no known early racing history. Offered for sale by Performance Cars Ltd in September 1957:

'DB3S September 1955, one owner, 6500 miles, little used, heavily silenced, unscratched BRG, indistinguishable from new. £2345.' Acquired by Hindes who used it lightly in competition.

By 1967 it was, apparently derelict, discovered by restaurateur Alan Greig and rebuilt by him. Thereafter has competed regularly in the UK.

DB3S/109

See DB3S/11.

DB3S/110

Registered SLC 625, but no known early racing history.

DB3S/111

Exhibited at the 1955 Earls Court Show. Logic (but not evidence) suggests that it was the car tested by John Bolster for *Autosport* (10 February, 1956) and *The Autocar* (20 April, 1956). Registered SLX 899. No known early racing history, but was driven by George Baird at the British Empire Trophy meeting at Oulton Park in 1959. Owned by Roger Forshaw.

DB3S/112

Sold in the United States and raced by Graham. Generally butchered and eventually crashed and written off.

DB3S/113

Fixed head coupé registered SXD 9 and sold to the Hon. Max Aitken. Featured in article by Tony Hogg in *Road & Track* April 1966. It was then (and still is) owned by First Lieutenant Earl Kelton (now Colonel, retired).

DB3S/111: George Baird in the unlimited capacity sports car race at the British Empire Trophy meeting at Oulton Park in 1959. He retired because of damper trouble. *(T. C. March)*

Originally had chrome body strips and rear wheel valances (both removed by Baring, who owned the car in 1957) and featured louvred openings in the sides of the front wings instead of the usual cutaway front wings. No racing history apart from a couple of minor events by Baring in 1957.

DB3S/114

Supplied to Lieutnant-Colonel Arthur Bryant, USN, in 1956, painted white and blue and registered PLU 305. Bryant, who was a great Aston Martin enthusiast and previously raced a DB2/4, only appeared twice with the DB3S in 1956. He finished 3rd in a race at a BARC Goodwood meeting and crashed with fatal results in the British Empire Trophy. The car was scrapped.

DB3S/115

No known racing history.

DB3S/116

Sold to J. Arthur Rank Organization, registered 88 HME and used in the film *Checkpoint*. No known racing history until acquired by the present owner, T. J. Henderson, in 1966.

DB3S/117

Sold to Moroccan driver Kerguen. Later fitted by Kerguen with twin-plug engine. Extensive racing history that included 6th by Kerguen in the Agadir Grand Prix, 1956, and 11th (and 1st in class) by Kerguen/Colas at Le Mans, 1957. Sold in the United States, rebuilt by present owner Newell, who has owned it since 1972.

DB3S/118

Sold to Dutch driver Hans David, who had previously raced an ex-Ecurie Ecosse C-type Jaguar. Fitted with a twin-plug cylinder head. Raced extensively in 1956–7 with some success, including a 4th place at Spa. Believed in 1959 that it was sold in the United States, subsequently butchered, crashed and scrapped.

DB3S/119

Registered 3 HMY this was one of the two fixed-head coupés retained by the company. It was advertised by Peter Sutcliffe in September 1964 (remarkably quoting the chassis number): 'Aston Martin DB3S coupé. One of three only built, chassis No. 3S/119. Two owners only, unraced, immaculate in light grey and maroon upholstery, fully tractable for road use. Offers around £1000 . . .'

This car is now in the United States.

DB3S/120

Registered 58 JHX, this was one of the two fixed ,head coupés retained by the company. Re-registered JB 16 when used competitively by Jean Bloxam in 1958. Offered by the Bloxam company in September 1958 as follows:

'Aston Martin DB3S Fixed Head Coupé

Luxuriously equipped grand touring car, Oyster grey with grey and red interior. This fabulous car now offered for sale. Built for David Brown and driven by Jean Bloxam this year. 12,000 miles since new. Immaculate. Works maintained and recent overhaul just completed. 22 mpg and perfectly tractable under all road conditions. Specification includes 40 DCO Weber carburettors with ram induction, oil cooler, special works turbo-finned brake drums, 3.9:1 axle ratio (de Dion), screen washers, twin-speed wipers, duo-tone horn, long range Le Mans headlamps, sunshine roof. This car must be the fastest closed car in the country, and one of the fastest in the world,

DB3S/114: After Arthur Bryant's fatal crash at Oulton Park in 1956. *(T. C. March)*

DB3S/120: Registered JB16, driven by W. Monk at the Clubmen's Championship at Silverstone in October 1966. *(The Author)*

occupying a unique place in the history of Aston Martin cars. Genuine reason for sale.

£2950

GORDON WHITE & CO. LTD., AUSTIN HOUSE, GERRARDS CROSS
TELEPHONE: GERRARDS CROSS 2077/8'

Subsequently offered by Coombs of Guildford (March 1959), Harold Smith (Motors) of Paddington at £875 (March 1963), acquired by Peter Sutcliffe, used competitively by him in 1963 and advertised by him in March 1964:

'JB16 DB3S coupé. Completely refurbished in body (first concours d'élegance) and soul (hill climb class record holder). In all respects perfect. Dark green, light green interior. Perfect road car.'

Owned by Mark Bamford for many years, then Sytner and now with Anthony Bamford.

DBR1

DBR1/1

Prototype car built for Le Mans 1956 with 2493cc engine (Parnell/Brooks retired). Raced early in 1957 with small engine. Salvadori 2nd in the Unlimited Capacity race at the British Empire Trophy and 2nd at the Easter Goodwood meeting. With 3-litre engine Salvadori finished 2nd at Spa, Salvadori/Leston finished 6th at the Nürburgring and retired at Le Mans, Salvadori finished 2nd at the Grand Prix meeting at Aintree and 4th in the RACB Grand Prix at Spa. Lewis-Evans finished 6th at the International Trophy meeting at Silverstone. In 1958 Salvadori/ Shelby retired at Sebring and the Nürburgring, while Lewis-Evans (co-driving with Salvadori) crashed at Le Mans. Salvadori/Brabham finished 2nd in the Tourist Trophy. The car was in effect the team spare in 1959. Salvadori/Shelby retired at Sebring, the car was the spare at Silverstone in May and Moss/Fairman won the Nürburgring 1000 Kms race. The car was not disposed of by the works until 1961, when John Ogier bought it for his Essex Racing Stable. Clark/McLaren retired at the Nürburgring and Salvadori/Maggs retired at Le Mans. In 1962 McLaren/Maggs finished 4th at the Nürburgring. Ogier had offered the car at £1950 as early as October 1961 and by August 1962 The Chequered Flag was asking £1750. The Hon. John Dawnay (now Viscount Downe) acquired it in 1962, it was crashed in 1965, eventually rebuilt and remains in Viscount Downe's ownership.

DBR1/2

Built for the 1957 season and first appeared at Spa with 3-litre engine in May, when Brooks won. Subsequently Brooks/Cunningham-Reid won the Nürburgring 1000 Kms race, Brooks (co-driving with Cunningham-Reid) crashed at Le Mans, Brooks won the RACB Grand Prix at Spa and finished 4th at

Silverstone in 1958. In 1958 Moss/Brooks retired at Sebring, Brooks/Lewis-Evans retired at the Nürburgring, Brooks/Trintignant retired at Le Mans and Moss/Brooks won the Tourist Trophy at Goodwood. Moss drove the car at the International Trophy meeting at Silverstone in 1959 and finished 2nd. Thereafter Salvadori/Shelby won at Le Mans and Moss/Shelby/Fairman won at the Tourist Trophy at Goodwood after the disastrous fire. It must be the most famous of all Aston Martins. In 1960 the car was sold to Major Ian Baillie of the Grenadier Guards (previously owner of a D-type Jaguar). At the Nürburgring in 1960 Baillie/the Hon. Edward Greenall finished, but so far down the field that no one any longer knows the general classification. Jack Fairman won his race at the Rouen Grand Prix with DBR1/2 and Baillie/Fairman finished 9th at Le Mans. Baillie owned the car through 1962 (Peter Jopp drove it at Brands Hatch in late May, finishing 7th overall). In February 1963 DBR1/2 was offered by Derek Spencer (Engineering) Ltd of Holland Park Mews, London W11, complete with spare gearbox and final drive assembly at £1295. The car was bought by David Ham (who had previously raced a DB3S) and he offered it at £1750 in May 1965. After a succession of owners, including Neil Corner, Chris Stewart and Geoffrey Marsh, the car is now in France.

DBR1/3

Built for 1958 season. Moss retired in the Targa Florio (before Brooks co-drove). Moss/Brabham won at the Nürburgring, Moss/Brabham retired at Le Mans and Shelby/Lewis-Evans finished 3rd in the Tourist Trophy. In 1959 Moss/Fairman retired at Le Mans and DBR1/3 was burnt out in the Tourist Trophy (Moss/Salvadori). After the Goodwood fire the car was rebuilt. In 1960 it was sold to the Border Reivers, converted to Appendix 'C' specification, painted blue and registered FSH 360. Jim Clark drove the car in 1960, finishing 3rd in the over 1100cc race at Oulton Park in April, retiring at the Easter Goodwood meeting and Silverstone in May. Clark/Salvadori retired at the Nürburgring and finished 3rd at Le Mans. In August 1960 DBR1/3 was offered for sale:

'BORDER REIVERS
offer for sale the famous
ASTON MARTIN DBR1/300
Completely rebuilt as new by factory since gaining 3rd 1960 Le Mans and unraced since. Complete with pneumatic built-in jacks and vast quantity spares (including gearbox/final drive unit and full range alternative ratios). Full current Appendix "C" specification. Driven previously by Moss, Brabham, Brooks, Salvadori and Clark. Spares alone worth £200.
Complete with spares, £3500
May be seen at and full particulars from:
JOHN McBAIN
The Cottage, Chirnside Duns, Berwickshire
(Telephone: Chirnside 357).'

DBR1/2: Tony Brooks leads Cunningham-Reid (DBR2/1) at the International Trophy meeting at Silverstone in September 1957. *(T. C. March)*

Note that the car retained the built-in jacks used by the works at Goodwood in 1959. With two DBR1s still unsold at the factory, there were no takers. The car was raced by Clark/Flockhart at Le Mans in 1961 (retired) and a couple of minor races. For 1963 it was acquired by Charles Sgonina, it was rebuilt at a later date and is now in France.

DBR1/4

Rebuilt for 1959 from DBR3/1 and raced only twice by the works, Trintignant/Frère finished second at Le Mans and fourth at Goodwood. The car was not sold by the works and was the car featured in *The Sound And The Fury*, by Christopher Nixon, a brilliant account of Jack Fairman driving the car on the road published in *Autosport* of 10 and 17 March, 1961. For reasons that are not clear the car was loaned to the Essex Racing Stable for them to run at Le Mans in 1961. It was driven by Salvadori/Maggs, but retired. In December 1962 the following appeared in *Autosport*: 'David Brown has presented the famous DBR1/300, which clinched the 1959 World's Sports Car Championship, to Lord Montagu of Beaulieu, who will give the green car a place of honour in his Museum. Aston Martin is the only British concern to have won the Championship. The car for the Museum is the actual machine with which Roy Salvadori and Carroll Shelby won the 1959 Le Mans 24-Hour race.' This was obviously repeated word for word from a press release. Apart from the fact that the Le Mans winner, DBR1/2, was owned and being raced by Ian Baillie and DBR1/4 went to

Beaulieu, the word 'presented' is of interest. The car remained in the museum only until 1968, it was rebuilt by Peter Brewer with 2.5-litre engine and remains in private ownership.

DBR1/5

Built for Graham Whitehead at the works by Arthur Birks for 1959, registered 900 BH and the only DBR1 in private ownership from new. In 1959 Whitehead crashed at the British Empire Trophy meeting at Oulton Park, finished 3rd at the Easter Goodwood meeting, 5th at Silverstone in May and 2nd at Elaintahanajo in Finland in May (it was a 2-kilometre course on which Whitehead was changing gear nine times a lap). Whitehead/Naylor retired at the Nürburgring and crashed at Le Mans. Whitehead withdrew DBR1/5 from the Tourist Trophy so that Aston Martin could use his pit after theirs had been destroyed by fire. In 1960 Whitehead/Taylor retired at the Nürburgring and Fairman won the larger-capacity class of the Rouen Grand Prix. By this stage Whitehead had taken delivery of a Ferrari 250GT and had largely lost interest in the DBR1. Fairman drove and retired the DBR1 in the Angolan Grand Prix. There is reason to suppose that it stayed in Africa. Whitehead drove the car at the Belvedere track at Salisbury and at the Marlborough meeting in 1961, retired at both and sold the car.

DBR2

DBR2/1

3.7-litre car built for Le Mans 1957 and based on the chassis of Lagonda DP166/1. G. Whitehead/ P. Whitehead retired at Le Mans, Cunningham-Reid crashed in practice at Spa and finished 3rd at Silverstone in September. Engine enlarged to 3.9 litres for 1958. In 1958 Moss won the Sussex Trophy at Goodwood and the British Empire Trophy; Brooks retired at Aintree and came 5th at Silverstone in May. DBR2/1 was used as the practice car at the Targa Florio and Shelby finished 3rd at Spa. The car was fitted with 4.2-litre engine shortly after Spa and loaned to Elisha Walker for George Constantine to drive. Amongst the car's performances were the following:

1958

Lime Rock, 7 September	G. Constantine 1st, 78.84 mph
Marlborough, Date not known	G. Constantine 1st, 62.5 mph
Nassau Tourist Trophy, Bahamas, 2 December	G. Constantine Retired, broken de Dion tube

1959

Montgomery, New York, 9 August	G. Constantine 1st, 76.90 mph
Wakins Glen, 26 September	G. Constantine 2nd
Los Angeles Times Grand Prix, Riverside Raceway, 11 October	S. Moss, Retired, oil pressure
Nassau Tourist Trophy, Bahamas, 6 December	G. Constantine 1st, 87.25 mph

The car was returned to Aston Martin and offered for sale in 1960. Acquired by Bill Aston, registered 778 BPH and driven in minor British events. Sold to R. H. Dennis, who fitted the gull-wing body from DB3/6. Restored and sold in the United States.

DBR2/2

3.7-litre car built for 1957 on chassis of Lagonda DP166/2. Salvadori won at Silverstone in September 1957 and the car was then shipped to Nassau, where it ran as a quasi-works car. Stirling Moss finished 24th in the Nassau Tourist Trophy (ignition problems), and 4th in the Governor's Trophy. Driven by Ruth Levy in two Ladies' races, crashing in the second. The car returned to the UK and in 1958 with 3.9-litre engine Brooks finished 2nd in the British Empire Trophy. Salvadori finished 2nd at Aintree, Salvadori finished 4th at Silverstone in May and Frère finished 2nd at Spa. A 4.2-litre engine was fitted shortly after Spa and the car was shipped to the United States to be raced by Bob Oker. Amongst the cars' performances were:–

1958

Lime Rock, June, 20 laps	R. Oker 2nd
Los Angeles Times Grand Prix, Riverside Raceway, 12 October	R. Oker Non-starter after 'irreparable damage' in practice

1959

Los Angeles Times Grand Prix, Riverside Raceway, 11 October	S. Moss Retired, oil pressure
Governor's Trophy, Bahamas, 4 December	S. Moss, 1st in heat and 1st in final; speed in final 90.95 mph. Car entered by works and fitted with twin-plug engine developing 315 bhp.

Car returned to the UK and offered for sale by Aston Martin in March 1960. Sold to S. J. Diggory, registered 7 BXH, driven for him by Bruce Halford and Colin Escott in 1960, and retained by Diggory through 1962. Offered by sale by Diggory in October 1962 at £2500. After passing through various owners, bought by Victor Gauntlett and sold at Auction in 1990 for £1,750,000.

DBR3/1

Built in 1958 with short-stroke 3-litre engine based on the DB4 unit. Moss drove the car at Silverstone in May (retired) and it was used in practice for the Tourist Trophy. Rebuilt for 1959 as DBR1/4; engine used in modified form in DB3GT DP199/1 at Le Mans in 1959.

DBR4

DBR4/1

Formula 1 car raced by works in 1959. Salvadori finished 2nd in the International Trophy at Silverstone, retired in the Dutch Grand Prix, finished 6th in the British Grand Prix and 6th in the Portuguese Grand Prix. Sold to Lex Davison in

DBR2/2: Salvadori during his epic fight with Scott-Brown (Lister-Jaguar) at the International Trophy meeting at Silverstone in 1957. Salvadori won by a narrow margin. *(T. C. March)*

Australia. Retained as spare and no racing record. Rebuilt in 1975 onwards by the late Hon. Patrick Lindsay. Owned by Geoffrey Marsh.

DBR4/2

Formula 1 car raced by works in 1959. Shelby retired in the International Trophy at Silverstone, the Dutch Grand Prix and the British Grand Prix, but finished 8th in the Portuguese Grand Prix and 10th in the Italian. According to official sources the chassis was scrapped at the end of 1959, but there is a feeling that this car formed the basis of DBR5/1.

DBR4/3

New car with stressed-skin centre-section driven by Salvadori in the 1959 Italian Grand Prix (retired). Salvadori retired with DBR4/3 in the 1960 International Trophy at Silverstone and used it during practice for the Dutch Grand Prix. The car was sold to Bib Stillwell in Australia with 3-litre engine, but apart from a win at Warwick Farm in 1961 little success was gained. Now in the Donington Collection.

DBR4/4

Built to the same specification as DBR4/3 and entered for Salvadori at the International Trophy at Silverstone. Badly damaged in the pits by Moss's spinning Cooper, non-started and never raced by the works. Sold to Lex Davison with 3-litre engine and Maserati gearbox. Many good places achieved in Australian races, including 2nd place in the 1960 Australian Grand Prix, where according to one report it was a works entry. Davison brought the car to the UK to race in Inter-Continental events in 1961, retiring in the British Empire Trophy at Silverstone and finishing 6th in the Guards Trophy at Brands Hatch. Jack Fairman tested the car for *Motor Racing* in December 1961 and commented: 'This year has seen one of these cars [DBR4s] in a few Inter-Continental races, with that tough Australian veteran Lex Davison in the cockpit. The contrast between the Aston and the average 1961 machinery has been even more marked, and in its latest form the DBR4 not only looks powerful, it really is powerful.

'Lex Davison brought the ex-works car to use for the Australian and New Zealand season last year. Most races are run to Formule Libre out there and Lex took the car with a 3-litre sports car engine installed – the unit used to successfully in the DBR1 sports/racing cars.

'For the 1961 European season, the engine was modified, the 95-degree head being replaced by the later 80-degree top, and the output boosted to a really useful 296 horsepower. Lex went back home some time ago, but the car, which he will be using again for the "winter" season's races, has only just left Britain, having been back at David Brown's Feltham works for pre-season preparation.

'A few days before it was crated and shipped to Australia, I slipped up to Silverstone to put the car through its paces, just to see that everything was running well . . .

'. . . I don't mind admitting that I was surprised by the amount of punch [the 3-litre engine] gave the single-seater.

Carroll Shelby with DBR4/2 in the 1959 British Grand Prix at Aintree. *(T.C. March)*

'Yet it is not a "knife-edge" engine, with all the power coming in with a bang over a narrow rev band. Unlike the 2½-litre GP unit, which revved to over 8000 rpm, this one peaks at 6000, but it retains the flexibility of a typical hot sports car unit, and the power is usable as low as 3500 rpm or so, if needs be . . .

'As I tested it, it was fitted with the 4:1 axle as used at Oulton Park, but this, of course, was too low for the Silverstone circuit, and I found that I was getting peak revs in top at Abbey Curve and under the Dunlop bridge at the end of the pits. But it also meant that I could circulate the lazy way, with the top gear sufficing everywhere except at Copse and Becketts, where I had to step down to third.

'The car is now equipped with a 5-speed Maserati gearbox, which has a really delightful right-hand change. First is to the left and back, second is centre forward, third centre back and so on with reverse immediately forward of first, but protected by a bar, so that it cannot be engaged accidentally . . .

'The DBR4's clutch was progressive, with a reasonably light action, while the Girling disc brakes (mounted outboard all round) were extremely powerful. There was some wheel patter under heavy braking, and due to the lack of a servo unit quite a heavy pedal pressure was needed.

'The Aston's suspension is surprisingly supple, with unequal-length wishbones and Armstrong dampers inside coil springs at the front, and torsion bars and dampers at the rear in conjunction with a de Dion axle layout. An anti-roll bar is used at the front only.

'As set up at Silverstone, the car had considerable understeer, but heavy work with the right foot soon altered that! The back end would break away quite quickly, calling for some quick work on the steering wheel, and I formed the impression that a bit too much throttle at Copse, for example, would soon have the driver taking a reverse look at the Dunlop bridge! This is not a car for the novice, and that to me is part of its appeal.

'I think that it is fundamentally wrong that a Grand Prix car, which after all is supposed to demonstrate the highest form of driving technique, should be a comparatively simple car to drive quickly. This Aston Martin could be driven moderately fast by most racing drivers with average competence, but it calls for more than ordinary skill to extract the most out of those 296 horsepower.'

'Being fairly big-built, I found that my left hip was sitting pretty close to the transmission shield, which runs down on the left side of the seat, but otherwise, the cockpit seemed quite comfortable. The seat position, of course, is much higher than is the current vogue, and it was quite a change to have a "bird's-eye-view" of what was in front of me!

'The instrument layout was sensible, with the oil pressure and temperature gauges to the left of the central rev counter, and the fuel pressure and water temperature gauges to the right of it, along with the dual ignition switches. The car sits fairly high off the ground, the 15-inch wheels having 5.50 Dunlop tyres on the front and 7.00s at the back, bags of rubber behind the cockpit, but not so much that the rear wheels couldn't be spun quite merrily, even though we were testing the car with a full load of fuel. That's power for you!

'Lex Davison, like me, has been racing for a good many years, and has driven cars with widely varying performances and characteristics. He has long ceased to be the ambitious up-and-coming young man, and he races today because he loves the sport and loves real racing cars. That's why he settled for the Aston Martin, which though it may have a tough time beating the latest lightweight machinery, will give him a lot more fun. In his place, I think I'd do precisely the same thing.'

Davison achieved no further success in Australia, the car was brought back to the UK, raced with immense success by Neil Corner in historic events, then by Alain de Cadenet, and is now in the United States.

DBR5

DBR5/1

Lighter car built for the 1960 season. Trintignant finished 10th in the International Trophy at Silverstone, Salvadori practised for but did not run in the Dutch Grand Prix and Trintignant finished 11th in the British Grand Prix. Car scrapped.

DBR5/2

Lighter car built for the 1960 season. Salvadori retired in the 1960 British Grand Prix. Car scrapped.

DB4 GT/0194/R: Entered by Colin Crabbe at the Clubmen's Championship at Silverstone in October 1966. The car was painted black and suffering from major rear end damage. *(The Author)*

DP212, 214 and 215

DP212/1

GT Prototype built for Le Mans 1962. Graham Hill/Ginther retired. Car used at the 1963 Le Mans Test Weekend with revised tail. In 1964 it was fitted with a 4.2-litre engine, sold to Viscount Downe for road use and registered AYN 212B (now, appropriately 212 DP). Driven in many events 1964–81 by Peter Salmon and still owned by Viscount Downe.

DP214: DB4/GT/0194/R

Homologated as GT car for 1963. Kimberly/Schlesser retired at Le Mans, Ireland finished 6th in the Guards Trophy at Brands Hatch and 7th in the Tourist Trophy at Goodwood. Salvadori won the Inter-Europa Cup at Monza, whilst Le Guezec won the Coupe de Paris at Montlhéry and finished 5th in the Coupe du Salon at the same circuit. For 1964 the car was sold to the Hon. John Dawnay's Dawnay Racing Team. Salvadori/Salmon retired at Daytona, Salmon finished second in the GT race at Silverstone in May, Salmon/Sutcliffe retired at Le Mans and Salmon won at the Martini Trophy meeting. Subsequently raced by Tom Rose, Colin Crabbe, Nick Cussons and remains in the UK.

DP214: DB4/GT/0195/R

Homologated as GT car for 1963. McLaren/Ireland retired at Le Mans, Kimberly retired in the Guards Trophy at Brands Hatch, McLaren retired in the Tourist Trophy at Goodwood and Bianchi finished third in the Inter-Europa Cup at Monza. Dewez finished second in the Coupe de Paris at Montlhéry and Schlesser won the Coupe du Salon at the same circuit. For 1964 the car was sold to the Hon. John Dawnay's Dawnay Racing Team. Brian Hetreed/Kerrison retired at Daytona and Hetreed crashed fatally in practice at the Nürburgring, following which the car was scrapped.

DP215/1

Prototype built for 1964. Phil Hill/Bianchi retired at Le Mans, Schlesser retired at Reims and the car was entered at the Guards Trophy but withdrawn. Following a crash on the M1 in 1966 the car was rebuilt and subsequently fitted with 4.2-litre dry sump engine that had been used in an attempt to qualify a Cooper-Aston Martin at Indianapolis in 1963.

Appendix 4

David Brown's Statement of 28 October, 1959

At a dinner held at 6 Hamilton Place, Park Lane, London W1, to celebrate Aston Martin's victory in the Sports Car World Championship, David Brown made the following statement:

I have often been asked, since winning the Sports Car Championship, 'What are your future plans?'

In answering this, I think it necessary to go back to our early days of racing, some ten years ago, when we were competing with more or less standard DB2 saloons. And to remind you just how standard these cars were, I used one of the team cars, VMF 64, for my own personal transport in between its racing appearances.

The whole character of racing has, however, changed, until today an ordinary production car would stand about as much chance in a race as the proverbial snowball of getting into hell! The sports-racing car of today has become a more complicated and expensive version of a Grand Prix car, with the addition of a self-starter, lighting, mudguards, two seats, windscreen, etc.

To remain in the hunt today it is necessary to design, build and develop completely new cars every few years.

This leads to the big question: what is the purpose of sports car racing? – and it seems to me that it has departed very much from the original intention when sports car racing first started. I would like to see sports car racing where the cars are closely allied to what the public can buy.

For Grand Prix racing, on the other hand, the problem should be of producing within a prescribed formula the fastest machine that is possible, regardless of other considerations. Both forms of racing serve a useful purpose but they should be complementary to one another and not merely variations of a theme.

I believe that sports car racing has reached an important cross-roads – and nobody appears sure which way to go. The regulations for Le Mans – only seven months away – are still unknown and the formula laid down in 1958 for World Championships, which was to run for three years, has already, before its third, year, been altered. Even the DBR1 on our stand [at the London Motor Show] is not eligible in its present form to race next year.

Furthermore, we have been racing continuously for something over ten years and during that period our production has remained fairly static. On the other hand we have developed, as a result of racing, a very fine product which seems to be very much in demand. We feel it is now time we devoted a greater part of our efforts to this commercial aspect of our business and a greater part of our technical resources to the more rapid development of our production cars.

I have strong views on what the future of sports car racing should be and it is with regret that I have to tell you that we do not intend to compete in sports car racing next year. Our own racing efforts in 1960 will be concentrated upon the Grand Prix field in this last year of the present Grand Prix Formula.

I should like to think that if, and when, we return to sports car racing, it will be something that more closely resembles our production car and what the public can buy.